KEYNES AND PUBLIC POLICY
AFTER FIFTY YEARS
VOLUME I: ECONOMICS AND POLICY

Keynes and Public Policy After Fifty Years
Volume I: Economics and Policy

Edited by
Omar F. Hamouda
John N. Smithin

NEW YORK UNIVERSITY PRESS
Washington Square, New York

© O.F. Hamouda and J.N. Smithin, 1988

First published in the USA by
NEW YORK UNIVERSITY PRESS
Washington Square
New York, N.Y. 10003

Library of Congress Cataloging-in-Publication Data

Keynes and public policy after fifty years.

   Papers from Conference on Keynes and Public Policy
after Fifty Years held in Sept. 1986, at Glendon
College, York University, Toronto.
   Bibliography: p.
   Includes index.
   Contents: v. 1. Economics and policy — v. 2.
Theories and method.
   1. Keynesian economics—Congresses.   2. Economic
policy—Congresses.   I. Keynes, John Maynard, 1883–
1946.   II. Hamouda, O. F.   III. Smithin, John N.
IV. Conference on Keynes and Public Policy after
Fifty Years (1986: Glendon College)
HB99.7.K3815   1987   330.15′6   87–20368

ISBN 0–8147–3444–8 (v. 1)
ISBN 0–8147–3445–6 (v. 2)

Printed and bound in Great Britain

Contents

Foreword

The Conference of which these volumes are the fitting outcome could not have been held at a more appropriate time: fifty years after the publication of the *General Theory*, and in honour of Lorie Tarshis's seventy-fifth birthday. Keynes's contributions, and especially the *General Theory*, are experiencing a proper reappraisal and revival following those lean years in which the modern purveyors of classical theory (in Keynes's sense) celebrated prematurely both his demise and their own ascendancy. Lorie Tarshis is a most distinguished expositor of Keynes's theories and their extensions, to which he himself has made substantial contributions. He has also always placed his own eminently sensible policy proposals on a secure Keynesian base, drawing on his thorough grounding in Keynesian principles first, at the University of Toronto, and then at Cambridge itself when Keynes was lecturing from the proof-sheets of the various stages of the development of the *General Theory* embryo.

Thanks to the energy and enthusiasm of Omar Hamouda, John Smithin and Bernard Wolf, a friendly and happy band were gathered together in the fine surroundings of Glendon College of York University in Toronto for an exhausting but exhilarating few days. It is splendid that the papers presented there should be preserved in more permanent form in these two volumes. And it is especially good that Richard Goodwin and Robert Skidelsky, those intrepid travellers on People's Express, should have their addresses – one after lunch, the other after dinner – printed in the volumes. Both were great occasions. The addresses were fitting climaxes to the fine meals and ample wines (for Canada) which preceded them. They will serve to recall to those who were there the standing ovation which Lorie Tarshis received when after dinner he was presented with the first published copy of the book of essays in his honour.

There is a wide range of topics and approaches covered in these volumes. I hope that the small band of original Canadian Keynesians who were present will be cheered to see in what capable hands their tradition is being carried on.

G.C. Harcourt, *Cambridge*

Acknowledgments

The editors of these volumes wish to express their thanks to Bernard M. Wolf, who played a leading role on the organizing committee of the original Glendon Conference (and is also the co-author of one of the contributed papers).

The organizing committee, *in toto*, would also like to thank the following individuals and organizations, all of whom have given invaluable support and encouragement in various ways, both for the Conference and the preparation of these volumes: President Harry Arthurs, York University; Principal Phillipe Garigue, Glendon College; Mr John Crow, Governor of the Bank of Canada; the Hon. Robert Nixon, Treasurer of Ontario; Mr Bryne Purchase, Ministry of Treasury and Economics, Government of Ontario; Professor Jon Cohen, University of Toronto; Dr Geoff Harcourt, University of Cambridge; Vice-President Ken Davey, York University; Associate Vice-President Paul Lovejoy, York University; Associate Principals Ian Gentles and Beth Hopkins, Glendon College; Dean David Bell, York University; Dean Yvette Szmidt, Glendon College; Ms Noli Swatman, Office of Research Administration, York University; Mr Tim Nau, Office of the Principal, Glendon College; Ms Danielle Comarmond, Budget Office, Glendon College; Professors John Buttrick, John Evans and Charles Plourde, Department of Economics, and Professor Bryan Massam, Department of Geography, York University; Professors Ian McDonald and David McQueen, Department of Economics, Glendon College; Glendon College Students' Association; and the Economics Graduate Students' Association, York University.

Financial support for the Conference was provided by the Ministry of Treasury and Economics, Government of Ontario; Office of the President, York University; the York University Ad Hoc Research Fund; and the Glendon College 20th Anniversary Celebration Committee.

First-class secretarial support has been provided by Mrs Paule Cotter, Research Office, Glendon College; Mrs Azi Subrahmanyam and Ms Christine Goary, Department of Economics, Glendon College; and Ms Svatka Hermanek, Faculty of Administrative Studies, York University.

Special mention must be made of the hard work put in during the Conference by M. Franque Grimard and his fellow undergraduate students in Economics at Glendon College; Louise Laliberté, Joanne

Castonguay-McNamee, Milos Kostich, Michèle Rioux, Todd Smyth, Charles Rouyer, David De Wees, Jim Lauer, Robert Najm and Eric Armour. It was largely thanks to their efforts that the meetings, out of which this collection of papers developed, were conducted so smoothly. Finally, we would like to express our appreciation for the enthusiasm and vision of our publisher, Edward Elgar, in guiding these volumes through to publication.

Introduction
Omar F. Hamouda and John N. Smithin

This collection of papers originated in a Conference on 'Keynes and Public Policy after Fifty Years', which was held in September 1986 at Glendon College, York University, Toronto, to mark the fiftieth anniversary of the publication of Keynes's *General Theory* (the actual date of publication being February 1936).

As well as commemorating the *General Theory*, the Conference participants were also able to honour Professor Lorie Tarshis, who is currently chairperson of the Economics Department at Glendon College and was celebrating his seventy-fifth birthday during 1986. Lorie was a pupil of Keynes at Cambridge during the crucial period 1932-6 in which the *General Theory* was being elaborated, and has since gained an international reputation for his many contributions to Keynesian economics. At the Conference dinner on the evening of 26 September, Geoff Harcourt presented Lorie with the first copy of a Festschrift, edited by Jon Cohen (University of Toronto) and himself, containing contributions by many of Lorie's old friends and admirers in the economics profession. Lorie received a standing ovation from the Conference.

We are also pleased to record the participation of two other students of Keynes, Robert B. Bryce and Walter S. Salant, who were classmates of Lorie Tarshis fifty years ago, and like Lorie, have gone on to distinguished careers: Bryce at the Ministry of Finance in Ottawa, and Salant in Washington, DC, latterly at the Brookings Institution. These volumes contain contributions by all three former pupils of Keynes: Bryce, Salant and Tarshis.

The anniversary happened to fall at a time of more than usual uncertainty in the realm of macroeconomic theory and policy. During the 1970s and early 1980s it seemed that Keynesian economics was rather out of fashion, and with the rise first of monetarism, and then the so-called 'new classical' school, more than one economist could be found to assert that the insights of Keynes into the functioning of the capitalist market economies of forty and fifty years ago were no longer relevant to the modern world. By 1986, however, things seemed to be much less clear-cut. The worldwide recession of 1981-2 (which some economists have blamed, at least partly, on monetarist policies designed to cure inflation) and the subsequent return to prolonged mass unemployment in many of the industrialized countries, have naturally evoked memories of the 1930s. Rising protectionist sentiment, particularly in the USA, reinforces this impression. Of course, circumstances are different, but it is hardly surprising that there has been renewed interest in the diagnosis and solutions offered by Keynes for an apparently similar set of problems.

In this situation, the objective of these essays is not merely, or not only, commemorative, but also to take the opportunity suggested by the anniversary to inquire to what extent we can learn from the past and to place Keynes's ideas in a present-day context. The contributors are a diverse group of scholars, practitioners and theorists, some of whom participated in the original Keynesian revolution, some who have established reputations in the development and interpretation of ideas originally suggested by Keynes, and a younger generation who feel that the study of Keynes remains relevant to the macroeconomics of the 1980s. The emphasis on public policy is natural, as Keynes was, *par excellence*, the economist for whom economic theory was only valuable in as far as it contributed to a sound basis for public policy.

Taken as a whole, these papers testify to the fact that Keynes's ideas continue to provide an intellectual challenge to the contemporary economist, and to an extent that would have seemed surprising at the zenith of the 'rational expectations revolution' only a few years ago. It is perhaps too soon to talk of a 'Keynesian recovery', to borrow Peter Howitt's (1986) phrase, but such a development no longer seems impossible.

The real reason for the continuing relevance of Keynesian ideas, we would argue, lies not so much in the text of the *General Theory*, or even the personality of Keynes himself, remarkable though that was in the testimony of those who knew him, but rather in the perennial and fundamental nature of the issues being discussed. These concern the deeply controversial questions of the nature and functioning of capitalist market economies, and the extent to which state intervention in economic affairs, particularly at the macroeconomic level, is necessary and desirable. As long as the real world economy fails to replicate the smooth functioning of an Arrow–Debreu type general equilibrium model, these issues of policy will continue to be debated. This is inevitably so, even if one takes the Hayekian view that it is (misguided) government intervention which causes macroeconomic problems in the first place.

At this date, it is possible to see that Keynes's original contribution was not so much in any specific policy proposal or theoretical construct, but in the notion that policy problems may be capable of rational thought and management. Before Keynes (and in many quarters after him), both the defenders of the economic system and its critics – the political forces of the right and the left – took what can only be described as an *alienated* view of macroeconomic problems. That is to say, that the economy is seen as an external force which determines the fates of those who live under it but is not amenable to conscious control by them. For the believers in *laissez-faire* this is not disturbing, because the market economy, while sometimes harsh in its judgements on individuals, is ultimately benign from the point of view of society as a whole. It is a natural organism which only has to be left alone to provide the best of all possible worlds, in a material sense, for its powerless participants. To the political left, the capitalist economy is equally an uncontrollable natural force, but in this case a demonic one, which leads only to misery and suffering for most of those in its power, and is proceeding via ever worsening crises to inevitable breakdown.

Keynes, who lived through World War I, Britain's economic stagnation and political crisis in the 1920s, and the worldwide depression of the 1930s, was certainly not able to believe in *laissez-faire*; but at the same time was not prepared to contemplate the ultimate collapse of the economic system and a totalitarian future, which would destroy the basis and values of civilization as he knew it. He came to believe that a third alternative was possible, that the system could be managed in order to retain the benefits and material standard of living that capitalism and the market system had made possible, and yet avoid its abuses. Not even the most ardent Keynesian could claim that Keynes fully spelled out the details of how this could be achieved in practice, and it is no doubt the case that Keynes's faith in governments was influenced by his position in the élite of British society, with its deeply ingrained paternalistic sense of public duty. It is also possible that observation of some attempts at economic management in the past fifty years would have made him more sceptical. None the less, the idea that society is not powerless in the face of the impersonal tides of the economy is Keynes's great contribution to the history of ideas.

Very clearly, after a period between World War II and the early 1970s, in which society and governments in the industrialized democracies seemed to accept something like Keynes's vision of the relationship between the public and private sectors, the later 1970s and early 1980s witnessed a strong revival of what we are calling here the 'alienated view'. Symptomatic of this was the prominence among theoretical economists of the famous 'policy irrelevance' proposition of the new classical school and, in the real world, the election to power in many jurisdictions of governments which explicitly rejected the apparent postwar consensus about the role of government in the management of the economy; in particular, the responsibility to maintain full employment.

As it has turned out, however, the events of the 1980s, including the

1981-2 recession, have rather seriously damaged the credibility of the view that government policy is powerless to influence (for good or ill) the course of the economy. It is simply not plausible to argue, for example, that there is no link between the monetary and fiscal policies of the British government since 1979, and the double-digit unemployment rate which has persisted in that country throughout the decade thus far. Or similarly, that the unbalanced US fiscal/monetary policy mix of the 1980s was not connected with the unwelcome rise of the exchange value of the dollar to late 1985, and the ensuing trade difficulties. Nor is it persuasive to invoke the rational expectations distinction between 'unanticipated' and 'anticipated' policy actions in an environment in which the break with traditional macroeconomic policy was much heralded, and actually a major plank of the political platforms of the governments concerned.

One potential response to recent events of course is that they reinforce the view that governments themselves are the source of the problem, and that the authorities should somehow disengage themselves from the economy, pursue a 'neutral' policy, adhere to 'rules rather than discretion', etc. But this view itself is not exactly 'policy irrelevance', and glosses over the fact that at least some of the responsibility for the dramatic policy shifts of recent years lies with the confident rational expectations arguments of the 1970s that there could be 'disinflation without tears' if only the commitment to reduce inflation was sufficiently credible. More fundamentally, the mere observation of policies that increase unemployment or cause trade difficulties leads one to suspect that the other side of the coin may be that policies which do the opposite are indeed possible.

Hence it is another rather natural corollary of the dislocations of the past few years that some economists are willing to take another look at Keynes's fundamental ideas. Few would argue that there are any ready-made formulas from the 1930s or 1940s which can be removed from the shelf, dusted off and applied without modification to contemporary problems. Each generation will clearly have to grapple with the issue of the extent to which conscious macroeconomic control of the economy is possible and desirable in the particular historical circumstances of its time. However, the widening gap between much contemporary economic theory and the 'facts of experience' does suffice to explain why Keynes's pragmatic and undoctrinaire approach to macroeconomic policy problems once again seems attractive and worthy of attention.

This collection of papers has been grouped into two volumes: Volume I contains three sections entitled 'Keynes and Public Policy in Britain and North America', 'Keynesian Economics Past and Present' and 'Impressions and Recollections of J.M. Keynes'. The first section, with contributions by Elizabeth Durbin, Susan Howson, Don Moggridge, Walter Salant and

Robert Skidelsky, deals with both the immediate and more lasting impact of Keynes's idea on public policy, political parties and political programmes on both sides of the Atlantic. We have also included here a brief comment by Alexander Dow on these issues. Part 2 contains papers by Brian Bixley, David Colander, Robert Clower, Sheila Dow and David McQueen, each of which from different points of view attempts to assess the current state of Keynesian economics and suggest directions for the future. Robert Dimand's chapter in this section has a more historical theme and traces the actual development of Keynes's original theory from 1932 to 1936 using the lecture notes of Keynes's students, including those taken by Bryce, Salant and Tarshis.

The final section of Volume I, 'Impressions and Recollections', includes Robert Bryce's paper and also a contribution by another distinguished Canadian public servant, Louis Rasminsky, a former Governor of the Bank of Canada, who came into contact with Keynes at an earlier stage in his career during the historic negotiations leading up to the Bretton Woods agreement in 1944. The chapters by Robert Skidelsky and Richard Goodwin in this section originated as dinner and luncheon speeches at the Conference respectively. Skidelsky's paper drew on his authoritative biography of Keynes, and Goodwin's on his participation in the Keynesian revolution on both sides of the Atlantic: first, as the pupil of Keynes's close colleague and disciple (and first biographer), Sir Roy Harrod, at Oxford, and later at Harvard.

Volume II contains chapters which focus on particular specific issues and is divided into six parts, including 'Keynes and Econometric Method', 'The Theory of Investment', 'Aspects of the Labour Market', 'Money and Interest Rates', 'International Trade and Finance' and 'Positional Goods and Growth: Analogies to Keynesian Economics'. The first of these, with contributions by Ingrid Rima and Robin Rowley, and the joint paper by Ronald Bodkin, Lawrence Klein and Kanta Marwah, is addressed to the current debate about Keynes's influence on the development of macro-econometric models. The authors take different positions on this issue, and the extent to which Keynes anticipated the criticisms of econometric methodology which are troubling today's practitioners. The chapters by Clarence Barber and Michael Perelman in Part 2 both deal with aggregate investment spending, the behaviour of which was a key element in the original Keynesian system. Alan Abouchar's chapter in this section has a more microeconomic focus and explores the implications of Keynesian ideas for the optimal level of public sector investment.

The third section of Volume II contains a number of contributions which address labour market issues. The chapters by Tom Asimakopulos and Paul Davidson are both critical of the recent widely publicized proposals put forward by M.L. Weitzman for the reform of labour market institutions (the 'share economy'). Both authors point out that the basic concepts were explored, and apparently discarded, by Keynes himself, even before the publication of the *General Theory*. In the other contributions in Part 3 Peter Howitt's chapter, using contemporary analytical techniques, revives the controversial argument of chapter 19 of the *General Theory* that a 'flexible wage policy' will not necessarily improve employment performance, while the contribution by Christopher Marme and Paul Wells criticizes Sir John Hicks's 'Wage Theorem' interpretation of the ch. 19 arguments. The final chapter in this part, by Serge-Christophe Kolm, explores the implications for employment of concern over relative wages and wage norms, a question originally broached by Keynes in ch. 2 of the *General Theory*. Various controversial topics involving monetary and interest rate policy are discussed in the contributions in Part 4 by Basil Moore, Thomas Rymes and Marc Lavoie and Mario Seccareccia. As there was considerable discussion of these issues at the original Conference, we have also included here written comments by Meyer Burstein and Nancy Wulwick.

Part 5 deals with various aspects of international trade and finance. Bernard Wolf discussed Keynes's attitude towards free trade and the tariff question and attempts to put into perspective Keynes's famous volte-face on the issue of tariffs in the 1930s. Lorie Tarshis's contribution addresses a policy issue of great current concern in the international debt crisis of the less developed countries (LDCs), and suggests a number of alternative methods of dealing with the problem. Bernard Schmitt, in a chapter which perhaps reflects the spirit rather than the letter of Keynes's approach to the problem of international monetary settlements, claims to find a major flaw in the current system, and suggests far-reaching reforms.

Finally, Part 6 in Volume II, contains just one chapter, prepared by Omar Hamouda and Lorie Tarshis, which is a summary of Tibor Scitovsky's contribution to the Conference. It is suggested that Hirsch's concept of 'positional goods' may in some sense be regarded as a generalization of Keynes's 'liquidity preference', and that an increase in the demand for such goods in an affluent society may have effects in retarding output and employment growth similar to those of an increase in liquidity preference in the Keynesian system.

The two volumes deal with a number of diverse topics, each of which is of intrinsic individual interest, but are also unified by the theme of the general approach to macroeconomic problems and policies pioneered by Keynes fifty years ago.

Reference

Howitt, P. (1986), 'The Keynesian recovery', The 1986 Innis Lecture. *Canadian Journal of Economics*, **XIX** (4), November, 626–41.

Contributors

Alan Abouchar, University of Toronto, Canada
Athanasio Asimakopulos, McGill University, Canada
Clarence L. Barber, Professor Emeritus, University of Manitoba, Canada
Brian Bixley, York University, Canada
Ronald G. Bodkin, University of Ottawa, Canada
Robert B. Bryce, Ex-Deputy Minister of Finance, Government of Canada
Meyer L. Burstein, York University, Canada
Robert W. Clower, University of South Carolina, USA
David Colander, Middlebury College, USA
Paul Davidson, University of Tennessee, Knoxville, USA
Robert W. Dimand, Carleton University, Canada
Alister Dow, University of Stirling, Scotland
Sheila C. Dow, University of Stirling, Scotland
Elizabeth Durbin, New York University, USA
Richard Goodwin, Professor Emeritus, Cambridge (UK) and Siena University, Italy
Omar Hamouda, York University, Canada
G.C. Harcourt, University of Cambridge, UK
Peter Howitt, University of Western Ontario, Canada
Susan Howson, University of Toronto, Canada
Lawrence R. Klein, University of Pennsylvania, USA
Serge-Christophe Kolm, ENPC, Paris, France
Mark Lavoie, University of Ottawa, Canada
David McQueen, York University, Canada
Christopher Marme, University of Illinois, USA
Kanta Marwah, Carleton University, Canada
D.E. Moggridge, University of Toronto, Canada
Basil J. Moore, Wesleyan University, USA
Michael Perelman, California State University, Chico, USA
Louis Rasminsky, Ex-Governor of the Bank of Canada
Ingrid H. Rima, Temple University, USA
Robin Rowley, McGill University, Canada
T.K. Rymes, Carleton University, Canada
Walter S. Salant, Senior Fellow Emeritus, Brookings Institution, USA
Bernard Schmitt, Fribourg University, Switzerland
Tibor Scitovsky, Professor Emeritus, Stanford University, USA

Mario Seccareccia, University of Ottawa, Canada
Robert Skidelsky, Warwick University, UK
John Smithin, York University, Canada
Nicholas P. Smook, York University, Canada
Lorie Tarshis, York University, Canada
Paul Wells, University of Illinois, USA
Bernard M. Wolf, York University, Canada
Nancy Wulwick, LeMoyne College, USA

PART I

KEYNES AND PUBLIC POLICY IN BRITAIN AND NORTH AMERICA

1 Keynes's political legacy
Robert Skidelsky[1]

Introduction

John Maynard Keynes often described himself as a man of the left. In 1926 he wrote 'the republic of my imagination lies on the extreme left of celestial space'.[2] The question, he told Kingsley Martin in 1939, was 'whether we are prepared to move out of the nineteenth-century *laissez-faire* state into that of liberal socialism'.[3] The problem with such self-perception is that Keynes rarely championed causes which were distinctively left-wing. Social democracy, then as now, was distinctively about equality. It aimed to bring about a more equal distribution of property, income, rights, life-chances, and circumstances. Redistributionary finance received powerful support from the Cambridge school of welfare economics. Keynes was almost completely silent on such issues. There are very few references to equality or social justice in his economic and political writings; and when they occur, they do so in much more limited contexts than has characterized even moderate socialist usage. What is missing from these writings, therefore, is that which is distinctively *ethical*.[4]

One may speculate on the reasons for this. Economics, like everything else, is subject to a division of labour. At Cambridge, Keynes taught the theory of money; the theory of value and distribution was in the hands of Pigou. At one point, Keynes invoked a political division of labour as well. Questions of social justice, he said, were best left to the 'party of the proletariat'; Liberals like himself should concern themselves with issues of 'economic efficiency' and 'individual liberty' (*CW*, IX, p. 292). Again, Keynes sometimes talked of socialism being for 'later', after the economic problem had been solved.[5] That is, he did not regard the question of the distribution of given resources to be as urgent as that of how to obtain full utilization of potential resources.

I doubt whether such reasons go to the heart of the matter. As Elizabeth Durbin has rightly pointed out, 'the focus on particular problems, the choice between different economic means, and even the use of one economic model rather than another, may ... be affected by the values of the policy adviser'.[6] Keynes's values were, in important respects, different from those of most socialists. Equality was never a passion for him, indeed Keynes's passions were not importantly political at all.

Any investigation of Keynes's political legacy has to start, then, from his philosophy of life. We start with his ethics, and then go on to trace the connections between his ethics, his politics and his economics. One preliminary point needs to be made straight away. Keynes was the child of the Cambridge revolt against Benthamite utilitarianism, the main *secular* philosophical system of Victorian Britain. Bentham sought to direct private and public conduct to the achievement of a single moral end: 'the greatest happiness of the greatest number' this end being held to be rationally deduced from a factual premise about individuals, namely, that they sought pleasure and tried to avoid pain. The difficulties with Benthamism accumulated during the nineteenth century and culminated in a frontal attack by G.E. Moore in his *Principia Ethica* (1902) – the most important philosophical influence on Keynes's life. In essence, Moore denied that goodness and happiness are the same thing; that what people *wanted* (happiness or pleasure) is necessarily good for them. Benthamism ceased to be serviceable as a moral philosophy, without necessarily ceasing to serve as a rational basis for politics and economics. This conclusion was fundamental to Keynes; his political legacy cannot be understood apart from it. He never regarded public life as an important arena for the achievement of ethical ends; this severely limited the ethical passion he invested in his politics and economics. Bertrand Russell put the matter with the utmost precision when he wrote of Keynes that 'when he concerned himself with politics and economics he left his soul at home'.[7]

Keynes had problems with another aspect of utilitarianism, its consequentialism. Actions can be justified only by results, i.e. by whether they increased the sum of utility. But how can we ever have enough advance knowledge of results to be able to say that this or that action is even probably right? Keynes's study of the connection between 'ought' and 'probable' culminated in his *Treatise on Probability*, published in 1921. His epistemology, in turn, suggested conclusions as to what constituted rational behaviour in politics and economics. His lifelong bias against *long-run thinking* can perhaps be traced to these epistemological investigations.

The Keynes we encounter is not someone whose life and thought were directed by a coherent, unified philosophy – such had become impossible to someone of his temperament and generation. His character and ideas alike were fragments of vanished wholes. He believed that each fragment could be rationally justified; but the task of putting them together was beyond him. He was both aesthete and manager, and his life was partitioned between the aesthetic and managerial passions. In this he was, as Alastair Macintyre suggested, a representative 'character' of modernity.[8] To the student of politics and economics his legacy lies in the mixture of scepticism and optimism, timidity and robustness, which he brought to the public questions of his day. His was the temper of the Middle Way.

Moore's ethics

In Benthamite ethics any increase in total utility (happiness) is equivalent to an increase in the sum of goodness. Cambridge welfare economics was explicitly Benthamite in this sense: 'welfare means the same thing as good', wrote Pigou in his *Wealth and Welfare* (1912). By increasing welfare one was increasing happiness; and by increasing happiness one was increasing goodness. It was along such lines that an economist could justify his work as a direct means to the good; and that social democracy could identify redistributionary politics with ethics.

For the philosopher, G.E. Moore, a proposition of the kind 'welfare means ... good' is an example of what he called the 'naturalistic fallacy'; the fallacy consisting in the attempt to identify 'good' with a natural property like 'pleasant' or 'agreeable'. To say that people want something is not to say that they *ought* to want it; rather they ought to want what is good. Moore was drawing attention to what has always seemed obvious to the moralist: that what people want is not necessarily good for them, nor does wanting it more intensely make it better. Want satisfaction and ethical goodness are separate things; the connection between them is at best indirect, and needs to be established by further argument.

It is important in what follows that Keynes's ethical beliefs were derived from Moore, whose *Principia Ethica* was published when he was an undergraduate at Cambridge. For Moore, the primary ethical question is 'what is good?' or 'what sorts of thing ought to exist for their own sake?'. The question: 'what ought I to do?' can be answered only by reference to this question, and to the probable consequences of actions. Moore's answer to the first question is that:[9]

> by far the most valuable things we know or can imagine are certain states of consciousness which may be roughly described as the pleasures of human intercourse and the enjoyment of beautiful objects, adding that 'it is only for the sake of these things – in order that as much of them as possible may at some time exist – that one can be justified in performing any public or private duty; that ... it is they ... that form the rational ultimate end of human action and the sole criterion of social progress.

Of course, Moore did not deny that there were other valuable ends, which it might be rational to pursue, provided these were consistent with, or could be shown to promote, the ultimate end. Thus it was ethically better that people should be good and happy than good and miserable. This opened the door to social reform as a rational activity, while leaving open the question of the nature of the connection between 'happiness' and 'goodness', the means appropriate to promote one or other or both, the adequacy of our knowledge to decide between different courses of action. The connection between ethics, politics and economics was evidently more problematic if one took Moore seriously than if one applied a common Benthamite reasoning to all three; yet the chief value of Moore for Keynes was that he had expelled Benthamism from ethics.[10]

To sum up: Moore's ethical system permitted social activism but did not entail it. No prima-facie case is made out that economic reform which produced more income on the whole or a greater amount of total satisfaction from a given income would increase the goodness of the universe. Moreover, against involvement in public affairs was an important consideration. Such involvement could lead to bad states of mind by diverting individuals from the pursuits of their own ethical goodness – from the cultivation of personal relationships and aesthetic pleasures. And this, in turn, might diminish the sum of ethical goodness in the universe, at least in the immediate future.

These ideas had a profound impact on Keynes at an impressionable period in his life. As late as 1938 he described the publication of *Principia Ethica* as 'the beginning of a new renaissance, the opening of a new heaven on earth'. The talk which preceded and followed it 'dominated, and perhaps still dominates, everything else' (*CW*, X, p. 435). The fundamental point to note is that Moore's ideal – and Keynes's – was a non-political ideal. It was the ideal of a civilized society; and Keynes would not have dissented from his friend Clive Bell's characterization of such a society as one containing highly civilized groups of men and women capable of 'passionate love, profound aesthetic emotion, subtle thought, charming conversation ... attractive vices'.[11] Bell makes the important point that there is no necessary connection between civilization and any particular political order. The great civilizations of the past have been oligarchies or tyrannies. Social justice is not an end in itself, but only a possible means to civilization; and Bell inclines to the belief that its pursuit would diminish the sum of civilization, since it involved taxation to squeeze out the leisured class for the benefit of wage-earners.[12]

We need to take this seriously, for it has become a cliché that the test of a civilized society is some political practice or condition – how it treats minorities, whether it provides 'social justice'. But as Moore reminds us in his quotation from Bishop Butler 'Everything is what it is, and not another thing'. A state of civilization is not the same as a state of happiness or equality, and does not necessarily imply either. Anthony Crosland admitted as much when he talked of the value of ends such as 'leisure, beauty, grace, gaiety, excitement ... variety' which are 'not to be subsumed under any defensible definition of socialism'.[13] Indeed it is not difficult to see how a conflict can arise between the kinds of social arrangement which, historically, have marked great periods of civilization and those intended to achieve 'social justice' or 'utility maximization'. When in his *General Theory* Keynes looked forward, incautiously, to the 'euthanasia of the rentier', his French friend Marcel Labordère wrote him reproachfully:

> The rentier is useful in his way not only, and not even principally, on account of his propensity to save, but for deeper reasons. Stable fortunes, the hereditary permanency of families and sets of families of various social standings are an invisible social asset on which every king of culture is more or less dependent. To entirely overlook the interests of the rentier class which includes benevolent, humanitarian, scientific, literary institutions and groups of worldly interests (salons) may, viewed in a historical perspective, turn out to be a short-sighted policy. Financial security for one's livelihood is a necessary condition of organised leisure and thought. Organised leisure and thought is a necessary condition of a true, not purely mechanical civilisation.

In his reply, Keynes wrote:[14]

> I fully agree with this, and I wish I had emphasised it in your words. The older I get the more convinced I am that what you say is true and important. But I must not allow you to make me too conservative.

We will return to the problem of the rentier in the next section.

Ethics and economics
Neither Marshall nor Pigou had the slightest difficulty in defining economic commitment in moral terms. This was because they regarded an increase in welfare as equivalent to an increase in goodness. Nor, unlike Mill, did they apparently feel that their pursuit of the world's happiness might be at the expense of their own. For a Moorean, the problem of finding a rational ethical justification for economic work was more difficult. Three kinds of such justification can be extracted from Keynes's writings.

First, Keynes added to Moore's cloistered list of ethical goods two others: states of knowledge, and what may be termed the satisfactions of citizenship. He felt, in 1938, that 'there are many objects of valuable contemplation and communion beyond those we know – those concerned with the order and pattern of life amongst communities and the emotions which they can inspire' (*CW*, X, p. 449). Knowledge, compassion and devotion to the public good can be attributes of good states of mind. This connects with an important strand in Keynes's thought – the high value he placed on the 'public service' motive for action. He was, after all, the child of Victorian parents in whom the sense of duty ran strong.

A second argument has to do with the *conditions* of good states of mind. The Cambridge in which the young Keynes passed his life offered an environment of leisure, beauty, knowledge, intelligence and charm. The ethically valuable life-style made possible by these things was supported by the wealth-creating and political mechanisms of bourgeois civilization which, however, did not impinge on it directly. After 1914, these mechanisms deteriorated. As Keynes put it, his generation had not realized that 'civilization was a thin and precarious crust erected by the personality and will of a very few, and only maintained by rules and conventions skilfully put across and guilefully preserved' (*CW*, X, p. 447). After World War I, social progress could no longer be safely entrusted to 'automatic forces' with the élite left free to cultivate good states of mind in Moorean seclusion. Even a follower of Moore could not go on fiddling while Rome was burning.

This links up with the third argument. Keynes repeatedly, but most emphatically in his essay 'Economic Possibilities for our Grandchildren', indicted capitalist civilization for overvaluing the economic criterion. The solution of the economic problem would cure mankind of that 'disgusting morbidity', love of money. In so far as the work of the economist helped free man from 'pressing economic cares', so that he would gain leisure to live 'wisely and agreeably and well', it could be justified in Moorean terms.[15]

This essay deserves more careful attention than it has received, not because it is very profound, but because of the light it sheds on Keynes's social values. The argument that the solution of the economic problem will free people from the 'love of money' is really very curious, since 'love of money' (by which Keynes meant something like the psychological propensity to save in excess of rational prudence for the pleasure it gave the saver) was hardly the most conspicuous moral blemish of the poor – those with the most 'pressing economic cares'. The point of the essay seems to be not that the solution of the economic problem will make the poor good, but that it will make the rich good; or more precisely, that section of the well-to-do which lived off rentier incomes, the class which embodied the great Victorian virtues of thrift and abstinence. This raises the question of what 'economic problem' Keynes thought he was solving.

Keynes's *ethical* indignation was aroused not by the degradation of the poor which inspired Marshall's work, but by the cultural deformation of his own class, the 'rentier bourgeoisie', as exemplified by the life-style of his parents' generation. He first launches into them in *The Economic Consequences of the Peace* (1919) – they are the class who have made saving 'nine-tenths of virtue', sacrificing the 'arts of enjoyment' to 'compound interest' (*CW*, II, pp. 12–13) – and he rarely left up thereafter. Keynes's attitude to this, his own class, is deeply ambiguous. That fraction of it known as Bloomsbury stood in his eyes for 'civilization', but he also recognized that the social function of this class was to accumulate; and the need for accumulation put a premium on the character-type of the miser, who could not enjoy the 'arts of life'. Thus he could at one and the same time look forward to the 'euthanasia of the rentier' and agree with Marcel Labordère that the rentier class was the source of civilization.

What is interesting is the way Keynes gradually brings his economic valuation of this class into line with his adverse ethical valuation. In 1919 he had no doubt about its economic utility: abstinence, however ethically unlovely, was the Victorian answer to Malthus. The decisive break comes with the *Treatise on Money* (1930) with its rejection of the abstinence theory of economic progress: 'For the engine which drives enterprise is not thrift, but profit' (*CW*, VI, p. 133). In *The General Theory* model abstinence or thriftiness is given a negative economic value for all conditions short of full employment. Keynes expects socially organized investment programmes to drive down the rate of interest, leading to the 'euthanasia of the rentier' (*CW*, VII, pp. 375–6). The abundance to which Keynes thus looks forward in 'Economic Possibilities for our Grandchildren' is *capital* abundance. This state of affairs does not mean that unearned income or saving will or should disapper. What it means is that the interest rate which is a function of capital scarcity will fall to zero; and that the social premium which capital scarcity gives to a certain character-type will disappear. It is in this sense, I think, that Keynes expects the 'solution' of the economic problem to enlarge the possibilities of civilization. But there is no indication that the locus of civilization will shift to the proletariat. The grandchildren he was thinking about were very much the grandchildren of the middle class, the class which had sacrificed its civilizing potential to compound interest.

What the above discussion has emphasized is the narrow ethical basis of Keynes's economic work. Keynes did good, but not because he was a do-gooder like Marshall or Pigou. He did not seek to build the New Jerusalems through economics and even less through politics, to which we now turn.

Politics: ends and means

The nearest Keynes got to expounding a theory of politics was in an undergraduate essay on Edmund Burke, which he successfully submitted for the University Members' Prize for an English essay in the summer of 1904.[16] Keynes showed himself to be largely sympathetic to the views of the founder of British Conservatism. There are at least two reasons for taking this youthful production seriously. First, Keynes evidently took a great deal of trouble with it. It came to 99 pages of manuscript, based on over 200 pages of notes. More important, his assessment of Burke is generally consistent with his general philosophy and later practice. He approved of Burke's separation of ethics and politics, also his preference for present over future goods. He criticized him for excessive timidity as a reformer, and for undervaluing the claims of truth and, in general, for carrying reasonable propositions too far. The date of Keynes's essay is important. He was in the first flush of excitement with G.E. Moore and the germs of his later probability theory were already present in a paper he read to the Cambridge Apostles earlier in the year.[17]

Burke's 'unparalleled political wisdom', according to Keynes, lay in the fact that he was the first thinker consistently to base a theory of politics on utilitarianism rather than on abstract rights, though it was a utilitarianism 'modified' by the principle of equity – governments should avoid artificial discrimination against individuals or classes. He quotes him approvingly: 'The question with me is, not whether you have a right to render your people miserable, but whether it is not in your interest to make them happy.' Keynes adds: 'This is not a very recondite doctrine, but to Burke must be given the credit of first clearly and insistently enunciating it' (*Burke*, pp. 42–3). Today this interpretation of Burke would be considered mistaken. Modern commentators say that Burke believed in natural law, the organic state and the religious foundations of politics. But it is what Keynes believed Burke to believe that is important for our purposes:

> He did not much believe [Keynes writes] in political ends good intrinsically and in isolation. The happiness of the people was his goal, and the science of government worthless except insofar as it guided him to that end. Whatever the doctrines of utilitarianism may be worth abstractedly [*sic*] . . . they do not form an unsatisfactory basis to a political theory. The tastes and the emotions, good feeling and right judgment, the government cannot directly do much to foster and develop on any scheme or theory. Physical calm, material comfort, intellectual freedom are amongst the great and essential means to these good things; but they are the means to happiness also, and the government that sets the happiness of the governed before it will serve a good purpose, whatever the ethical theory from which it draws its inspiration . . . To clear away the divine right of Kings and the French rights of man . . . [was] of the utmost importance for all clear and rational thinking on questions of government. (*ibid.*, pp. 93–4)

The key point here is Keynes's endorsement of utilitarianism as a political, though not an ethical, doctrine. Indeed he specifically denied that Burke was an *ethical* utilitarian like Bentham (*ibid.*, p. 7), i.e. that he identified happiness with goodness. An important conclusion follows. If the government's business is want satisfaction, it follows that promotion of economic prosperity is a proper concern of statesmanship. Moreover, a government which promotes welfare in this sense will run little risk of diminishing goodness for, up to a point, the requirements of both coincide.

Keynes also endorses another key principle of Burke's: that the happiness or utility which governments should aim to maximize is *short run* not *long run*. The following portmanteau quotation gives the gist of Keynes's argument:

> Burke ever held, and held rightly, that it can seldom be right ... to sacrifice a present benefit for a doubtful advantage in the future ... It is not wise to look too far ahead; our powers of prediction are slight, our command over remote results infinitesimal. It is therefore the happiness of our own contemporaries that is our main concern; we should be very chary of sacrificing large numbers of people for the sake of a contingent end, however advantageous that end may appear ... We can never know enough to make the chance worth taking ... There is this further consideration that is often in need of emphasis: it is not sufficient that the state of affairs which we seek to promote should be better than the state of affairs which preceded it; it must be sufficiently better to make up for the evils of the transition. (*ibid.*, pp. 16–17, 95)

Keynes's handling of Burke's views on property and democracy in the light of such 'maxims' of statesmanship is worth particular notice. Burke defended existing property rights on the double grounds that redistribution of wealth would make no real difference to the poor, since the poor greatly outnumbered the rich, while at the same time it would 'considerably reduce in numbers those who could enjoy the undoubted benefits of wealth and who could confer on the state the advantages which the presence of wealthy citizens always brings'. Keynes felt this argument 'undoubtedly carries very great weight; in certain conceivable types of communities it is overwhelming; and it must always be one of the most powerful rejoinders to any scheme which has equalisation as its ultimate aim'. But its validity is 'very much less' if directed against (1) 'any attempt to influence the channels in which wealth flows', and (2) the relief of starvation or acute poverty. Burke's method was not valid, Keynes wrote, against estate duties 'whose object is to mulct great masses of accumulation', nor against the expropriation of feudal estates during the French Revolution (*ibid.*, pp. 28–9). The argument is that where there is great degradation, and subsequent discontent, the balance of expediency shifts towards redistribution: Burke is often so concerned to defend the 'outworks' that he does not see that this might endanger the 'central system' itself (*ibid.*, p. 49).

Keynes never believed that the maintenance of the 'central system' of

Britain in his day required large-scale confiscation of property. In *The Economic Consequences of the Peace* he wrote of prewar Britain that 'The greater part of the population, it is true, worked hard and lived at a low standard of comfort, yet were, to all appearances, reasonably contented with this lot. But escape was possible, for any man of capacity or character at all exceeding the average, into the middle and upper classes' (*CW*, II, p. 6). At the same time, he insisted that governments must have discretion to revise contracts between the living and the dead since 'the powers of uninterrupted usury are too great'. It was the 'absolutists of contract', he wrote in his *Tract on Monetary Reform* (1923), 'who are the parents of Revolution' – a good Burkean attitude, though one that Burke sometimes ignored (*CW*, IV, pp. 56–7).

The issue of democracy, Keynes insisted, involved two separate questions. Has the mass of people a right to direct self-government? Is it expedient and conducive to good government that there should be more self-government? To both questions, Burke returned an 'uncompromising negative'. On the first, Keynes stood solidly with Burke. Government is simply a 'contrivance of human wisdom' to 'supply certain ... wants; and that is the end of the matter'. People, that is, are entitled to good government, not self-government. The more difficult question is whether self-government is a necessary means to good government, and here Keynes is more open than Burke. He agree with him that 'the people' are incompetent to govern themselves. and that Parliament must always be prepared to resist popular prejudice in the name of equity between individuals and classes. But he criticizes Burke's 'dream of a representative class' which underpinned his defence of rotten boroughs and restricted franchise, on the ground that no one class can adequately represent the feelings or interests of the whole. Burke also underestimated the educative value of self-government.

Nevertheless, Keynes doubted whether any 'rational or unprejudiced body of men' would have ever dared to make the experiment in universal suffrage had they not been 'under the influence of a fallacious notion concerning natural political rights'. But whatever the ultimate fate of this experiment, so far democracy had not disgraced itself. This was because its 'full force had not yet come into operation'. First, 'whatever be the numerical representation of wealth, its power will always be out of all proportion'. Secondly, 'the defective organisation of the newly enfranchised classes has prevented any revolutionary alteration in the pre-existing balance of power' (*Burke*, pp. 60–9).

Running through Keynes's commentary is a utilitarian attitude to rights. If people are made discontented by the absence of 'rights', then rights should be conceded – but as a means to good government. It was the typical Whig attitude to reform.

Keynes's criticisms on Burke issued on three main points: 'his preference for peace over truth, his extreme timidity in introducing present evil for the sake of future benefits, and his disbelief in men's acting rightly, except on the rarest occasions, because they have judged that it is right to act.' As Keynes notes, these contentions are all related to Burke's central epistemological position, that we can never be certain enough of the truth to choose rationally between different courses of action. This being so, it is better to fall back on tradition (*ibid.*, pp. 11–12). In other words, Burke denied the value of the pursuit of truth on the ground that it would disturb the peace of the Commonwealth (a present good) without giving any assurance of a greater benefit in the future.

This was a conclusion which Keynes wanted to resist. As he put it: 'It is usually admitted that, whatever the immediate consequences of a new truth may be, there is a high probability that truth will in the long run lead to better results than falsehood.' He conceded, however, that 'the modern prejudice in favour of truth [may be] founded on somewhat insufficient bases' (*ibid.*, p. 14). He had nothing more to add to this in his essay on Burke. But he had already started to develop a theory of probability explicitly designed to improve the epistemological foundations of rational choice; it is to this that we now turn.

The influence of Keynes's theory of probability on his economics is at last starting to be discussed;[18] but there has been no attempt to relate it to his theory of politics. The problem with which Keynes grappled is inherent in any consequentialist theory. If the rightness of actions is to be judged by their effects, action must be informed by a knowledge of probable consequences. This immediately raises the question of our power to predict future events. Statistical or empirical probability is part of our predictive system. It tells us that an event A will occur in a certain ratio to event B. The basis for such predictions lies in the high degree of regularity exhibited by certain natural and artificial arrangements. The existence of statistical probability is what makes possible insurance against risk. But the theory is much less relevant when applied to most *social* arrangements where, as Keynes remarked, our power of predicting all but the most immediate consequence of our actions rapidly dwindles to zero either because there are no statistical probabilities or because we lack knowledge of them. The conclusion Moore drew from this is that we ought to obey the law and follow the 'rules' of correct behaviour, since the adverse consequences of disregarding them, from the individual point of view, are likely to be high, while the benefits are indeterminate. Moore's consequentialism led him towards conservative morality, Burke's towards conservative politics.

Keynes wanted to escape from a train of argument which put an excessive premium on tradition. The only way he saw doing so was to disconnect the notion of probability from that of prediction. He did this by developing his *logical* theory of probability. There could be probabilities, Keynes argued, without frequencies, or knowledge of frequencies. The probable is not what is likely to happen, but what it is rational to believe will happen given our information. It has to do with the bearing of evidence on conclusions; we can say that our actions are probably right independently of whether our expectations are realized or disappointed. Probability is thus not a prediction ('This will happen more or less often if that happens'), but a logical judgement about the relationship between the premiss (evidence) and conclusion of an argument ('It is reasonable to believe *that* conclusion to *this* extent'). This formulation opened up a wide field to *rational* discretionary action which both Moore and Burke seemed to have closed off. To make an estimate of a probability was simply to think rationally about consequences when there were no frequencies. Rational judgement was not so easily defeated as Moore (or, for that matter, Burke) believed.

The policy conclusion which Keynes attributed to Burke – that 'it is the happiness of our own contemporaries which should concern us' – is not thereby upset, since Keynes's probabilities are based on circumstances which change by the very fact of us acting on them. But Keynes believed that he had developed a more rational theory of means, one that allowed greater scope for reason, judgement and discretion than Burke was willing to concede. If Burke was sceptical about reform, Keynes was sceptical about tradition. He took the distinctively Enlightenment position that tradition was a repository of falsehood, which could be dissipated by allowing reason to play on facts. His theory of probability was thus designed to strengthen the claims of reason against those of tradition.[19] For these reasons, Keynes cannot be classified as a Burkean Conservative, much as he sympathized with Burke's general position. His 'prejudice' in favour of truth was too great. This was to dominate the work of his maturity.

The reconstruction of liberalism

Keynes was a lifelong liberal (with both a small and large 'l'). By the interwar years the tasks of liberal statemanship had emerged with painful clarity: to stave off revolution from left and right and to make the economic system (or 'capitalism') work more efficiently and humanely. The two tasks were connected, the second being a means to the first, for by the 1930s both communism and fascism were staking their claim to power on liberal capitalism's inability to provide full employment. This premiss Keynes set out to refute.

'The authoritarian state systems of to-day', he wrote in the *General Theory*,

> Seem to solve the problem of unemployment at the expense of efficiency and freedom. It is certain that the world will not much longer tolerate the unemployment which ... is associated – and, in my opinion, inevitably associated – with present day capitalistic individualism. But it may be possible by a right analysis of the problem to cure the disease whilst preserving efficiency and freedom. (*CW*, VII, p. 381)

Taking a broad historical view, the Keynesian revolution in economics was a key part of what emerged as the dominant Western intellectual response to the rise of the totalitarians and, more generally, to the 'rise of the masses'. Keynes's reconstruction of economics, Schumpeter's reformulation of democratic theory, Mannheim's programme for the social sciences and Popper's work on the logic of scientific discovery can all be seen as part of the intellectual re-equipment of liberalism to meet the threats to it. Keynes's achievement is the more impressive as being, uniquely, that of a non-emigré – someone who had not suffered personally from the breakdown of the liberal order.

This intellectual movement may be called the second liberal revival. Unlike the 'new' liberalism of the turn of the century, it made no serious attempt to reshape the philosophical foundations of liberalism. 'New' liberals like Leonard Hobhouse were concerned chiefly with the justifications of existing property relations, from the point of view of efficiency and equity, and as affecting the moral growth of the individual. By contrast, the second wave of liberal thinkers took the existing property relationships as given: what they did was to superimpose a managerial philosophy on the theory and practice of 'classic' liberalism. This reflects, on the one hand, a much greater institutional timidity, in face of the violent rearrangement of property relations which had taken place in Russia and, on the other, a faith that existing institutions could be made to work, provided that government intervened in certain key areas and that the social sciences could provide an ideologically neutral logic of intervention – a faith which may have been born of desperation. A philosophy of *ad hoc* intervention based on disinterested thought was thus twentieth-century liberalism's answer to the faith of early-nineteenth-century liberals that institutional reform could secure the conditions of minimalist government – a belief, or course, which Marx also shared. It reflects the extent to which utilitarianism had lost its radical cutting edge.[20]

In Keynes's updated version of liberalism the intellectual has a key part to play in stabilizing society – as social scientist and as manager. Keynes believed that the economic problem of his day was an intellectual and not a structural or institutional problem: the slump was the result of a 'frightful muddle' (*CW*, IX, p. xviii) – whose cure lay, first, in the realm of thought, and secondly, in that of management.

Keynes has often been criticized for exaggerating the importance of ideas, relative to power, especially class power. According to the Marxist, John Strachey, his *Essays on Persuasion* were so 'uniformly unpersuasive' because he ignored the fact that unemployment was a necessary feature of capitalism.[21] Keynes compounded his political naïveté, from this point of view, by writing in the *General Theory*: 'But soon or late, is its ideas, not vested interests, which are dangerous for good or evil' (*CW*, VII, p. 381).

It is a facile misinterpretation of Keynes's position to say that he believed that ideas triumph by a kind of natural magic. Successful ideas succeed because they have more political utility than the alternatives on offer; smaller interests yield to larger interests, or survive only if they can plausibly attach themselves to coalitions of interests. Here public opinion, as filtered through the electoral process, is ultimately decisive in a democracy. Far from believing in the unsupported power of ideas, Keynes wrote in 1922: 'Even if economists and technicians knew the secret remedy, they could not apply it until they had persuaded the politicians; and the politicians, who have ears but no eyes, will not attend to the persuasion until it reverberates back to them as an echo from the great public.'[22] Politicians, being in the business of want satisfaction, have to attend to public opinion sooner or later, if they are to win or retain power; and public opinion will not stand indefinitely for policies which they perceive as bringing about impoverishment. Having said this, it is also true that Keynes was the last person to deny the power of persuasive utterance. He was himself a master of it, and it was through journalism that the educated public, at any rate, became familiar with his general approach to curing the slump.

With intellectuals (and in this case economists) the process of acceptance of new ideas is admittedly more complicated. Economists too have political purposes, and are open to non-rational 'persuasion'. But genuine intellectual conversion also has to take place. Theories must possess formal properties of logical consistency which commend them to specialists. However, it would be wrong to say that Keynes attached excessive importance to this factor. What he tended to require of fellow economists was the power of 'seeing the world' as he saw it; minds must meet intuitively before logical discussion could become fruitful. But such 'meeting of minds' was never for him simply or largely a matter of psychological affinity. His faith was that all rational (and competent) persons confronted with the same evidence will attach the same values to various possible conclusions to be drawn from it.

For Keynes, therefore, the success or failure, as well as the truth or falsity, of ideas was always connected to the facts. Those ideas win which have a perceived tendency to maximize contentment; for intellectuals the probable rightness of a theory is a matter of logical intuition applied to the evidence. These are straightforward deductions from his political utilitarianism and from his theory of probability. It is significant that Marxists, who started in the 1930s by saying that Keynes's ideas could not possibly be implemented under capitalism, ended up by explaining that they 'fitted the needs' of capitalism. Keynes could not, I think, have asked for more.

Keynes has also been criticized for his belief in the possibility of disinterested economic argument. Seymour Harris accused him of failing to 'reconcile his dislike and distrust of politicians with his determination to thrust upon government serious additional responsibilities'.[23] Altern-atively, he has been attacked for believing that economic management could be 'insulated' from political pressures.

In considering such criticisms it is important to be clear about what Keynes wanted his 'managers' to do. Keynes's (not Keynesian) policies for securing a high, continuous, non-inflationary level of output and employment can be divided into two main parts: 'a somewhat comprehensive socialisation of investment' (*ibid.*, p. 378), and monetary fine-tuning.[24] Fiscal fine-tuning was not part of his design; budget deficits were to be resorted to only to pull an economy out of a slump. The postwar reliance on managing the economy through budgetary policy, with monetary policy either ignored or reduced to a subsidiary role, was not part of Keynes's original intention. The short answer to Seymour Harris, therefore, is that Keynes did not wish to thrust large extra responsibilities on politicians as such. He can still be held to be politically naïve in supposing that they could be prevented from using the potential instruments for manipulating demand to their own political advantage.

In trying to understand how Keynes visualized the political economy of the future a key problem of interpretation is posed by the phrase 'a somewhat comprehensive socialisation of investment'. It is clear enough that Keynes means that *the state* will become responsible for a major part of total investment. Thus he writes in the *General Theory* 'I expect to see the State, which is in a position to calculate the marginal efficiency of capital-goods on long views and on the basis of the general social advantage, taking an ever greater responsibility for directly organising investments' (*ibid.*, p. 164). The problem here is to determine what Keynes means by 'the State'. It is highly improbable that Keynes wants to identify the state with the government of the day since he can hardly have supposed that politicians elected to govern on the basis of renewable popular consent would be best placed to take 'long views'. At the very least, we must supposed Keynes to mean the permanent officials; but by the state he seems to mean something wider still. Take, for example, the following letter he wrote to *The Times* on 25 March 1925 (italics added):

> So far from wishing to diminish the authority of the Bank of England I regard that great institution as a heaven-sent gift, ideally suited to be the instrument of the reforms I advocate. We have here a semi-independent corporation *within the state*, with immense prestige and historical tradition, not in fact working for private profit, with no interest whatever except the public good, yet detached from the wayward influence of politics ... The Bank of England is a type of that *socialism* of the future which is in accord with the British instincts of government, and which – perhaps one may hope – our Commonwealth is evolving within its womb. The Universities are another example of the semi-independent institutions divested of private interest which I have in mind. *The state* is generally sterile and creates little. New forms and modes spring from the fruitful minds of individuals. But when a corporation, devised by private resource, has reached a certain age and a certain size, it *socialises* itself, or falls into decay. But none perhaps, except the Bank of England – and (should I add?) *The Times* newspaper – has yet completed the process. I differ from the immediate policy of the Bank of England; but it is on the greatness and prestige of this institution ... that I rest my hopes for the future. (*CW*, XIX, p. 347)

The clarity of language in this letter is not ideal, but the gist of what Keynes is saying is both understandable and interesting. He means by the state that sector of the polity not working for private self-interest, but for the public good. This cuts across the division between the public and private sectors; the state includes bodies which are legally private, but which in the course of their evolution have come to acquire a sense of public purpose. In so far as politicians were motivated by public purposes, they were part of the state; in so far as they pursued their own interests through politics, they were part of the non-state. Governments were presumably a mixture of both.

All this may sound very strange, but Keynes's language has its roots in the past, when the sovereign, or prince, was both ruler and private landlord, with public and private interests inextricably intertwined. The difficulty Keynes found in expressing his thoughts in clear language also testifies to the lack in Britain of any adequate modern theory of the state. In constitutional law the State in Britain is the Crown-in-Parliament and its servants; but in mediaeval times sovereignty was fragmented through the system of vassalage by which grants of land were invested with juridical and political powers. In the capitalist era property escaped from vassalage to become fully 'privatized'; with its public functions taken over by the Crown-in-Parliament. In effect, Keynes suggested that this tendency was now reversing itself. The state was no longer rigidly separated from private property and private enterprise, rather the two were forging or re-forging a corporate relationship. 'Time and the Joint Stock Company and Civil Service have silently brought the salaried class into power', Keynes wrote in 1934.[25]

It was through the forging of a new relationship between the civil service and the joint-stock companies that Keynes expected the 'socialisation of investment' to come about. He never supposed that the Prince, in his modern guise of congeries of competing politicians, had divested himself of all private interest. That is why he supported Beveridge's proposal for an Economic General Staff: 'We shall never enjoy prosperity again', he wrote, 'if we continue indefinitely without some deliberate machinery for mitigating the consequences of selecting our governors on account of their gifts of oratory and their power of detecting in good time which way the mind of uninstructed opinion is blowing'.[26] Similarly, Keynes argued before the Macmillan Committee that the principles of central banking should and could be 'utterly removed from popular controversy and ... regarded as a kind of beneficient technique of scientific control such as electricity or other branches of science are' – which prompted one of his fellow commissioners to remark 'You are a very sanguine man' (*CW*, XX, p. 263).

On the other side, Keynes saw the public service motive growing at the industrial level through the emergence of the 'semi-autonomous' corporation: in 1927 he estimated that two-thirds of the capital of large-scale undertakings could not be classed as private any more.[27] The central thread of his argument has to do with the tendency of large-scale industry to 'socialise' itself. By this he meant the divorce of management from ownership, and the transformation of the money-making into the 'public service' motive. He wrote of 'the trend of the Joint Stock Institutions, when they have reached a certain age and size, to approximate to the status of the public corporations rather than that of individualistic private enterprise'.[28] Keynes welcomed these developments as ridding capitalism of its 'casino' features, while avoiding the dead hand of bureaucratic governmental controls. Interestingly, while left-wing commentators saw in this concentration of private capital a powerful argument for public ownership, Keynes believed it made it unnecessary since the 'managers' were no longer short-term profit maximizers. The same argument was later to be used by Anthony Crosland.[29] If large-scale industry was already 'socialised', public ownership was superfluous.

The final assumption which underlay Keynes's vision of the political economy of the future was that all these different parts of the state would be controlled by much the same kind of people. The 'semi-autonomous' corporations would be run neither by Cabinet ministers nor by town councils, but by boards chosen for business ability, adequately remunerated and free from bureaucratic interference. 'I do not see', he wrote, 'why we should not build up in this country a great public service running the business side of public concerns recruited from the whole population with the same ability and the same great tradition as our administrative Civil Service' (*CW*, XIX, p. 697). Keynes undoubtedly saw the 'socialisation' of large parts of the economy, in the form of legally private, but public-spirited, corporations, run by university high-fliers and generating their own investment funds as providing the essential guarantee of a stable high level of investment since it was this development which would mitigate the large-scale *fluctuations* of investment associated with the psychology of the stock market. Monetary fine-tuning and residual fiscal policy would be in the hands of different members of the same élite at the Bank of England and the Treasury. Thus he saw science, expertise, and public spirit gradually ousting politics and self-interest as governors of a system which remained largely unchanged in its legal, institutional forms.

Keynes's intellectual and managerial élitism left little room for what we would now call 'participatory democracy'. In a revealing passage from a speech to the Liberal Summer School of 1925 (left out in the printed version published in his *Essays in Persuasion*) he stated his 'fundamental' objection to the Labour Party:

> I believe that the right solution [to the economic question] will involve intellectual and scientific elements which must be above the heads of the vast mass of more or less illiterate voters. Now, in a democracy, every party alike has to depend on this mass of ill-understanding voters ... Nevertheless there are differences between the several parties in the degree to which the party machine is democratised in its details. In this respect the Conservative Party is in much the best position. The inner ring of the party can almost dictate the details and technique of policy. Traditionally the management of the Liberal Party was also sufficiently autocratic. Recently there have been ill-advised movements in the direction of democratising the party programme ... The Labour Party, on the other hand, is in a far weaker position. I do not believe that the intellectual elements in the party will ever exercise adequate control; too much will always be decided by those who do not know *at all* what they are talking about. (*CW*, IX, pp. 295–6)

Keynes and socialism

There is little in Keynes's ethical or political beliefs which is distinctively socialist and much that is anti-socialist. It is not difficult to imagine him supporting the 'enlightened' Conservatism of Macmillan and Butler in the 1950s: indeed, he once remarked that it was the task of the Liberal Party to provide the Labour Party with ideas and the Conservatives with Cabinets.

But we must remember that for a Liberal of Keynes's generation, the Conservative Party was the historic enemy, and remained so throughout the interwar years, despite the 'decency' of Stanley Baldwin. It was the party of stupidity and prejudice, standing pat on the old ways, and he habitually wrote about it in these terms, e.g. it 'ought to be concerning itself with evolving a version of individualistic capitalism adapted to the progressive change of circumstances. The difficulty is that the capitalist leaders in the City and in Parliament are incapable of distinguishing novel measures for safeguarding capitalism from what they call Bolshevism' (*CW*, IX, p. 299). The other problem with the Conservative was that they were the guardians of the reactionary codes of morals against which Keynes was in revolt: he could not more look to them to support 'scientific' birth control than 'scientific' monetary control, though there is nothing specifically 'socialist' about these things.

With the historical Liberal Party in decline, Keynes came to see the Labour Party as the most plausible vehicle of the reforms he wanted. In most of his political writings he is engaged in a dialogue with the Labour Movement. This involved him in very ambiguous use of language as he tried, at one and the same time, to distinguish his position from that of socialism and also to stress the compatibility between Liberal and Socialist aspirations.

Keynes had three fundamental objections to socialism as he understood it. First, he challenged the doctrine that socialism was the only remedy for the ills of *laissez-faire*. That is, he objected to it as a mechanism for securing economic reform on the grounds that its doctrines were ideological, obsolete, irrelevant and inimical to wealth creation and likely to involve gross interferences with individual freedom. State socialism, he wrote in 1926, 'misses the significance of what is actually happening ... There is, for instance, no so-called important political question so really unimportant, so irrelevant to the reorganisation of economic life in Britain as the nationalisation of the railways' (*ibid.*, p. 290).

Secondly, Keynes objected to socialism's stress on the class basis of politics and thought: 'I can be influenced by what seems to me to be justice and good sense; but the class war will find me on the side of the educated bourgeoisie' (*ibid.*, p. 297). Against the class analysis of socialists he always emphasized the importance of individual choice and character; the role of intelligence (Keynes only really recognized one class war, that between the clever and the stupid); the autonomy of ideas; and the potential harmony of interests between capitalists and workers. These were the classic liberal positions.

Finally, Keynes did not believe in equality as an ethical or political goal. He believed in equality of opportunity, but thought that this state of affairs already largely existed in the England of his day (see above, p. 12). As for social justice, although Elizabeth Johnson goes too far when she writes that it 'existed [for Keynes] only in there not being enough jobs to go round',[30] his redistributionary aims, as we have seen, were largely confined to limiting the incomes from the lending of money.

Keynes's hostility to Marx and Marxism is too well-known to require extensive quotation: 'Marxist Socialism', he declared in his Sidney Ball lecture of 1924, 'must always remain a portent to the historians of thought – how a doctrine so illogical and so dull can have exercised so powerful and enduring an influence over the minds of men and, through them, the events of history' (*ibid*, p. 289). He believed that his *General Theory* would 'knock away' the intellectual foundations of Marxism.[31] Yet the similarities between Marx and Keynes are worth exploring: their joint belief that capitalism was a stage in history that would end when capital was plentiful, their moral and aesthetic distaste for the 'money-motive' and the resemblance of their Utopias.

Despite his contempt for socialism as a system of ideas, Keynes was always careful to endorse a certain range of socialist ideals. The atheist who thought Christianity a lot of 'hocus-pocus' sympathized in 1925 with the 'religious' appeal of communism, so superior to the 'money-making' purposes which was all that Western capitalism had to offer.[32] The author of the *General Theory* could declare in 1939 that 'there is no one in politics today worth sixpence outside the ranks of liberals except the post-war generation of intellectual Communists under thirty five' (*CW*, XXI, pp. 494–5). The mandarin civil servant had little difficulty in subscribing to the Fabian ideal of public service. The well-endowed Cambridge aesthete looked forward to the abolition of the 'money motive' (Keynes never used the phrase 'profit motive') as the basis of human activity.

Yet the main characteristic of the political writings that Keynes addressed to Socialists is the separation between the present and the future. Managed capitalism ('what is economically sound') is for now; what Keynes calls 'socialism' ('what is economically unsound') is for later – once the economic problem has been solved. The only real bridge he offers is the growth of the 'public service' motive in capitalism's womb – which means that actual public ownership is not needed (*CW*, XXI, pp. 33–48). By these means, Keynes set out to woo – and tame – the left.

The Keynesian logic of intervention

The Keynesian Revolution in economic policy was a particular manifestation of the general trend towards collectivism which distinguished the first half of this century from the first half of the nineteenth century. Its success derives from the fact that it offered a logic of collective action within the framework of liberal democracy. It did not raise in acute form issues which liberal democracy cannot easily handle – distributional questions, questions of property rights and questions about the relationship between liberty and legal coercion. The Keynesian logic of intervention offered the benefits of collectivism without any of its costs.

Collectivism is the belief that individual and/or social well-being cannot be achieved by individuals pursuing their own interests within the law, but must be willed and brought about by the action of collective bodies, embodying the 'common will' of their members. The dominant forces behind collectivist surge in our century are generally taken to be: the quest for economic security by individuals, firms, trade unions and states; the quest for social and/or national efficiency; efforts to control the abuse of private power; and the quest for justice between classes. Twentieth-century collectivism has ranged all the way from centrally planned and owned and politically controlled economies to milder forms of planning and selective public provision of goods and services which have been adovocated not only as good in themselves, but as inoculations against the more virulent forms of the disease.

Keynes was certainly a collectivist in the latter sense, but of a very precise kind. 'I come next', he wrote in 1924,

> to a criterion of the *Agenda* which is particularly relevant to what is urgent and desirable to do in the near future. We must aim at separating those services which are *technically social* from those which are *technically individual*. The most important *Agenda* of the State relate not to those activities which private individuals are already fulfilling, but to those functions which fall outside the sphere of the individual, to those decisions which are made by *no one* if the State does not make them. The important thing for government is not to do things which individuals are doing already, and to do them a little better or a little worse; but to do those things which at present are not done at all.

Examples of the agenda of government were: (1) control of the business cycle by the central bank; (2) control of the amount of savings and their flow as between domestic and foreign uses; and (3) population policy, including attention to 'quality' as well as to mere numbers (*CW*, IX, pp. 291–2).

The main charge against *laissez-faire* capitalism was not that private self-interest allocated resources inefficiently or unjustly as between different uses – Keynes specifically denies that it does (*CW*, VII, pp. 378–9) – but that it failed to ensure full use of the potential resources. This suggested a quite different logic of intervention from that of the reigning socialist and national socialist models, directed as they were to 'planning' for efficiency or national power, or the achievement of distributional justice.

Pre-Keynesian economics had no theory capable of explaining persisting mass unemployment. The fact of such unemployment was attributed to contractual, institutional or legislative obstacles to the formation of market-clearing prices for labour. The only advice economists had to offer governments was to remove these obstacles, so that the instutitional setting would once more be 'appropriate' for the achievement of full employment. Governments naturally shrank from dismantling most of the social and trade union legislation they had passed in the previous fifty years.

Keynes's earliest analysis of the unemployment problem – in terms of fluctuations in the quantity of money – had the great political merit of by-passing this set of problems. Given the institutional setting, and particularly the wages policies of employers and unions, the quantity of employment depended (within limits) on the quantity of money supplied by the central bank. If the operations of the gold standard prevented the central bank from supplying the appropriate quantity of money, then it should be jettisoned in favour of the 'labour standard', which would be maintained by varying the exchange rate.

Keynes clearly thought it was good economics to tackle unemployment on the least-cost principle. 'When we have got unemployment down to 4 or 5 per cent', he declared in 1924, 'then there are other causes which also have to be tackled by other methods, but, if you have financial factor responsible for the difference (say) between 5 and 12 per cent, then ... it is a matter well worth bending our energies to get rid of' (*CW*, XIX, p. 184). Behind every monetary radical, as Galbraith has acutely remarked, lurks a social conservative. Behind Keynes's concentration on the monetary factor as a cause of unemployment lay a great deal of institutional timidity; he often expressed the view that an old, inflexible economy like England's could not take the classical medicine without the risk of grave social disorder.

Although in Keynes's mature theory, the quantity of employment was made to depend (again within limits) on the level of demand (particularly investment demand) rather than on the quantity of money, prevention and cure remained, at least for shallow fluctuations of market demand, the task of monetary policy. Collectivism is confined to two points: provision by the central bank of an appropriate quantity of money, and by the 'state' of an appropriate level of investment. Nothing else is to change. In the mature Keynes, the picture of a sluggishly self-healing economy has given way to one in which an economy which experiences a decline in investment demand subsides, if left to itself, into a state of permanent illness. Yet Keynes remained confident that a change in ideas superimposed on a natural evolution towards corporatism could cure the disease without any need for institutional change.

Conclusion

Both Keynes's economic research programme and the way he 'modelled' the unemployment problem can be said to have been influenced by his ethical and political values in two ways – one negative and the other positive. On the negative side it was important that he did not come to economics with a prior commitment to achieving social justice through economic reform. As we have pointed out, his ethical commitments were personal, and were not importantly related to economics or politics. That is to say, his commitment to the civilized ideal did not imply any particular political or economic order. This meant that he had no initial bias towards seeing the unemployment problem as an effect of an unjust social order, as was general among thinkers on the left. A comparison with J.A. Hobson, whom Keynes came to admire, is illuminating at this point. The weakness in Hobson's analysis, according to Keynes, was that he lacked an 'independent theory of the rate of interest', leading him to place too much emphasis on underconsumption, to be cured by redistributing wealth and income from the rich to the poor (*CW*, VII, p. 3). For Hobson, economic analysis had to be adapted to ethical commitment. The one important case with Keynes where ethical and economic values come into (somewhat tortured) relationship concerns the role of the rentier.

On the positive side is Keynes's political utilitarianism, as influenced by Burke and also by his own theory of probability. This led him to emphasize the connection between economic prosperity and political contentment/social order. But at the same time, it was the 'happiness of our contemporaries' that he chiefly sought. He was not prepared to risk too much of the present for the sake of a better future since 'our powers of prediction are too slight'. This institutional timidity was reinforced by the rise of communism and fascism. However, Keynes's theory of probability gave him a justification for breaking with Moore's moral and Burke's political conservatism since it purported to show how individuals and governments could within a short time range act rightly for the right (rational) reasons. From this followed his preference for discretion over rules; and his faith in intelligence and the rule of experts. He felt that industrial and political evolution was on the side of this development by making markets in capital and politics less important. The economy would be stabilized by being 'socialised', which meant that it did not have to be nationalized.

It remains to consider what is left of Keynes's political legacy today. Is it depleted beyond replenishment? Or does it still have the power to invigorate our thinking? Keynes raises in a variety of ways the central political question of our time, and perhaps all times: what we think a 'central authority' can or should do to bring about a more desirable state of affairs. Three issues deserve particular attention.

The first concerns the relationship between goodness and utility and more generally between ethics and politics. The classical tradition, which runs deep, is that politics is a means to, and part of, the 'good society'. Political utilitarianism broke finally with this by seeing government as a mere contrivance to satisfy certain wants. But much political practice, and the political vocation itself, rests on the older assumption. People may go into politics because they are ambitious, or because they feel that government should be as competent as possible; but they normally feel the need to justify their choice by saying that they aim to 'do good'. Keynes's political thought is for the cool hour, when politicians ask themselves what they really think they are doing, rather than for the platform where they trumpet their faiths.

The second issue concerns the relationship between élites and masses. Keynes's thinking challenges the ideal of a participatory democracy – whether in the form of consumer sovereignty which the right offers or in the form of popular decision-making advocated by the left. Keynes clearly saw a conflict between direct government and good government; and while he would not have denied the educative value of popular democracy, he would not have taken too many risks for what would be at best a long-run benefit. It may be we are in a position to go further than Keynes by taking into account different levels of decision-making; direct democracy may be appropriate in some places and not in others. A related question is this: if Keynes was wrong in thinking that certain kinds of high-level decision-making could be insulated from vested interest or vote-catching, how does this affect our judgement about the proper sphere of public action? Is the Prince inevitably and irretrievably tainted by corruption? Or is he our main safeguard against it?

Thirdly, there is the relationship between management and reform. Keynes's approach, and that of his generation of liberals, was heavily infected by institutional timidity. This gave a 'demand-side' bias to his economics, which became even more pronounced in the postwar Keynesian regime. Have we now reached the end of this road? Keynes saw institutional reform as fraught with danger for social stability. Moreoever, he saw institutions evolving in a manner helpful to his macroeconomic purposes. But to what extent is institutional reform, in Britain today and in the near future, a necessary condition of fuller employment? To put it concretely: are the wage-determining and political institutions such that any Keynesian policy is bound to generate, at an early date, unacceptable levels of inflation? It may be that reform has become a less risky option than reliance on unaided management, though management will still be needed. Keynesian liberalism, in other words, may need some of the cutting edge of an earlier, less embattled, liberalism, if good government is to be preserved.

Notes and references

1. I would like to thank the following for comments on an earlier version of this paper: Mrs Jean Floud, Professor Partha Dasgupta, Dr Larry Siedentop, the Political Theory Group at the University of Warwick and the SDP Philosophy Group.
2. J.M. Keynes 'Liberalism and labour', *Nation*, 9 February 1926; in *The Collected Writings of John Maynard Keynes* (hereafter *CW*), Vol. IX, p. 309. All references to Keynes's printed works will be in the *CW* edition, preceded by place and date of original appearance.
3. Keynes, 'Democracy and efficiency', *New Statesman*, 28 January 1939; in *CW*, XXI, p. 500.
4. Keynes does talk from time to time about 'arbitrary and inequitable' distribution (see esp. the *General Theory*, 1973 edn, p. 372); but he characteristically uses phrases like this when discussing the effects of an unstable value of money (e.g. *CW*, XIX, p. 160). There is nothing I have found in his work to suggest that he held the long-run distribution of wealth and income ground out by capitalist society to be unjust. Keynes's use of social and political language always needs to be subjected to the closest textual, and contextual, scrutiny.
5. Notably in 'The dilemma of modern socialism', *Political Quarterly*, April–June 1932; in *CW*, XXI, pp. 33–48.
6. Elizabeth Durbin, *New Jerusalems* (London: Routledge and Kegan Paul 1985), p. 11.
7. Bertrand Russell, *Autobiography* (London: Allen and Unwin 1967), Vol. I, p. 71.
8. Alastair Macintyre, *After Virtue* (Notre Dame: University of Notre Dame Press 1981), pp. 23–9.
9. G.E. Moore, *Principia Ethica* (Cambridge: CUP 1903), pp. 188–9.
10. Keynes, 'My early beliefs', paper read to the Memoir Club, 9 September 1938; in *CW*, X, p. 445.
11. Clive Bell, *Civilisation*, (London: Chatto and Windus 1928), p. 43.
12. *Ibid.*, pp. 166–7.
13. C.A.R. Crosland, *The Future of Socialism* (London: Cape 1964 edn), p. 353.
14. This correspondence is in the Keynes Papers at King's College, Cambridge, under Labordère, Corr. III. Labordère to Keynes, 4–21 January 1937; Keynes to Labordère, 7 May 1937.
15. 'Economic possibilities for our grandchildren', a talk first given in 1928, published in *Essays in Persuasion*, 1931; in *CW*, IX, pp. 321–32.
16. Keynes, 'The political doctrines of Edmund Burke', 1904; in Keynes Papers, Marshall Library.
17. Keynes, 'Ethics in relation to conduct', paper read to The Apostles on 23 January 1904; in Keynes Papers, box 1, King's College, Cambridge. For an account see R. Skidelsky, *John Maynard Keynes* (London: Macmillan 1983), pp. 152–4.
18. See, for example, Tony Lawson and Hashem Pesaran (eds), *Keynes' Economics: Methodological Issues* (London: Croom Helm 1985).
19. Whether it succeeded is open to question. The trouble with his theory of probability is that knowledge of probabilities (in his sense) is a matter of logical intuition. This exposed him to Ramsey's famous retort: '[Keynes] supposes that, at any rate in certain cases, [probability relations] can be perceived; but speaking for myself I feel confident that this is not true. I do not perceive them ...' (F.P. Ramsey, *The Foundations of*

Mathematics and Other Logical Essays, ed. R.B. Braithwaite, London: Routledge and Kegan Paul (1931), p. 161).

20.   This interpretation of Keynes's work was first suggested to me by Maurice Cranston who wrote: If we consider the line of British liberal theorising that goes from J.S. Mill through T.H. Green to L.T. Hobhouse, we can see how the central idea of liberty is first transposed from the idea of individual freedom into one of social freedom, and then transformed from social freedom into social justice ... we find liberalism ... to be mainly a doctrine of social and economic betterment and hardly at all a doctrine of individual rights ... But Keynes stands apart from this endeavour to modernise liberalism by transforming its philosophy. What he tried deliberately, if somewhat deviously, to do, was to preserve the essential core of classical liberalism by attaching to it certain practical policies which he chose to call socialistic. Yet in doing this, Keynes seems to me to go straight back to the simple liberalism of Locke, and not in any way to subscribe to the idealistic and metaphysical philosophy of radical liberalism which emerged after J.S. Mill ... The sort of "state control" Keynes envisaged was always organisational and not confiscatorial' (Maurice Cranston, 'Keynes's political ideas and their influence' in A.P. Thirwall (ed.), *Keynes and Laissez-Faire*, London: Macmillan 1978), pp. 110–12.

   For a different view see Peter Clarke, 'The politics of Keynesian economics, 1924–1931' in Michael Bentley and John Stevenson (eds), *High and Low Politics in Modern Britain* (Oxford: OUP 1983), pp. 155–81. Clarke writes: 'Keynes's political outlook ... remained in essentials that of the new Liberalism which had flourished in the Edwardian period when he was a young man' (p. 175).

21.   John Strachey, *The Coming Struggle for Power* (London: Gollancz 1933), p. 200 f.

22.   Keynes, 'Reconstruction in Europe: an introduction', *Manchester Guardian Commercial*, 18 May 1922; in *CW*, XVII, p. 427.

23.   Seymour Harris, *John Maynard Keynes*, (New York: Scribner 1955), p. 79.

24.   For example, Keynes to E.F.M. Durbin, 30 April 1936; in *CW*, XXIX, p. 235. However, the idea of monetary fine-tuning comes mainly from the *General Theory*.

25.   'Mr. Keynes replies to Shaw', *New Statesman*, 10 November 1934; in *CW* XXVIII, p. 32.

26.   Keynes, Letter to the *Westminster Gazette*, 17 July 1926; in *CW*, XIX, pp. 567–8.

27.   Keynes Address to the Liberal Summer School, *Manchester Guardian*, 1 August 1927; in *CW*, XIX, p. 696.

28.   Keynes, 'The end of laissez-faire'; in *CW*, IX, p. 289.

29.   Crosland, *op.cit.*, p. 15 f.

30.   Elizabeth Johnson, 'John Maynard Keynes: scientist or politician?', in Joan Robinson (ed.), *After Keynes* (Oxford: Basil Blackwell 1973), p. 24.

31.   Keynes to G.B. Shaw, 1 January 1935; in *CW*, XIII, p. 492.

32.   Keynes, *A Short View of Soviet Russia* (London, Hogarth Press, December 1925); in *CW*, IX, pp. 253–71.

2 Keynes, the British Labour Party and the economics of democratic socialism
Elizabeth Durbin

The future economists among our grandchildren may well decide that news of the death of the Keynesian era was vastly exaggerated in the 1980s. They are still likely to conclude that the Keynesian revolution played a crucial role in building the consensus among Western democracies in favour of the mixed economy after World War II. In Britain the 1945–51 Labour governments introduced a programme of industrial and social legislation, which had been thrashed out during the 1930s and which ushered in the British version of the mixed economy. Their Chancellors of the Exchequer were the first to practise a conscious policy of Keynesian demand management as an essential ingredient of socialist planning. By the early 1950s Keynes had completed his elevation to the pantheon of democratic socialist gods. John Strachey (1952) claimed that the *General Theory* had converted him from a Marxist revolutionary to a proper social democrat. He explained that Keynes had shown that 'a way through did exist' in choosing between fascist corporatism and Soviet communism, which seemed to be the only alternatives for dealing with the devastation wrought by capitalism in the 1930s.

The purpose of this chapter is to explore the influence of Keynes himself and of his economic ideas on the prewar formation of the Labour Party's economic programme and policies, and on the economic and political thinking of the party's socialist intellectuals, in particular, the younger generation of economists who did the party's background research under the direction of Hugh Dalton, the chief economic spokesman. These included Colin Clark, Evan Durbin, Hugh Gaitskell, Douglas Jay and James Meade among others. There are those who feel that this group reflected the party's postwar right-wing position, that they had simply 'swallowed Keynes whole', as G.D.H. Cole (1950) put it, and had given up on the earlier commitment to take over the economy through the common ownership of the means of production. However, as in most matters, the real story is both more complex and more interesting. For although all democratic socialists were in a sense natural allies with Keynes in his call for active government intervention in the economy, they were also in

29

profound disagreement on many basic issues.

Keynes himself worked most closely for the Liberal Party. Indeed he helped to design the radical economic programme stressing expansionary investment policy and public works, which Lloyd George took to the country in 1929. He also co-authored the party pamphlet, 'Can Lloyd George Do It?'. However, he was scarcely an orthodox party man, and was fully aware that the Liberal Party left much to be desired. Yet, when it came down to a choice between the Conservative Party of die-hards and Labour, 'the Party of Catastrophe' as Keynes (1932a) designated it, he felt that 'my true home, so long as they offer a roof and a floor, is still with the Liberals'. But on economic questions, especially on the critical problems of unemployment and exchange rates, Keynes was willing to work with, to comment upon and to persuade whomever he possibly could. Thus he not only played an active role in the Economic Advisory Council (EAC) set up by the Labour Prime Minister, James Ramsay MacDonald, in 1930, but he was also asked for confidential advice at critical moments and he never ceased to offer his opinion publicly throughout his life.

In many ways Keynes was an unlikely socialist hero. As Donald Winch (1969) has pointed out, his general attitude to political parties and his contempt for the common herd made it unlikely that he would ever win a popular following among the working class. At another level his impatience with cautious politicians often antagonized his less brilliant brethren. Indeed, on one occasion he tactlessly hurt MacDonald's feelings at an EAC meeting by describing himself as 'the only Socialist present' (Marquand, 1977; Dalton 1953). In an article 'The Dilemma of Modern Socialism', Keynes (1932b) argued that socialists were drawn into advocating unsound economic policies, first, in their pursuit of equality and justice, and secondly, in their challenge to the existing system. He believed that: 'the first task of the Labour Party, if it is to be effective is, as I see it, to become intellectually emancipated as to what is economically sound, without losing either its political strength and its political organisation, which goes so deep into the social and economic life of England, or its ideals and ultimate goals.'

The great depression threatened both the political and economic stability of capitalist systems. In Britain the Labour Party came to power in 1929, but it suffered its own climactic defeat as a direct result of the collapse of the world economy and its impact on the already overvalued pound. In August 1931 the Cabinet split on the question of cutting unemployment benefits to secure foreign loans with which to stem the outflow of British reserves. When MacDonald formed a National government, the Labour Party expelled him as a traitor to the socialist cause, but then suffered a humiliating defeat in the October election. The party remained out of power throughout the decade, until Churchill brought the leaders into the wartime coalition. However, the Labour government's failure to cope with either unemployment or the financial crisis and its inability to introduce any significant socialist measures precipitated a systematic search for a practical set of specific proposals to meet its political goals. *Labour's Immediate Programme*, the result of these efforts, was adopted at the 1937 Annual Conference. It formed the basis of the party's 1945 election platform, and thus the reforming programme of the 1945–51 Labour governments.

The first part of this chapter traces the influence of Keynes on official party policy before the war. The second part discusses in greater depth his intellectual relations with the younger democratic socialist economists. Until 1933 Keynes advocated an actively managed monetary policy, and was increasingly forceful in demanding expansionary policies to combat unemployment in the face of the orthodox deflationary policies pursued by successive governments. In March 1933 he published a series of articles for *The Times*, 'The Means to Prosperity', where he first proposed the unorthodox budgeting with which his name has since been associated. While the Labour Party did not officially endorse Keynesian full employment policy until 1944, most of the important economic leaders had been convinced that Keynes was right about policy much earlier. However, among the party's professional economists, there remained a group sceptical of the extent to which Keynesian arguments provided the appropriate analysis for a socialist state.

Keynes and official Labour Party policy

Keynes's connection with the Liberal Party and its charismatic leader, Lloyd George, made him doubly suspect in the eyes of most Labour Party supporters. The Liberals were their political rivals for the anti-Tory vote, and Keynes's economics seemed both dangerously appealing and dangerously unsound. In the circumstances of the 1920s there were conflicting views within the Labour Party on the appropriate economic policy for a Labour government (Durbin, 1985). On the one hand, there was the strong political urge, one might say necessity, to appear respectable and able to govern. Philip Snowden, Labour's first Chancellor of the Exchequer, epitomized this viewpoint; he strongly supported the return to the gold standard in 1925, he believed in free trade and out-Treasuried the Treasury in his adherence to the principles of 'sound finance'. On the other hand, the radical left wing, represented in Parliament by the militant 'Clydesiders', believed that socialists must proceed with a rapid takeover of the economy and a broad expansion of social services. In between were those who opposed confrontations with capitalism, but who wanted more systematic intervention than Snowden. They were most ambivalent about Keynes; they were attracted to the activist Liberal platform, but anxious to maintain a distinctive programme for the Labour Party. Furthermore, public works were not popular with the working class, for whom they raised ancient spectres of outdoor relief. Thus, as unemployment persisted in Britain in the late 1920s, trade unionists sought to improve unemployment benefits for their members, rather than to promote make-work jobs.

In the late 1920s these conflicts surfaced publicly at the annual conference in debates over the party platform; later they helped to precipitate the 1931 crisis. Hugh Dalton and Oswald Mosley pushed hard for specific measures to deal with unemployment along contemporary Keynesian lines; Dalton (1953) later noted that he had been particularly impressed with Keynes's 'lucid positive Employment Policy'. However, in a crucial debate on whether the joint-stock banks should be nationalized (all agreed that the Bank of England should be publicly owned), Dalton sided with the more cautious leaders against the radical left. In the event, the official platform fudged the issues in vague promises. G.D.H. Cole (1929) wrote the official reply to Keynes's pamphlet, which criticized the Liberal plan as insufficient and based on 'madcap finance'.

Soon after the Labour government was installed, the New York stock exchange collapsed and any attempts to put the party's economic programme into effect were swamped by daily events. None the less, Mosley persisted in trying to get a Keynesian public works system; when he failed, he left the Labour Party to form the New Party, Britain's version of a European fascist party. Meanwhile Keynes himself continued to exert his energies as a member of the EAC, as Susan Howson and Donald Winch (1977) have revealed in their study of its deliberations.

The EAC itself has been judged as largely ineffective both because it was deadlocked between the businessmen and the bankers, who supported deflationary policies, and the expansionists led by Keynes, and because Snowden was totally opposed to any protective measures to support the pound. When Keynes came out publicly for a revenue tariff *and* expansionary policies in March 1931, he shocked and antagonized many thrifty working-class socialists, as well as Liberal economists, because they believed in free trade and balanced budgets. Dalton, who had known Keynes since Cambridge days where they vied for the attentions of Rupert Brooke, was equally appalled. He had been getting inside information on the deliberations of the EAC from Colin Clark, its research assistant, and he hurried to console Lionel Robbins after a particularly bruising encounter with Keynes on the Council's committee of economists. He even supported Philip Snowden's position.[1]

Keynes was far more successful in educating Cole and Ernest Bevin, the influential leader of the Transport and General Workers' Union and a member of the General Council of the Trades Union Congress. As a result, both Cole and Bevin understood the political and economic implications of the government's policy options in 1931. Indeed Bevin's intervention in the crisis of August was crucial in refusing to allow the Labour government to acquiesce in the demands of the international banks, the Treasury and the opposition parties. He had first understood the effect of the overvalued pound on unemployment when Keynes had fulminated against the return to gold in 1925; he stood firm for devaluation and against cuts in unemployment benefits in the crisis, thus precipating the Cabinet split.

In his pioneering study, *Politicians and the Slump*, Robert Skidelsky (1967) argued that the Labour government was unable to act upon Keynes's unorthodox economic policies because of the party's commitment to unrealistic 'Utopian Socialism'. David Marquand (1977) has even suggested that 'the most tragic, as well as the most disastrous, mistake of MacDonald's life' was his failure to follow Keynes's advice to devalue. However, Keynes's own recommendation for a revenue tariff was itself quite unrealistic given the implacable opposition of Snowden and Liberal supporters of the minority government; it appeared to the uninitiated to support Tory demands for protectionism. Furthermore, Keynes did not advocate devaluation publicly in the summer of 1931, indeed he argued *against* it in the Macmillan Commitee report, and his private letters to the Prime Minister in August were equivocal. Labour's suspicion of Keynes throughout this period is well captured in the satirical 'New Left Wing Creed on Unemployment', composed by M. Philips Price, a Labour MP, which Dalton copied into his diary in August 1930. It began: 'I believe in one Lloyd George, the Father Almighty/The Giver of political wisdom,/And in all his promises; possible and impossible./And in one Lord Oswald Mosley,/The only begotten Son of the Father,/From whom all Yellow Books are made', and continued 'And I believe in one J.M. Keynes, Lord and Giver of Inflation,/Who with Lloyd George and Sir Oswald together is worshipped and glorified:/Who spoke through *The Nation*'.

After the crisis, Hugh Dalton emerged as the party's chief economic spokesman. In consultation with Bevin, and with Colin Clark's assistance, he hurriedly put together a statement on economic policy for the Annual Conference. He arranged a meeting between Keynes, who renounced the revenue tariff as soon as Britain left the gold standard, and the new party leader, Arthur Henderson. Apparently it was a great success; at a lunch Keynes presented his views urging a stable common currency between a group of nations headed by a united British Empire. Then according to Dalton (1953), Keynes turned to Henderson and said: 'Here's a good ending for your next speech! "A week ago the pound looked the dollar in the face. Today it is kicking it in the arse".' Afterwards an obviously pleased Henderson told Dalton: 'And when I quoted the chap in the Cabinet, Snowden said he was a fool!'

The party's official statement unanimously adopted at the Annual Conference condemned the gold standard, tariffs and deflationary policies, and 'currency inflation', which meant Keynesian expansion. It resolved to bring 'the banking and credit system of the country ... under public ownership', to create a national investment board, to stabilize wholesale prices and to nationalize the most important basic industries.[2] When a left-wing group tried to introduce an amendment to nationalize the joint-stock banks, Bevin rose to condemn the motion. He also pointed out that for many years he had tried to persuade the authorities to abandon the gold standard, but 'even Mr Keynes and other Professors refused to look at an alternative'. Despite its emphasis on nationalization, under Bevin's leadership the party's financial policy in 1931 closely resembled Keynes's advocacy of monetary management – even though it hedged on forceful expansion.

However, in 1932 the left-wing triumphed; despite the pleas of Dalton, Bevin and other moderates, the party voted to amend the national executive's resolutions and to nationalize the joint-stock banks, as well as the Bank of England.[3] This remained the party's official policy, although it was dropped from the list of immediate proposals at the 1937 conference. In many ways, this issue symbolized the dividing-line between traditional socialists, who looked to the public ownership of financial institutions as the means to direct the economy, and the new breed of economic planners, who focused upon the proper policy and different forms of control to ensure aggregative efficiency and growth in the socialist economy. It was Keynes who gave the latter group their ideas about how to accomplish these goals with limited direct administration.

Interestingly, Keynes (1932c) himself was one of the first to make this distinction clear in two articles which he wrote for the *New Statesman* in September 1932: these reviewed the national executive's proposals published before the conference in a penny pamphlet entitled *Currency, Banking and Finance.* Keynes believed that the party was making 'the right decision' to opt for 'a managed sterling currency'. Furthermore, the party had 'wisely and prudently' left in abeyance the question of nationalizing the joint-stock banks, because it was not necessary for 'handling the vital controls'. However, Keynes did not think that the proposals for the National Investment Board, to 'exercise control over all new public issues on the capital market', went far enough. As he had originally proposed for the Liberal Party, he wanted the board to have the power to control the total volume of all investment, public and private, and the amount of new lending going to foreign and domestic borrowers. Indeed he asserted that 'grappling with these central controls is the rightly conceived socialism of the future'. Naturally, he lost sympathy when the party did vote to nationalize the joint-stock banks, and reverted to what he called 'moss-grown, demi-semi, Fabian Marxism'.

However, the moderate leadership had not given up on Keynesian ideas. In 1933 Dalton included expansionary policies in *Socialism and the Condition of the People*, referring specifically to Keynes's articles, 'The Means to Prosperity'; but these references were deleted at the next conference. He tried again in 1937, but once more explicit mention of budget deficits was deliberately removed in the drafting stages. Thus the party officially continued to oppose orthodox deflation, but to avoid 'inflationary' expansion. However, in 1939 the national executive did formally endorse a finance and trade committee proposal to expand the role of the National Investment Board, thus meeting Keynes's earlier criticism; the matter was not taken to conference.[4] The party's official unemployment policies stressed structural issues, the raising of the school age, the lowering of retirement age, old-age pensions and public works developments in the distressed areas.

However, in the unofficial memoranda for the party's Finance and Trade Committee, chaired by Dalton throughout the 1930s, the full impact of the Keynesian revolution can be traced. Beginning in 1932 when James Meade wrote a paper on financial panic, Dalton kept what he described as his 'live pigeon-hole' on all aspects of monetary, fiscal and exchange rate policy.[5] In the early years these memoranda focused on expansionary policies and the danger of capital flight when a socialist government took office; later they dealt with budget deficits, cheap money, fluctuating exchange rates, trade policy and the details of the institutional reforms necessary to implement all these policies effectively. Susan Howson's research on the continuing debates over wartime finance, full employment and postwar monetary policy provides the links between this prewar story, the Labour Party's official adoption of Keynesian employment policies in 1944 and government policy after the war.

Keynes and the democratic socialist economists
In March 1931, G.D.H. Cole founded the New Fabian Research Bureau (NFRB) to provide the background research necessary to help the Labour Party to come up with a practical programme to introduce socialism.[6] In committee work and conferences the New Fabian economists thrashed out

their policy differences. Durbin and Gaitskell were largely responsible for organizing the economic research programme. Clark ran a subcommittee on capital supply in Cambridge with G.F. Shove and Joan Robinson among others. Meade organized a similar group of Bureau sympathizers at Oxford, of which Roy Harrod was the most influential Keynesian. At the same time as professional economists, these socialist researchers also made important contributions to both the macro and microrevolutions of the 1930s.

There are two quite distinct aspects to the influence of Keynes on the work of democratic socialist economists. One is reflected in the disputes over the diagnosis of the unemployment problem and consequent prescriptions for its cure. The other emerges from the ways in which the Keynesian revolution was integrated into overall conceptions of the workings of the socialist economy, that is, its part in the economics of democratic socialism. It is now more apparent than it was in the 1930s that these economists differed with each other on both aspects, as well as with Keynes to varying degrees, even though they were all at one in demanding active government intervention to deal with unemployment.

On the question of unemployment policy James Meade and Colin Clark, who both worked closely with Keynes, were already convinced expansionists by late 1931, and after 1936, Meade became one of the important evangelists for the *General Theory*. G.D.H. Cole, who worked closely with J.A. Hobson during the 1920s, was very sympathetic to his views on underconsumption, although under Keynes's influence he was less suspicious of 'monetary palliatives'. Thus he too was an expansionist in the early 1930s, and greeted the *General Theory* enthusiastically, especially Keynes's acknowledgement of the importance of Hobson's work. Evan Durbin and Hugh Gaitskell, by contrast, were deeply suspicious of both underconsumption and 'inflationary' expansionism. In the early 1930s, they were strongly influenced by the Austrian school, particularly by Hayek's trade cycle theories as propounded at the London School of Economics.

At the NFRB, Durbin convened a subcommittee on Industrial Fluctuations and the Price Level, where he and Meade argued and disagreed in a series of memoranda; unfortunately, most of them have been lost. One interesting exception is a memorandum from Richard Kahn to Meade reporting on Keynes's reactions to one of the lost documents in April 1932. The 'angel messenger' reported that Keynes was 'very much interested', but had criticized Meade's neglect of the relationship between the rate of interest and the price level of securities; Keynes acknowledge that he had not dealt with this question either, and indeed Kahn believed he did not know how to.[7] What does emerge from the remaining records is that, using the theoretical framework of *The Treatise*, Meade had convinced Durbin by 1933 that expansionary policy was the appropriate solution, and by 1935, as the implications of the multiplier became clearer, he had also persuaded him that budget deficits were a necessary tool. In short, Durbin also agreed to Keynesian policy prescriptions well before the *General Theory* was published (Durbin, 1985). After its publication, Meade converted Douglas Jay as well, who became one of the party's leading advocates of economic management. In an influential book, *The Socialist Case*, published in 1937, Jay has been credited with completing the process of 'dressing up Keynes in socialist clothes' (Pimlott, 1977).

The work of Durbin, and Gaitskell is particularly interesting for illuminating the complexities of developing a distinctive socialist approach to the problems of macroeconomic policy in the pre *General Theory* era, and why they were so dubious about Keynesian expansionism. First, given the appeal of various 'funny money' theories to left-wingers in the Labour Party, they believed that it was important to refute simplistic underconsumption arguments, such as Major Douglas's social credit scheme, because they raised unrealistic hopes that unemployment could be easily cured. Secondly, they explored the application of Austrian theory to the problems of trade cycles and capital formation, because they were convinced that the socialist state must overcome these problems if it was to claim the successful overthrow of capitalism. In his first book Durbin (1933) showed that underconsumption theories led to mistaken attacks on saving and on monetary policy in general. He also concluded that expansionary policies would only bring about the recurrence of the trade cycle, for which underconsumption theories provided no explanation.

By late 1933, again under Meade's influence, Durbin had developed a new approach to these problems using the savings/investment analysis developed by Robertson and Keynes in the late 1920s. He submitted a more academic version of his argument to the *Economic Journal* in early 1934. Although the paper is lost, correspondence with the editor reveals that Durbin criticized a number of points in the *Treatise on Money*. Therefore, Keynes wrote to Dennis Robertson asking for his reactions, explaining that he needed his help on the passages dealing with Hayek: 'Here I am left feeling like Sidgwick examining the Hegelian candidate. I can see that it is nonsense, but is it the right nonsense?'[8] Although Robertson said it was the right nonsense, Keynes eventually decided against publication.

Meanwhile Durbin had refined and expanded his arguments. In *The Problem of Credit Policy* (1935), published a few months before the *General Theory*, he completed his break from Hayek by declaring that in the midst of mass unemployment deflation was 'a pedagogical impertinence'. He remained cautious about the inflationary effects of prolonged government expansion, but concluded optimistically that under socialism the central planning authority would have the means and the will to cure the trade cycle: 'It should be possible to banish unemployment forever. It should be possible to double the standard of living in thirty years. These are reasonable expectations.'

Durbin's concern with the appropriate supply policies for the socialist state made him critical of some aspects of *The General Theory* from the start. On 20 April 1936 he wrote to Keynes:[9]

> May I say how very much I have enjoyed 'The General Theory'. I have read almost nothing else since it came out and I have immensely enjoyed my labours. I find myself in profound disagreement with the political notes in the last chapter and I do not understand which monetary policy you are advocating for the trade cycle – but the main argument of the book has been most stimulating to me.

In a subsequent letter he described its 'aesthetic thrill that I last remember at Oxford when I was reading Berkeley's *Theory of Vision* – deep insight and clear logic expressed with an economy of words and a sense of prose rare indeed in the sloppy literature of our subject'. For the socialist readers of *Labour*, however, he elaborated on his disagreements with Keynes's defence of capitalism. While socialists would agree with Keynes's conception of a 'somewhat comprehensive socialization of investment', his reasons for refusing further public ownership were 'bizarre and unconvincing', according to Durbin, particularly when it came to harmless tyrannies over bank balances.[10] Under R.H. Tawney's influence, Durbin believed that 'the necessary relation of employee to private employer may be, and too often is, oppressive to the one and degrading to the other'. Furthermore, he argued that 'freedom of enterprise is freedom to combine, monopolise and exploit as much as it is freedom to compete'.

In responding Keynes agreed that economists 'are entitled, as well as likely, to differ à l'outrance amongst themselves' about non-economic factors. But he protested that Durbin inaccurately portrayed his economic views, in particular, by describing his cure for unemployment as an attempt 'to force the rate of interest sufficiently low and maintain it there'; in fact it was precisely the ineffectiveness of the rate of interest and the inadequacy of private investment which had led him to conclude that investment 'cannot be left solely to private decision(s)'.

In a lengthy reply Durbin elaborated his opposition to private enterprise on microeconomic grounds and to capitalism on social and political grounds. He also explained why he did not think that Keynes's measures to increase the private propensity to consume and the level of public investment would cure the trade cycle: 'you have given no reason for supposing that your "cure" would not simply lead to an accelerated inflation, an ultimate rise in prices and the continuous dilemma between allowing the movement to gain further impetus or checking it. And if the movement is checked the disappointment of expectations is the crisis and produces the depression.' In a final letter Keynes conceded that he would not use any further expansion once full employment was reached and 'that our methods of control are unlikely to be sufficiently delicate or sufficiently powerful to maintain continuous full employment'. However, he concluded: 'You seem to argue that because a further dose of expansionist expedients would merely lead to a rise of prices when the existing dose is sufficient to maintain full employment, therefore they would have the same effect when the existing measures were not sufficient to maintain full employment.' Only later would it become clear that their economic differences arose from Keynes's short-run approach to unemployment problems, in contrast to Durbin's continued concern with long-term growth problems once full employment was achieved, a perspective he never lost.

Nevertheless, the *General Theory* did have an important effect in finally persuading Durbin that the nationalization of the joint-stock banks was not an immediate priority to gain financial control of the economy. In pointed contrast to Dalton, Meade and others, he and Gaitskell had agreed with the radical left-wingers that the government must control the direction of short-term credit through public ownership of banks and of long-term credit through the NIB. However, he had modified his views somewhat in light of the National government's experience with a cheap money policy in the early 1930s (Durbin, 1935). By the summer of 1935 he only supported nationalization if the banks refused to give the loans necessary to implement a budget deficit policy. Keynes had now demonstrated that what mattered was total investment and business expectations, shifting the problem of implementation from commercial banks to government policy and the central bank. In December 1936 Durbin wrote to Dalton that he no longer believed that nationalization of the joint-stock banks was necessary, one step in the widespread agreement to drop this item in the party platform from *Labour's Immediate Programme* (Dalton, 1957).

However, the influence of Keynes should not be overstated; there remained fundamental differences. While Durbin and Gaitskell had concluded that 'prosperity' measures would be necessary if the party came to power in a depression, they were adamant that full employment was not 'the distinguishing characteristic of the socialist ideal', as Gaitskell put it in

1932.[11] In joint work on the appropriate economic strategy for the next Labour government they concluded that the financial controls outlined above and the nationalization of basic industries must precede expansion of social services and large-scale redistribution. Even Meade, who was in total agreement with Keynes's unemployment policy and its priority as a matter of strategy, also advocated a substantial nationalization programme. As socialists, they were all united on the importance of equality, and they agreed that substantial redistribution would follow after full employment and nationalization goals had been met. Despite Keynes's assertion in the *General Theory* that the other 'outstanding fault' of society (besides unemployment) was 'its arbitrary and inequitable distribution of wealth and incomes', to socialists in the 1930s he appeared to be less committed to eradicating inequality than they were.

Conclusion

Keynes's 'rightly conceived socialism of the future' included as necessary elements: (1) nationalization of the Bank of England; (2) a National Investment Board with authority to issue guaranteed public and private loans; and (3) active monetary and fiscal policies to maintain effective demand. In the early 1930s the Labour Party only endorsed the first; it agreed to a more limited role for the NIB and it was opposed to 'inflationary' policies. Against Keynes's explicit advice it voted to nationalize the joint-stock banks in 1932. However, before war broke out, this proposal had been relegated to the back-burner and the role of the NIB had been broadened.

As an advocate for his policy ideas to the Labour Party, Keynes was most active before 1933, in other words, well before the *General Theory* came out fifty years ago. He was most successful in converting the influential leaders, Ernest Bevin and Hugh Dalton, to a managed monetary policy, to expansion and eventually to deficit finance. He was least successful in persuading Snowden how to mitigate the financial crisis of 1931.

Keynes's most profound influence was upon the new generation of professional economists, who worked for the Labour Party. When he became the party leader in 1955, Hugh Gaitskell identified Dalton, Keynes, Cole and Tawney as their mentors in thinking through the principles of their brand of democratic socialism; he believed that they had managed to incorporate Keynes's economics without his social philosophy (Gaitskell, 1955). However, during the 1930s this conversion was more limited than it appeared to be after the war. In the *General Theory* Keynes advocated government intervention to deal with the macroeconomic problem; as Durbin had pointed out, he did not believe that large-scale unemployment necessarily implied microeconomic misallocation. The democratic socialist economists were convinced that the monopoly aspects of capitalism, the need for public goods, the growth of externalities and socialist demands for equality provided further ground for systematic government intervention. In their own work they made important contributions to the postwar consensus among economists for this broader rationale for the mixed economy.

The British version of the mixed economy combined the socialist programme of nationalization, the Beveridge Report's recommendations for comprehensive social services and Keynesian macroeconomic policy. Once the nationalization programme was completed, the prewar distinction between liberal and socialist approaches became blurred. In 1950 Cole even suggested that the postwar position, which Gaitskell was propounding, represented 'little more than Keynesian Liberalism with frills'. Anthony Wright (1984) has recently pointed out that, in the realm of social policy, the view of equality as the provision of services and the redistribution of income rests upon an individualistic liberal ethos, in sharp contrast to Tawney's relational concept of equality based on equal worth as fellow citizens. A similar distinction can be made in the economic realm. As a liberal, Keynes viewed unemployment as the key economic problem; once that was solved, market capitalism would be restored as the efficient allocator. Lacking faith in capitalism, socialists viewed the economic problem in both macro and micro terms, and advocated socialist planning to integrate efficiency and egalitarian policies. Those economists, whose socialist faith was animated by Tawney's egalitarianism, further believed that capitalist institutions must be fundamentally transformed to equalize the relations between classes.

Notes

1. Hugh Dalton, Diary, 28 October 1930, to be found in the British Library of Political and Economic Science, London School of Economics.
2. Labour Party, *Annual Conference Report*, 1931, pp. 321–2, 191–2.
3. For the entire debate see Labour Party, *Annual Conference Report*, 1932, pp. 182–94.
4. Finance and Trade Committee, 'Heads of a Bill on Finance', Labour Party, Finance Policy No. 3, December 1938, and Labour Party, National Executive Committee, *Minutes*, 21 and 22 February 1939.
5. Hugh Dalton to James Meade, March 1933, in Meade Papers, folder 1, British Library of Political and Economic Science, London School of Economics.
6. See Margaret Cole, *The Story of Fabian Socialism* (London, Heineman, 1961). Keynes was later enrolled as an 'Associate' member since he would not pledge to support the Labour Party.
7. Richard F. Kahn to Meade, 18 April 1932, in Meade Papers (see no. 5, above).
8. For the full correspondence see John Maynard Keynes Papers, file EJ/13, Marshall

Library, Cambridge.

9. E.F.M. Durbin to J.M. Keynes, 20 April 1936, in Keynes's and Durbin's personal papers; also reprinted in *The Collected Writings of John Maynard Keynes* (London, Macmillan, 1979), Vol. XXIX, pp. 231–4.

10. E.F.M. Durbin, 'Professor Durbin quarrels with Professor Keynes', *Labour* (undated copy in Keynes's papers, *op. cit.*). A footnote states: 'The following article is not a review of Mr Keynes' new book ... but reflections suggested by the final chapter on the Social Philosophy towards which the General Theory might lead.'

11. H.T.N. Gaitskell, 'Socialism and Wage Policy' (n.d.), mimeo., Fabian Society Papers, box J24/2, Nuffield College, Oxford.

References

Cole, G.D.H. (1929), *How to Conquer Unemployment: Labour's Reply to Lloyd George*, London: Labour Party.

Cole, G.D.H. (1950), *Socialist Economics*, London: Gollancz.

Dalton, H. (1953), *Call Back Yesterday: Memoirs*, London: Muller, Vol. 1.

Dalton, H. *Fateful Years: Memoirs,* London: Muller, Vol. 2.

Durbin, E.F.M. (1933), *Purchasing Power and Trade Depression*, London: Cape.

Durbin, E.F.M. (1935), *The Problem of Credit Policy*, London: Chapman and Hall.

Durbin, E. (1985), *New Jerusalems: The Labour Party and the Economics of Democratic Socialism*, London; Routledge and Kegan Paul.

Gaitskell, H. (1955), 'The ideological development of democratic socialism in Great Britain', *Socialist International Information*, 5 (52–53), December.

Howson, S. and Winch, D. (1977), *The Economic Advisory Council 1930–1939*, Cambridge: Cambridge University Press.

Keynes, J.M. (1932a), 'The end of laissez-faire' and 'Am I a liberal?', in *Essays in Persuasion*, New York: Harcourt and Brace.

Keynes, J.M. (1932b), 'The Dilemma of Modern Socialism', *The Political Quarterly*, 3 (2).

Keynes, J.M. (1932c), 'Monetary policy of the Labour Party', *New Statesman and Nation*, 17 and 24 September.

Marquand, D. (1977), *Ramsay MacDonald*, London: Cape.

Pimlott, B. (1977), *Labour and the Left in the 1930s*, Cambridge: Cambridge University Press.

Skidelsky, R. (1967), *Politicians and the Slump: The Labour Government of 1929–31*, London: Macmillan.

Strachey, J. (1970), 'Tasks and achievements of British labour', in R.H.S. Crossman (ed.), *New Fabian Essays*, London: Dent.

Winch, D. (1969), *Economics and Policy*, London: Hodder and Stoughton, 1969.

Wright, A. (1984), 'Tawneyism revisited: equality, welfare and socialism', in B. Pimlott (ed.), *Fabian Essays in Socialist Thought,* Aldershot: Gower.

3 Monetary policy and the Labour Government in the 1940s
Susan Howson[1]

The research, on which what I want to present here is based, was not intended to be about Keynes, but about what I called with tongue in cheek, 'socialist monetary policy', that is, the ideas on the objectives and practice of monetary policy held in the Labour Party in Britain in the 1940s. But it is a measure of Keynes's influence that it is not possible to write about British economic policy or policy-making in the 1930s or 1940s without frequently mentioning his name. So let me extract from my work on monetary thought in the Labour Party in the 1940s that which relates to Keynes and his influence on monetary policy and the Labour government in those years. I shall concentrate on *domestic* monetary policy not only because of the constraints of space, but also because I have so far found more new material on this topic than in the area of international monetary policy – where the extent of Keynes's influence is, anyway, better known.[2]

The first majority Labour government in Britain was elected in July 1945 and not defeated in a general election until October 1951. It came to office pledged to reform the UK financial system and to nationalize the major industries, and thus to maintain full employment and promote economic growth as well as to redistribute income and wealth. The desired financial reforms were nationalization of the Bank of England and establishment of a National Investment Board; the Bank and the Board together were to control short- and long-term interest rates, bank lending, the securities markets, and real investment (public and private) by a mixture of conventional monetary policy and more direct control. The Labour government did nationalize the Bank of England, on 1 March 1946, but did not set up a National Investment Board. Their monetary policy first took the form of trying to reduce interest rates on government debt from 3 to 2½ per cent for long-term bonds and then reverted to the 'cheap money policy' that had been pursued by previous governments since 1932.

Most of the programme of the 1945 Labour government had been adopted by the party in the 1930s, notably in *Labour's Immediate Programme* (1937), prepared when Hugh Dalton, who became Chancellor of the Exchequer in 1945, was chairman of the party's National Executive Committee. But Dalton's policy of trying to drive down long-term interest rates did not follow from the published policy statements of the party and was soon criticized. Dalton himself said he had had the support of his Treasury and Bank of England advisers, including Keynes and Sir Richard Hopkins (Permanent Secretary of the Treasury, 1942–5), and admitted to official criticism only from Evan Durbin (who was his Parliamentary Private Secretary in 1946).[3] Hence an important part of my research on the monetary policy of the 1945–51 Labour governments has been directed to the issue of why Dalton tried to reduce already low interest rates, where he got the idea from and what was Keynes's role in the policy – if any: Keynes died on 12 April 1946, a few months after the Labour government took office:

There are three possible sources of Dalton's cheaper money policy:

(1) Dalton himself, since he was professional economist, but he had been more concerned as an economist with public finance than with monetary theory or policy;[4]
(2) the younger economists in the Labour Party such as Colin Clark, Evan Durbin, Hugh Gaitskell, Douglas Jay, James Meade and Joan Robinson;
(3) Dalton's official advisers who included, as I have already mentioned, Keynes.

Elizabeth Durbin has told the story of the contribution of the 'young economists' to the programme of the Labour Party in the 1930s in her book *New Jerusalems*. In chapter 2 of this volume, she has also pointed out the extent of Keynesian influence on the party through those young economists.[5] By the end of the 1930s the resulting financial policy for the next Labour government included the taking of emergency measures such as exchange control to prevent financial panic and capital outflows on the election of a Labour government; legislation to nationalize the Bank of England and to set up a National Investment Board; and, most important, the reduction of unemployment by means of public works, conventional monetary policy and countercyclical budgetary policy, of which the last was seen as the most promising permanent weapon. A Labour government coming to power in a depression might have to pursue a policy of very low interest rates, but such a cheaper money policy was only recommended for depression conditions, not a time of full employment such as 1945.[6]

The threat of war in 1938 led the younger Labour Party economists into making proposals for financing the war effort; during the war they were involved in making plans for postwar policy. Both sets of proposals had some impact on the 1945–51 Labour governments' monetary policy, and the wartime proposals for postwar monetary policy show a strong Keynesian influence.

The proposals of the War Finance Group were published as *How to Pay for the War* under Evan Durbin's name in late 1939. The group included Durbin, Gaitskell and Jay of the economists I have already mentioned: Meade was *not* involved as he was in Geneva from 1937 to 1940 and then in the government's Economic Section where he resolved to behave as a civil servant and stay out of political activities. They were justifiably annoyed when Keynes produced his pamphlet of the same title in February 1940 – though they did in fact strongly support his proposals. Their proposals were: large-scale government borrowing at low interest rates from the banks, whose other lending would be controlled, and also low interest rates on other government borrowing, with controls, rationing and high taxation to keep down consumption and inflation. Bank rate should be reduced to 2 per cent and yields on long-term government bonds lowered to less than 3 per cent. They took it for granted that exchange control would be instituted on the outbreak of war as it was on 4 September 1939.[7] But there was little discussion of these proposals in the party once Keynes's proposals had been published. The next stage in the story comes three years later, when Dalton got the party's postwar finance subcommittee down to work.

Wartime monetary policy had not in fact differed greatly from the Labour economists' hopes: there was large-scale borrowing from the banks at low rates of interest (but as 1 per cent rather than the ½ per cent they desired), bank lending and capital issues were controlled and interest rates on long-term government borrowing were kept down to 3 per cent though not pushed down below that.[8] As Dalton told the party's Reconstruction Committee at the end of 1942:[9]

> The Bank of England has now become a mere branch of the Treasury, and the Joint Stock Banks mere collecting agencies for Government finance. [This] is a wartime invention of great value, and we must seek, after the war, to be most conservative as regards financial institutions, and to hold fast what we have won.

The other Labour Party economists agreed, but in the postwar finance committee Joan Robinson proposed going further – that the wartime methods of monetary control could be used to lower interest rates permanently, to encourage long-term investment and to reduce rentier incomes. Interest rates on the floating debt should, therefore, be reduced to their prewar level of ½ per cent and gilt-edged yields reduced gradually towards 2½ per cent for long-term bonds in the first instance. This would necessitate the maintenance of exchange controls to prevent capital flows. It would also involve 'abandoning altogether the traditional use of the rate of interest as a check to inflation', but that would not matter, since 'the rate of interest would be much too weak a defence to use against inflation in the post-war situation' when rationing and controls would be needed anyway. Robinson's views seem to have dominated this meeting. Dalton recorded that 'though most of the men don't like Mrs Robinson [she] seems to be extremely able and to have the right approach'.[10]

The idea of a permament low interest rate policy derived from the *General Theory* (Keynes, 1936) and appeared in other publications in the 1940s such as Strachey (1940) and Beveridge (1944). Many Labour economists were, however, suspicious of the idea, either because it seemed too much like a panacea to preserve capitalism or because they did not share Keynes's scepticism about the utility of variations in interest rates. Meade and Durbin were in the latter category.

The party's document on *Full Employment and Financial Policy* published in April 1944 was written by Dalton, who described it as 'largely Keynesian' with 'some socialist additions'. Budgetary policy was to maintain purchasing power in the context of continued wartime controls, a nationalized Bank of England and a National Investment Board. Price controls would prevent inflation in the immediate postwar period, exchange control would prevent capital outflows and, along with large-scale government borrowing from the banks as in wartime, would prevent interest rates from rising and thus allow the government to borrow cheaply to finance its expenditure, both in the transitional period and in the longer term when unemployment was feared. As in the coalition government's White Paper on Employment Policy published a few weeks later, monetary policy was to play a subordinate role.[11]

When Dalton arrived at the Treasury in 1945, he immediately told his advisers he wanted to do something about monetary policy, and they produced plans they had already drawn up earlier in 1945. Those plans were thoroughly and explicitly Keynesian; despite objections from James Meade and Lionel Robbins to Keynes's attitude to monetary policy, Keynes had dominated the committee which produced the report, to the extent that the author of the report, Sir Richard Hopkins, adorned it with quotations from the *General Theory*. The report of the 'National Debt Enquiry' proposed essentially to maintain fixed low interest rates by the wartime methods of control, for 'as far ahead as can reasonably be the subject of discussion'. It recommended that short-term interest rates should be reduced by ½ per cent (from 1 per cent) while long-term interest rates were maintained at their wartime 3 per cent.[12] Note that there was no recommendation to reduce long-term interest rates below 3 per cent, partly because the immediate postwar period would hardly be a suitable time to do so, and anyway Keynes, Bursar of King's College, Cambridge, was not in 1945 particularly anxious to reduce rentier incomes.[13]

Dalton, however, did want to reduce long-term interest rates as well as short-term interest rates by ½ per cent. He had drawn the 'Keynesian' conclusion from wartime financial arrangements that interest rates could be set wherever the authorities wanted them, an argument put to him by Joan Robinson in 1943 and again by Keynes and the National Debt Enquiry in 1945. He chose 2½ per cent for several reasons: 'to save public expenditure on interest, to improve the distribution of income, to encourage investment ... to help the local authorities to keep down the cost of housing programmes, and thus to keep down rents ... [and] to prepare the way for the series of nationalisation Bills which ... we intended to pass.'[14] The Treasury and the Bank readily agreed to reducing short-term rates and, less readily, they agreed in 1946 to try to lower long rates to 2½ per cent too. (I am not going to say anything here about the progress of the cheaper money policy in 1945 and 1946 (or its failure in 1947) except for Keynes's role as Dalton's personal adviser.)

Although Keynes did not himself favour 2½ per cent for long-term interest rates, once he realized Dalton was quite determined on this, he began to provide him with technical advice on how to do it. This was in March and April 1946, the last weeks of Keynes's life, and when the attempt to issue long-term government debt at 2½ per cent later in 1946 was made, it was not carried out in the way that Keynes had recommended. But Dalton was none the less quite correct to claim that Keynes had supported him in his cheaper money campaign.[15]

An epilogue to the story of the influence of Keynes on monetary policy and the Labour government, in the 1940s, occurred in 1951. The Labour government were still in power and short-term interest rates were still tied down by a ½ per cent Treasury Bill rate but long-term interest rates had risen to 3½ per cent, the attempt to keep them down to 2½ per cent having been given up by the end of 1947. Many economists, including the young economists in the Labour Party, for example, James Meade (now back in academic life) and Anthony Crosland were arguing that short-term interest rates, at least, should be raised to more realistic levels. Dalton (still in the government although he had resigned as Chancellor of the Exchequer in 1947) disliked this 'dear money heresy', and re-read the *General Theory* (as he had done in 1946) to reinforce his argument for the 'euthanasia of the rentier' by means of a permanent low interest rate policy. But Crosland, in particular, managed to persuade Dalton that since low interest rates led to large capital gains, it would not necessarily be bad on distributional grounds or 'unKeynesian' to raise interest rates in the 1950s.[16]

Notes

1. I should like to thank Stephen Bird, Colin Clark, Marjorie Durbin, the Fabian Society, J.S. Fforde and the Bank of England, the Labour Party, James Meade, Angela Raspin, and the Controller of Her Majesty's Stationery Office for access to or permission to cite the unpublished sources on which most of my findings are based. I also wish to thank Elizabeth Durbin for her enthusiastic encouragement of my research and Donald Moggridge for delivering this paper for me at the Glendon Conference on 27 September 1986.
2. See Gardner (1956) and (1980a).
3. Dalton (1962); pp. 124–5, 160–1, 182–3; Dalton to the Editor, *The Economist*, 3 February 1951, p. 256.
4. See Dalton (1922) and (1953), ch. VI.
5. Durbin (1985), chs 4, 10, 12; 'Keynes, the British Labour Party and the economics of democratic socialism'.
6. S. Howson, '"Socialist" monetary policy: monetary thought in the Labour Party in the 1940s', paper presented to History of Economics Society Meetings, New York, June 1986, pp. 7–8.
7. *Ibid.*, pp. 9–10; Durbin (1939); Keynes (1940) and (1978), ch. 2.
8. Sayers (1956), chs V–VII.
9. Dalton Diary, vol. 27, 20 December 1942, British Library of Political and Economic Science.
10. RDR 133, Robinson, 'War-time control of the rate of interest', September 1943, and 'Note to be appended to RDR 133 – Wartime control of the rate of interest', Minutes of the fourth meeting of the post-war finance subcommittee on Thursday, 25 March 1943, Labour Party Archives; Dalton Diary, vol. 28, 25 March 1943.
11. Howson, '"Socialist" monetary policy', pp. 15–16.
12. Howson, 'The origins of cheaper money 1945–47', Economic History Workshop, University of Toronto, November 1985, pp. 7–13; National Debt Enquiry, First Report, 'The question of future gilt-edged interest rates', May 1945, T230/94, Public Record Office. Para. 18 of the report read: 'It is understood that the following extract from Lord Keynes' work, The General Theory of Employment, Interest and Money (1936) page 203, would now command a wide measure of agreement among economists: "A monetary policy which strikes public opinion as being experimental in character or easily liable to change may fail in its objective of greatly reducing the long-term rate of interest, because (the amount of cash held to satisfy the 'speculative' motive) may tend to increase almost without limit in response to a reduction in (the rate of interest) below a certain figure. The same policy, on the other hand, may prove easily successful if it appeals to public opinion as being reasonable and practicable and in the public interest, rooted in strong conviction, and promoted by an authority unlikely to be superseded.

    "It might be more accurate, perhaps, to say that the rate of interest is a highly conventional, rather than a highly psychological phenomenon. For its actual value is largely governed by the prevailing view as to what its value is expected to be. *Any* level of interest which is accepted with sufficient conviction as *likely* to be durable *will* be durable; subject, of course, in a changing society to fluctuations for all kinds of reasons round the expected normal".'
13. Keynes's preference for 3 per cent as a 'socially desirable reward of saving' was made clearer in the meetings of the committee than in his notes before the meeting (National Debt Enquiry, 2nd meeting, 8 March 1945, T230/94, Public Record Office; Keynes, 1980b).
14. Dalton (1954), p. 235.
15. Howson, 'The origins of cheaper money 1945–47', section III.

16. Dalton Diary, vol. 39, 21 March 1951; Dalton to Piercy, and Dalton to Crosland, 22
     May 1951, Dalton, 'Note on rate of interest, etc.' and and 'Rate of interest postscript',
     Dalton Papers 9/19, British Library of Political and Economic Science; Dalton Diary,
     vol. 41, 30 May and 26 June 1951; Dalton to Lady Keynes, 30 May 1946, Keynes
     Papers; see also Crosland (1956), pp. 409–15.

References

Beveridge, William (1944), *Full Employment in a Free Society*, London: Allen and Unwin.

Crosland, C.A.R. (1956), *The Future of Socialism* (1st edn), London: Cape.

Dalton, Hugh (1922), *Principles of Public Finance* (1st edn), London: Routledge.

Dalton, Hugh (1953), *Call Back Yesterday: Memoirs 1887–1931*, London: Muller.

Dalton, Hugh (1954), *Principles of Public Finance* (4th edn), London: Routledge.

Dalton, Hugh (1962), *High Tide and After: Memoirs 1945–1960*, London: Muller.

Durbin, E.F.M. (1939), *How to Pay for the War, an Essay on the Financing of War*, London:
     Routledge.

Durbin, Elizabeth (1985), *New Jerusalems: The Labour Party and the Economics of
     Democratic Socialism*, London: Routledge and Kegan Paul.

Gardner, R.N. (1956), *Sterling–Dollar Diplomacy*, London: Oxford University Press.

Keynes, J.M. (1936), *The General Theory of Employment, Interest and Money*, London:
     Macmillan.

Keynes, J.M. (1940), *How to Pay for the War. A Radical Plan for the Chancellor of the
     Exchequer*, London: Macmillan.

Keynes, J.M. (1978), *The Collected Writings of John Maynard Keynes. Vol. 22, Activities
     1939–1945: Internal War Finance*, London: Macmillan.

Keynes, J.M. (1980), *The Collected Writings of John Maynard Keynes. Vol. 25, Activities
     1940–1944: Shaping the Post-War World: The Clearing Union*, London: Macmillan.

Keynes, J.M. (1980), *The Collected Writings of John Maynard Keynes. Vol. 27, Activities
     1940–1946: Shaping the Post-War World: Employment and Commodities*, London:
     Macmillan.

Sayers, R.S. (1956), *Financial Policy 1939–45*, London: Longman.

Strachey, J. (1940), *A Programme for Progress*, London: Gollancz.

4 The Keynesian revolution in historical perspective
D.E. Moggridge[1]

Fifty years ago Keynes's *General Theory of Employment, Interest and Money* appeared in British bookshops priced at five shillings, to encourage student purchases. Since then it has been continuously in print, and it still sells respectably despite changing fashions.[2] Presumably it still gets read. So too if one judges from publishers' lists, do books about Keynes. The journals still have room for Keynes as well. With every passing year come guides for the interested student, surveys of the state of play in debates between Keynesians of various stripes and their opponents (who, to add to the confusion, sometimes also call themselves Keynesians) and appraisals of Keynes's relevance or irrelevance to contemporary economic theory and economic policy. More recently, historians of various sorts have also discovered Keynes the economist in contexts other than the reparations discussions after 1918 – in Britain in sufficient numbers that the Economic History Society is producing one of its survey pamphlets devoted exclusively to the expanding literature on Keynes and British macroeconomic policy (Peden, 1986).

In this chapter, I do not intend to give yet another interpretation or appraisal of the *General Theory*. Instead, as it is now fifty years since the publication of the book and over forty since many of its modes of analysis and preoccupations began to penetrate the world of economic policy-making, I think it would be useful to go back and look at the reception of the book and its ideas. In particular, I want to look at the rhetoric of the book and the way it shaped subsequent discussion in the hope that such an exercise might prove useful in understanding the past and, perhaps even in informing our present preoccupations.

In his book, and in many of his preceding and subsequent discussions of its ideas, Keynes self-consciously employed a rhetorical device. To differentiate his theoretical views – and to a lesser extent his policy positions – he created the notion of an established orthodoxy. In theory, he called it 'classical economics'. He was clear about the purpose of the exercise. As he told Roy Harrod:

> My motive is, of course, not in order to get read. But it may be needed in order to get understood ... I expect a great deal of what I write to be water off a

duck's back. I am certain that it will be water off a duck's back unless I am sufficiently strong in my criticism to force the classicals to make rejoinders. I *want*, so to speak, to raise a dust; because it is only out of the controversy that will arise that what I am saying will get understood. (*CW*, XIII, p. 548)

With hindsight and a little more distance, he was more explicit in print about the exercise. As he told French readers of the book:

For a hundred years or longer English Political Economy has been dominated by an orthodoxy. This is not to say that an unchanging doctrine has prevailed. On the contrary. But its presuppositions, its atmosphere, its method have remained surprisingly the same, and a remarkable continuity has been observable through all the changes. In that orthodoxy, in that continuous tradition, I was brought up. I learnt it, I taught it, I wrote it. To those looking from the outside I probably still belong to it. Subsequent historians of doctrine will regard this book as in essentially the same tradition. But I myself in writing it, and in other recent work which has led up to it, have felt myself to be breaking away from this orthodoxy, to be in strong reaction against it, to be escaping from something, to be gaining in emancipation. And this state of mind on my part is the explanation of certain faults in the book, in particular its controversial note in some passages, and its air of being addressed too much to the holders of a particular point of view and too little *ad urbem et orbem*. (*CW*, VII, p. xxxi)

The rhetoric of theoretical revolt raised some dust. It irritated Roy Harrod and Dennis Robertson, as well as reviewers such as Joseph Schumpeter (1936) and Frank Knight (1937), and so offended A.C. Pigou as to result in an unusually petulant review (1936). Yet, for Keynes at least, the results of the irritation were not productive. As he remarked to Dennis Robertson:

What some of you think my excessively controversial method is really due to the extent that I am bound to my teachers and earliest pupils; which makes me want to emphasise or bring to a head all differences of opinion. But I evidently made a mistake in this, not having realised either that the old ones would be merely irritated or that to the young ones, who have been, apparently, so badly brought up as to believe nothing in particular, the controversy would mean practically nothing. (*CW*, XIV, p. 87)

Yet the rhetoric had one effect on the young: it raised the issue of 'Keynes vs the classics' which rumbled on in the literature for over a decade before becoming encapsulated in the textbooks with results I will discuss below.

The rhetoric over policy also had long-term effects. Here the source of the problem was not the *General Theory* itself, for Keynes's published writings show that he had ceased promulgating such a view in the early 1930s. Nevertheless, perhaps because he did not explicitly repudiate it, the view developed that Keynes prior to 1936 was alone (or almost alone) in fighting for countercyclical macroeconomic policies while his classical economist colleagues argued for wage cuts or more deflation as the appropriate cures for the slump of the 1930s. By the time of Keynes's death, this view was well on its way to orthodoxy (Klein, 1947 (1966), pp. 46–7; Hansen, 1947, pp. 201–2). It was to recur again and again in the ensuing years – not least in the writings of some of Keynes's most enthusiastic followers (Stewart, 1964, p. 66; Robinson, 1967, pp. 650–1; Robinson and Eatwell, 1973, pp. 41–8; Robinson, 1975, pp. 128–9).

These two rhetorical residues from Keynes's attempted revolution subsequently caused problems. The Keynes vs the classics discussion inevitably evolved into an examination of the few strategic assumptions which separated the two. As a result, by the time of Keynes's death the view had emerged that his contribution to pure theory was relatively minimal. This was not to deny that his innovations in substance (aggregation, for example) and emphasis were unimportant, if only because they were related to policy, or because they forced others to think matters through yet again (Samuelson, 1946; Haberler, 1946). However, the stage was set for further attempts to downplay the book's importance.

To see what happened over the ensuing three decades or so, one must inevitably rely on the scholarly equivalent of snapshots and hope that the selection does not distort the underlying realities. My selection from the 1950s comes from a twentieth anniversary assessment of the *General Theory*, where J.R. Schlessinger argued:

> (a) Keynes' original thesis, based in no considerable measure upon a misinterpretation of his predecessors, has now become qualified almost to the point of non-existence. (b) In the area of methodology and terminology, the Keynesian approach was notably triumphant; this should not, however, be confused with a theoretical victory. (c) With respect to public policy, Keynes and his followers scored a signal victory over the 'price flexibility school', but contrary to popular impression (carefully nurtured by Keynes' disciples) the latter was a small and relatively powerless group. (Schlessinger, 1956, p. 581)

The next decade or so was to provide confirmation for Schlessinger's last point for many scholars, for there was much more work on the actual policy advice of British and American economists during the 1930s. This revealed that the advice they offered was much more heterogeneous than the myth suggested and that countercyclical fiscal policy recommendations were relatively common before 1936 on both sides of the Atlantic (Hutchison, 1968; Stein, 1969; Davis, 1971). This emerging evidence led at least one economist to assert that 'among economists there was no Keynesian revolution' (Tulloch, 1971, p. xiv). In 1975, Harry Johnson pushed this trend to its limit:

> Had policy-makers of the 1930s really understood what was occurring in the international monetary system and their own part in it, or had economists of

the time understood it (as they could have by developing available monetary theory) and explained it effectively, the great depression of the 1930s would have been nipped in the bud and the *General Theory* either not written or received as one eccentric English economist's rationalization of his local problems. (Johnson, 1975, p. 112)

Of course, there was dissent from these views. For example, in Keynes's Cambridge some of those intimately involved with Keynes in the 1930s (and some of their students) protested against bastard Keynesianism, or the contemporary Keynesian orthodoxy whose development had accompanied and aided the emphasis on the theoretical unimportance of the *General Theory*. Yet some of these protesters, concerned with threats to the 'old time religion' and calling for a return to a correct reading of the appropriate sacred texts,[3] were not always that convincing defenders of Keynes. Despite the accumulating evidence they continued, as we have noted above, to promulgate the myth of Keynes the lonely policy adviser. As well, as Leijonhufvud has suggested (1981, p. 177), with their emphasis on the theoretical insights of Kalecki, Joan Robinson and her followers often gave the impression that Keynes was little more than a rather important pre-Kaleckian (or post-Kaleckian if they argued that Kalecki preceded Keynes in developing the theory of employment and that he developed more powerful tools) (Robinson, 1978, p. 55). In this version of events all that Keynes contributed were 'his wide sweep, his brilliant polemic, and, above all, his position within the orthodox citadel' (*ibid.*, p. 58), useful attributes for a publicist. Others, less sympathetic to Kalecki, might grant Keynes more of a contribution, but it was still played down.

If these were the trends up to the mid-1970s, one would have expected a decline in interest in Keynes, despite centenaries and other anniversaries. Yet, to judge by the literature, there has been a revival of interest in Keynes. A glance at this literature, varied as it is, suggests to me that there has also been a change of focus in that literature. There are still, it is true, essays examining Keynes's contemporary relevance, essays which use Keynes to justify positions taken up on other grounds and essays which use Keynes as a stick to attack one's opponents. The enterprise of economics in the spirit of Keynes – an enterprise which has always has its adherents – continues. But I think it can be argued that much of the revival has been concerned with the historical Keynes. It has attempted to fix Keynes's work more firmly within the wide-ranging enterprise that was interwar monetary economics and to examine its impact.

Several factors have doubtless played a role in this revival of interest. New materials have played a role. After all, Don Patinkin's *Keynes' Monetary Thought* (1976), which has itself stimulated a large literature, started life as a request for a review article for the *Economic Journal* of six volumes of *The Collected Writings of John Maynard Keynes*. Similarly, the availability of the papers of Keynes's contemporaries, most notably Ralph Hawtrey and Dennis Robertson, have helped the study of Keynes in context (Black, 1977; Davis, 1981; Deutscher, 1984; Howson, 1985; Presley, 1978), as has availability of material in official archives. However, the disarray of contemporary monetary theory, which has its parallels with the 1920s and 1930s, has also helped send many scholars back to the past.

Inevitably the quality of the literature has been mixed, but it has shed considerable light. For example, after Don Patinkin's *Anticipations of the General Theory* (1982), the case for Kalecki as a precursor or multiple will never be the same again, as some post-Keynesians have noted (Asimakopulos, 1983; Harcourt and O'Shaughnessy, 1985). Similarly, recent work on Keynes and expectations has made it clear that much of what might be called Shackle's Keynesianism – Coddington's fundamentalism (1983, ch. 6) – is a misrepresentation of Keynes's position, for Keynes's *General Theory* expectations were far from irrational, as Allan Meltzer and others have pointed out (Meltzer, 1981; O'Donnell, 1982; Carabelli, 1986). And similarly recent reconsiderations of the Keynes–Tinbergen discussions of 1939–40 have thrown considerable light on Keynes's views and made them look less silly than previously thought (Pesaran and Smith, 1985). One could go on, but my point should be clear. There are gains in looking back at Keynes and his contemporaries as historical figures, taking full advantages of the materials available. In doing so we will probably shed some light.

In the space remaining I should like to take this argument a bit further by looking at one area which is related to my introductory discussion of the rhetorical myths associated with the *General Theory*. I am doing so in rather summary fashion in the hope of stimulating further discussion rather than settling any issues. I want to look yet again at the literature on the Keynesian 'revolution' in economic policy.

In the discussion of the Keynesian revolution in economic policy the recent conventional wisdom follows Keynes, who commenting on Pigou's *Socialism versus Capitalism* (1937) remarked:

> As in the case of Dennis [Robertson], when it comes to practice, there is really extremely little between us. Why do they insist on maintaining theories from which their own practical conclusions cannot possibly follow? It is a sort of Society for the Preservation of Ancient Monuments. (*CW*, XIV, p. 259)

If one needs further evidence for agreement on practice, one needs only to look at *The Times* for 1932 and 1933, where both Keynes and Pigou signed joint letters advocating counter-cyclical fiscal policy (*CW*, XXI, pp. 126, 137–40), and Keynes wrote to the editor explicitly denying a difference in view between them on loan-financed public works (*ibid.*, pp. 200–1) or the comments on the unusual position of Lionel Robbins in the *General Theory* itself (*CW*, VII, p. 20n). I think it would now be almost unanimously agreed among historians of economic thought that proposals for countercyclical public works were hardly peculiarly Keynesian. One could go even further and argue that Pigou and Robertson were more consistently in favour of such policies than Keynes, whose interwar support for them waxed and waned with his evolving theoretical position. This same consensus, albeit with exceptions, could also be observed among Keynes's Anglo-American contemporaries concerning the utility of deliberately engineering further wage cuts as a cure for depression.

This leaves us with a problem: what was all the fuss about? This was the position taken up by some in the late 1960s and early 1970s, as I have noted above. If one looked to Keynes's own practice, one would get two answers. This first was not peculiar to the *General Theory*, for it was also a part of the style of the *Treatise on Money*. This practice, taken on board by most of the economics profession, saw the use of Keynes's set of macroeconomic categories and their supposed interrelationships because they made it: (1) easier to reach conclusions on public works, for example, which might previously have been reached by other means, and (2) possibly, in conjunction with evolving statistics and statistical techniques, to reach more informed policy judgements. The clearest example here in Keynes's lifetime came in the British wartime budget judgements, such as that for 1941 (*CW*, XXII, ch. 3). The second, according to Keynes, related to monetary policy, for if his *General Theory* approach to the theory of the rate of interest was correct, the authorities had some degree of freedom in the use of interest rate policy in the pursuit of economic stability. Interestingly enough, none of Keynes's Cambridge contemporaries – Pigou, Robertson or Henderson – was completely happy with the first, in either its *Treatise* or *General Theory* forms (Howson and Winch, 1977, esp. p. 64.7; *CW*, XXII, pp. 325–54; Sayers, 1956, pp. 55–6, 67–74).[4] As regards the second, Keynes and Robertson were in conflict over this in meetings of the Economic Advisory Council early in 1937 (Howson and Winch, 1977, pp. 140–1 and later).

As far as the literature on those matters goes, I will concentrate on that for the UK, for not only is the American literature thinner, although of high quality, but it only deals with the first aspect of Keynes's practice. In Britain, leaving aside Richard Sayers's masterly Official Civil History of wartime *Financial Policy* (1956), the first serious examination of the public records for the relevant period were by Susan Howson (1975), and with Donald Winch (1977). Their work centred primarily on the Treasury and its reactions to outside influence in the 1930s and to the deliberations of the Economic Advisory Council and its committees, particularly the Committee of Economists, and was concerned with both monetary and fiscal policy. On the basis of the materials they examined, they were prepared to argue that on the matter of budgetary policy, some senior Treasury officials had come to join the economists' consensus by the late 1930s. The war brought further developments, notably the 1941 budget, the 1944 Employment Policy White Paper and the 1945 National Debt Enquiry. By 1945 they argue that the '"conversion" of the Treasury to Keynes's ideas on economic management was apparently complete' (*ibid.*, pp. 162, 152). Some were prepared to go even further. In 1978, Terrence Hutchison, largely on the basis of his own work on the published views of economists in the 1930s (1968), of Howson and Winch, and of Richard Sayers's *The Bank of England 1891-1944* (1976), was arguing that 'not only among top Treasury officials, but at *the top of the Bank of England*, the conversion to Keynesian ideas had taken place *well before the publication of The General Theory*' (1978, p. 194; italics in original). Keynesian ideas in this case, however, only concerned public expenditure. Inevitably there was a reaction. Throughout the emphasis was on the Treasury, as work by George Peden (1979, 1980, 1983, 1984), Roger Middleton (1981, 1982, 1985) and Alan Booth (1983) attempted to take the arguments of Howson and Winch and, more important, Hutchison apart. In the process a number of important issues were raised, particularly the role of ideas other than those of economists in the process and the role of economic analysis underlying the classical Treasury view, as well as whether any Keynesian conversion occurred at all, or if it did, whether it should be moved to later years – 1947 or 1949 being the candidates settled. Throughout, although Peden is a partial exception, the emphasis has been on fiscal policy, and in all cases the emphasis has rested mainly on the views of senior administrative class Treasury civil servants, none of whom were trained economists.[5] Finally, the starting-point for defining the Treasury's views in the literature has been mid-1929 or later; there has been no thorough examination in the critical literature as to what the Treasury might have believed as it put together its classic 1929 condemnation of loan-financed public works, perhaps because of gaps in the public records. Rather the starting-point for most discussions has been Sir Richard Hopkins's evidence before the Macmillan Committee, where after the discussions of the previous year, Hopkins might have been expected to have been more elusive.

In the process, I believe several things have been lost. First, as I have suggested, monetary policy has dropped almost completely out of the picture, even though if one compares Treasury thinking on the determinants of interest rates in 1945–6 with that of, say, 1935–9, it is clear that a dramatic change has occurred (Howson, 1987). Secondly, I think that many of the critics have ignored, in their reading of the documents, an important aspect of the successful mandarin's style noted by James Meade when he spoke of Sir Richard Hopkins:

> He talks and writes so intelligently on the most difficult financial problems and has so acute an understanding of the practical and now[6] of the theoretical issues involved; and yet, where an academic would attempt to state precisely and pungently the points at issue where agreement could not be reached, he instinctively, and, indeed, avowedly attempts to find a meaningless form of words with which everyone can agree. (Meade Diary, 27 April 1945)

This is not an undesirable skill in a civil servant. It saw Hopkins through almost twenty years of senior Treasury service, including major roles in preparing every major Treasury document from its contribution to the 1929 *Memoranda on Certain Proposals Relating to Unemployment* to the 1945 *First Report of the National Debt Enquiry*. It also meant, not infrequently, that the resulting documents were internally inconsistent, giving critics, such as Keynes, a field day on occasion.[7] Yet if one stands back from the details of documentary drafting and looks at the broader picture, one can see changes at work. This leads me to a third point. For the past two years I have spent some of my time preparing an edition of the professional diary kept by James Meade between November 1944, when he agreed to succeed Lionel Robbins as Director of the Economic Section of the Cabinet Office, and September 1946. Meade, of course, was hardly a disinterested observer in the progress of the changes under discussion and, like Keynes, he would fasten on impediments to the movement towards the new order. Yet Meade's diary and the mass of documentation I have gone through in the process of annotation, especially for one who cut his first teeth on documents from the Treasury of the 1920s, do reflect a world where the changes documented by Howson and Winch have left a powerful mark, even if senior Treasury civil servants remained non-economists. The whole structure of interdepartmental committees was changing along Keynesian lines. Even within the Treasury, all one needs to do is look at the Chancellor's Budget Committee. Not only was Keynes a member after 1940, joined by Meade in 1945, but also the types of document produced, considered and even passed up to the Chancellor were markedly different in their orientation. The National Debt Enquiry was set up not because the Treasury needed to know anything about a capital levy – Hopkins knew all about that from last time – but because Hopkins believed that in connection with the government's employment policy commitments Keynes had important and useful ideas about debt management policy.[8] All in all, the evidence would seem to confirm Richard Sayers's observation that 'views from academic sources always reach Whitehall sooner or later' (1956, p. 153).[9] In Keynes's case the views seem to have travelled very quickly, despite the fact that implementation took a bit longer.

This is probably the best place to end my discussion. I hope that the preceding pages have emphasized that, most important, Keynes's views and his influence are now perhaps best regarded as historical questions. The serious study of Keynes in context – increasingly shorn of the rhetoric of revolution or religion – can throw useful light on our past, and even our present. In this light something significant did happen forty to fifty years ago. We may still be uncertain as to exactly how or why it occurred, but it is worthwhile to devote still more historical attention to sorting out our past.

Notes

1. Throughout all references to *The Collected Writings of John Maynard Keynes* (London, 1971—) are referred to in the form *CW*, together with volume number and page numbers.
2. Every 12–18 months, to service markets outside the USA, the Royal Economic Society find itself reprinting 5000 copies of the paperback edition.
3. Joan Robinson would speak of John Hicks's 'repenting' his invention of IS/LM: see Robinson (1970), p. xiv.
4. This is not to say that, for example, Pigou became more at home with aggregation over time. The structure of his *Employment and Equilibrium* (1941) clearly shows the influence of the *General Theory* and contemporary discussions. Yet even here, the influence does not seem to have taken all that much hold in his applied work; one need only look at the structure of the arguments in his *Aspects of British Economic History 1918-1925* (1947) to see what I mean.
5. One might argue that R.G. Hawtrey was a senior administrative class civil servant and an economist, but his views have not been the main subject of discussion, except for attempts to minimize the influence of his classic 1925 article, 'Public Expenditure and the Demand for Labour'. For a discussion of Hawtrey's views and influence see Howson (1985).
6. Hopkins had just reported to Meade that he had read the *General Theory* and Robertson's *Essays in Monetary Theory* for the first time during the previous month.
7. See, for example, his comments on what became the 1944 Employment Policy White Paper (*CW*, XXVII, pp. 364–72). Yet he prefaced these remarks with one on the document as a whole: 'an outstanding State Paper which, if one casts one's mind back ten years or so, represents a revolution in official opinion' (*ibid.*, p. 364).
8. See the documents on PROT273/389, originally Hopkins's own file on the Enquiry, subsequently passed to his successor, Sir Edward Bridges.
9. I am indebted to Susan Howson for this reference.

References

Asimakopulos, A. (1983), 'Anticipations of Keynes's *General Theory?*', *Canadian Journal of Economics*, **XVI**, August, 517–30.

Black, R.D.C. (1977), 'Ralph George Hawtrey, 1879–1975', *Proceedings of the British Academy*, **LXIII**, 363–97.

Booth, A. (1983), 'The "Keynesian revolution" in economic policy-making', *Economic History Review*, 2nd ser., **XXXVI**, February, 103–23.

Bryce, R.B. (1935), 'An introduction to a monetary theory of employment', reprinted in *CW*, **XXIX**, 132–50.

Carabelli, A. (1986), 'On Keynes's method', PhD dissertation, University of Cambridge.

Coddington, A. (1983), *Keynesian Economics: The Search for First Principles*, London: Allen and Unwin.

Davis, E.G. (1981), 'R.G. Hawtrey, 1879–1975', in D.P. O'Brien and J.R. Presley (eds), *Pioneers of Modern Economics in Britain*, London: Macmillan.

Davis, J.R. (1971), *The New Economics and the Old Economists*, Ames, Ia.: Iowa State University Press.

Deutscher, P. (1984), 'R.G. Hawtrey and the development of macroeconomics in the interwar period', PhD dissertation, University of Toronto.

Haberler, G. (1946), 'The place of the general theory of employment, interest and money in the history of economic thought', *Review of Economics and Statistics*, **XXVIII**, November, 187–94.

Hansen, A.H. (1947), 'The *General Theory* (2)', in S.E. Harris (ed.), *The New Economics: Keynes's Influence on Theory and Public Policy*, London: Dobson.

Harcourt, G.C. and O'Shaughnessy, T.J. (1985), 'Keynes' unemployment equilibrium: some insights from Joan Robinson, Piero Sraffa and Richard Kahn', in G.C. Harcourt (ed.), *Keynes and his Contemporaries*, London: Macmillan.

Hawtrey, R.G. (1925), 'Public expenditure and the demand for labour', *Economica*, **V**, February, 38–48.

Howson, Susan (1975), *Domestic Monetary Management in Britain, 1919–38*, Cambridge: Cambridge University Press.

Howson, Susan (1985), 'Hawtrey and the real world', in G.C. Harcourt (ed.), *Keynes and his Contemporaries*, London: Macmillan.

Howson, Susan (1987), 'Cheap money and debt management in Britain, 1932–1951', in P.L. Cottrell and D.E. Moggridge (eds), *Money and Power*, London: Macmillan.

Howson, Susan and Winch, Donald (1977), *The Economic Advisory Council 1930–1939: A Study in Economic Advice during Depression and Recovery*, Cambridge: Cambridge University Press.

Hutchison, T.W. (1968), *Economics and Economic Policy in Britain 1946–1966: Some Aspects of their Inter-relations*, London: Allen and Unwin.

Hutchison, T.W. (1978), *On Revolutions and Progress in Economic Knowledge*, Cambridge: Cambridge University Press.

Johnson, H.G. (1975), 'Keynes and British Economics', in Milo Keynes (ed.), *Essays on John Maynard Keynes*, Cambridge: Cambridge University Press.

Klein, L.R. (1947), *The Keynesian Revolution*, New York: MacMillan; 2nd edn, 1966.

Knight, F.H. (1937), 'Unemployment and Mr Keynes' revolution in economic theory', *Canadian Journal of Economics and Political Science*, **III**, February, 100–23.

Lawson, T. and Pesaran, H. (1985), *Keynes' Economics: Methodological Issues*, Armonk, NY: M.E. Sharpe.

Leijonhufvud, A. (1981), *Information and Coordination: Essays in Macroeconomic Theory*, Oxford: Oxford University Press.

Meltzer, A. (1981), 'Keynes's *General Theory*: a different perspective', *Journal of Economic Literature*, **XIX**, March, 34–64.

Middleton, R. (1981), 'Fiscal policy and economic management in the 1930s', PhD dissertation, University of Cambridge.

Middleton, R. (1982), 'The Treasury in the 1930s: political and administrative constraints to the acceptance of the "New" economics', *Oxford Economic Papers*, n.s., **XXXIV**, March, 48–77.

Middleton, R. (1985), *Towards the Managed Economy: Keynes, the Treasury and the Fiscal Policy Debate of the 1930s*, London: Methuen.

O'Donnell, R.M. (1982), 'Keynes: philosophy and economics – an approach to rationality and uncertainty', PhD dissertation, University of Cambridge.

Patinkin, D. (1978), *Keynes Monetary Thought: A Study of its Development*, Durham, N.C.: Duke University Press.

Patinkin, D. (1982), *Anticipations of the General Theory?, and Other Essays on Keynes*, Chicago: University of Chicago Press.

Peden, G. (1979), *British Rearmament and the Treasury, 1932*-1939, Edinburgh: Scottish Academic Press.

Peden, G. (1980), 'Keynes, the Treasury and unemployment in the later nineteen-thirties', *Oxford Economic Papers*, n.s., **XXXII**, March, 1–14.

Peden, G. (1983), 'Sir Richard Hopkins and the "Keynesian revolution" in employment policy, 1929–1945', *Economic History Review*, 2nd ser., **XXXVI**, May, 281–96.

Peden, G. (1984), 'The "Treasury view" on public works and unemployment in the interwar period', *Economic History Review*, 2nd ser., **XXXVII**, May, 167–81.

Peden, G. (1986), *Keynes, the Treasury and British Economic Policy*, London: Macmillan.

Pesaran, H. and Smith, R. (1985), 'Keynes on econometrics', in T. Lawson and H. Pesaran (eds), *Keynes' Economics: Methodological Issues*, Armonk, NY: M.E. Sharpe.

Pigou, A.C. (1936), 'Mr J.M. Keynes' *General Theory of Employment, Interest and Money*', *Economica*, n.s., **III**, May, 115–32.

Pigou, A.C. (1937), *Socialism versus Capitalism*, London: Macmillan.

Pigou, A.C. (1941), *Employment and Equilibrium*, London: Macmillan.

Pigou, A.C. (1947), *Aspects of British Economic History 1918–1925*, London: Macmillan.

Presley, J.R. (1978), *Robertsonian Economics*, London: Macmillan.

Robinson, E.A.G. (1967), 'Review of *The Age of Keynes*', *Economic Journal*, **LXXVII**, September, 650–1.

Robinson, Joan (1964), *Economic Philosophy*, Harmondsworth: Penguin.

Robinson, Joan (1975), 'What has become of the Keynesian revolution?', in Milo Keynes (ed.), *Essays on John Maynard Keynes*, Cambridge: Cambridge University Press.

Robinson, Joan (1978), *Contributions to Modern Economics*, Oxford: Blackwell.

Robinson, Joan and Eatwell, John (1973), *An Introduction to Modern Economics*, London: McGraw-Hill.

Samuelson, P.A. (1946), 'Lord Keynes and the *General Theory*', *Econometrica*, **XIV**, July, 187–200.

Sayers, R.S. (1956), *Financial Policy 1939–1945*, London: Longman/HMSO.

Sayers, R.S. (1976), *The Bank of England, 1891–1944*, Cambridge: Cambridge University Press.

Schlessinger, J.R. (1956), 'After twenty years: the *General Theory*', *Quarterly Journal of Economics*, **LXX**, November, 581–602.

Schumpeter, J.A. (1936), 'The general theory of employment, interest and money', *Journal of the American Statistical Association*, **XXXI**, December, 791–5.

Stein, H. (1969), *The Fiscal Revolution in America*, Chicago: University of Chicago Press.

Stewart, M. (1964), *Keynes and After*, Harmondsworth: Penguin.

Tulloch, G. (1971), 'Foreword' to J.R. Davis, *The New Economics and the Old Economists*, Ames, Ia.: Iowa State University Press.

5   The spread of Keynesian doctrines and practices in the United States
Walter S. Salant

This chapter attempts to identify the main channels through which Keynes's major book, *The General Theory of Employment, Interest and Money* (hereafter called *GT*), influenced economic policy and practice in the USA.

The subject obviously implies that Keynes did greatly influence doctrine and policy in the USA, so I should say at the outset that this implication has been questioned. While it struck me at first as absurd to question it, I have concluded, on reflection, that it is not absurd to do so, especially as doubts have been expressed by responsible people. Two are former chairmen of the Council of Economic Advisers, Leon Keyserling and Herbert Stein. Their views about economic policy could hardly be further apart. Stein's book, *The Fiscal Revolution in America*, all but says there was no fiscal change that can properly be regarded as a revolution and associated with Keynes, since the fiscal policies he advocated had earlier been advocated by others. Keyserling explicitly denied that Keynes had anything to do with the Truman administration's economic policy.

I will say now only two things on this subject. One is that their view deserves serious consideration, both because it has some merit and because such consideration forces one to think hard about what is meant by Keynesian doctrines and policies. The other is that, while I think they are both correct as to particular acts of policy, I think them wrong about the broad point: Keynes's ideas and the ferment they created did change the intellectual climate. I proceed on the assumption that Keynes's ideas really did affect doctrines and policies in the USA.

An attempt by any one person to give a detailed account of the channels through which writings influenced events is bound to be affected by the window through which the writer has seen the developments he describes; they would undoubtedly look different to someone who had seen them from a different view.

In the case of 'Keynesian doctrines and policies', it makes a difference not only who does the writing, but what the subject is. There is a difference, as is well known, between what one calls Keynesian economics and the economics of Keynes. This chapter could be about either or both. At the narrowest extreme, one could interpret Keynesian doctrines and practices as being confined to the adoption of countercyclical fiscal policies or policies designed to combat supposed longer-run tendencies for the economy to operate at less than the full potential of its labour and capital stock. At the other extreme, the term 'Keynesian doctrines and policies' could be broadly interpreted as rejection of the paradigm according to which market forces can be relied on to maintain or restore high output and employment and the replacement of that paradigm by another.

What is at issue could be any of these questions or all of them. To understand why Keynes's ideas were a novel contribution it is necessary to know the ideas about both theory and policy, especially fiscal policy, that were accepted before the *General Theory* was published.

Pre-Keynesian ideas about theory and policy

The widely accepted view of professional economists before the depression of the 1930s was that in a free market economy unemployment would be limited to the frictional and casual kind. Displacement of workers caused by structural changes would be overcome by the operation of market forces, such as the competition of workers for jobs. When expenditure on capital goods was too little to use all the saving that would be done at high levels of income, interest rates would fall enough to stimulate greater capital expenditure. According to this view, there could be overproduction of specific goods or types of good, but there could be no general overproduction, except as a temporary result of frictions, including lack of knowledge due to imperfections of communication and similar obstacles to adjustment that would be overcome in time.

At the same time, it was recognized that actual economic activity exhibited fluctuations. During the 1920s and 1930s there were intensive efforts to explain cyclical fluctuations in output and employment. This body of business cycle literature and the classical view that there could be no persistent failure of markets to clear were quite incompatible, as was noted by two observers commenting on Keynes's *General Theory* twenty years after its publication.

William A. Salant observed:

> It was in the spirit of classical and neo-classical analysis that a smoothly working economic system would tend toward equilibrium at full employment. The automatic mechanism by which full employment was maintained or restored was not very clearly spelled out ... Students of the saving–investment process, beginning with Wicksell ... dealt with disturbances in the equilibrium of the classical system. Some of them adovcated intervention by the monetary authority in order to offset these disturbances rather than reliance on the automatic self-correcting forces inherent in the system. They did not, however,

provide an alternative theory of the determination of the level of output. The Keynesian system did provide such a theory. (Salant, *American Economic Review*, May 1957, p. 91)

And Tibor Scitovsky said that 'Keynes coordinated already known bits of economic theorizing, supplied some missing links, and created a coherent theory of employment out of it'. He then went on to say:

> Let us bear in mind that before the *General Theory* unemployment was regarded as the result of friction, temporary disequilibrium, or the monopoly power of labor unions. This meant that the business cycle had to be explained within a theoretical framework that made no allowance for the possibility of variations in employment and income. It also meant that business cycle policy had to be formulated without the benefit of a conceptually satisfactory measure of prosperity, such as the level of income or output or employment. This may sound absurd to us today; but it was Keynes's *General Theory* that made us realize its absurdity. (Scitovsky, *American Economic Review*, May 1957, p. 93)

The views about what came to be called 'macroeconomic theory' and about policy that most of the established or rising economists held before publication of the *General Theory* were well indicated in the book by a group of Harvard economists, including Schumpeter, in *The Economics of the Recovery Program*, published in 1934. An example of their orthodox theory is the proposition that saving is simply an indirect form of expenditure, so that a cut in consumption automatically caused an increase in investment (in the sense of increased spending on capital goods or inventory accumulation).

With regard to policy, the prevailing orthodoxy was that the government should not interfere with the working of the market, or should do so only in limited ways. Some of the injunctions against propping up markets through creation of what was regarded as 'artificially' easy money were based on the view that depressions grew out of the excesses or at least mistakes of the preceding prosperities or booms, and that the resulting mistakes had to be liquidated before a recovery could be 'sound'. This view, associated with Austrian theorists, notably von Hayek in *Prices and Production*, and ridiculed by some of its opponents as the 'Crime and Punishment Theory' of the business cycle, regarded demand stimulation through either expansionary monetary policy or government budget deficits as positively harmful because it tended to impede 'liquidation' of the mistakes of the preceding prosperity, which was a necessary part of the therapy, and perhaps sufficient.

The *General Theory* attacked the theoretical propositions underlying those beliefs. The view that Keynes's important contribution was his attack on the validity of classical and neo-classical theory and the offering of an alternative theory has been strongly advanced by Patinkin (1977), who has emphasized that the *General Theory* is a book about theory, with only incidental references to policy. This view was in fact supported by Keynes himself; in the Preface he says, 'its main purpose is to deal with difficult questions of theory, and only in the second place with the applications of this theory to practice'.

The more widely held and less sophisticated understanding of Keynesian doctrine is much narrower: that it consisted of advocacy of countercyclical fiscal policy; i.e. that when business is slack and there is substantial unemployment, the government should increase its expenditure and/or reduce taxes so as to run a budget deficit, financing it by borrowing, and that during periods of prosperity it should do the opposite.

Prevailing orthodoxy of opinion leaders and the general public prior to the Great Depression held, to the contrary, that the government's budget should be balanced every year, but not for the reasons advanced by professional theorists mentioned above. The reasons more commonly given were that budget deficits were *necessarily* inflationary regardless of the extent of unemployment of labour, plant and equipment, and/or that increases in the public debt (or the payment of interest on it?) involve a loss of real national income. These reasons were supplemented by the naïve application to the whole economy of 'common-sense' precepts of 'sound' individual finance. Many other opponents of deficits merely accepted the view of established authority figures.

It should be recognized that before publication of the *General Theory*, and even before publication of Keynes's 1933 pamphlet, *The Means to Prosperity*, some established and outstanding economists, such as J.M. Clark, James Harvey Rogers and Jacob Viner understood that recovery required an expansion of aggregate demand and understood clearly the argument for a planned expansion of loan-financed expenditure, but in 1932 and even later they nevertheless thought such a programme unwise.

The reason was their judgement that, in the shaky financial situation that prevailed after the summer of 1931, the fears of and opposition to such a programme on the part of domestic and foreign bankers, businessmen and others would lead to an outflow of capital and declines in security prices, including a fall in the value of collateral for bank loans, that would aggravate the banking crisis and prevent or greatly restrain a recovery of investment. In the *General Theory* (pp. 119–20) Keynes himself mentions the possibility of such confidence-shaking effects.

Even before the economic situation deteriorated from an ordinary cyclical downturn into devastating depression, there were advocates of countercyclical spending. Indeed there was professional and some official support for such spending during the prosperity of the 1920s. Herbert

Stein documents this fact fully with respect to the USA in *The Fiscal Revolution in America.* And George Garvy (1973) shows that countercyclical fiscal policy was actively supported by some economists of pre-Hitler Germany. But in both countries these supporters either did not have answers to the theoretical objections of classical and neo-classical economists or, if they had such answers, were unable before the *General Theory* to make them persuasive to supporters of financial orthodoxy.

It is clear that Keynesian doctrine, even on the narrowest definition of it as countercyclical fiscal policy, was not accepted or even generally respectable up to and through the first Roosevelt administration. Roosevelt himself denounced the budget deficit and advocated balancing the budget during his first (1932) presidential campaign and made moves to cut government expenditures during his first year in office.

In fact the early New Deal, at least during Roosevelt's entire first term, was not an exercise in Keynesian economics. The centre-piece of the recovery programme in the early years was the National Recovery Administration (NRA), established under the National Industrial Recovery Act, which, among other things, put floors under prices and hourly wages. That legislation did not expand demand for goods and services, and it was the deficiency of demand that was the actual problem. Most of the federal budget deficits during the first years of the New Deal were the result of the depression, and the resulting fall in tax revenues and the expansions of relief and other depression-related expenditures. Although some economists supported monetary and fiscal expansion, only a few who did so were prominent in the FDR administration before 1937. The original New Deal intellectuals were not mainly economists, and of the economists among them only a few were students of economic fluctuations, or of money or of what we now call macroeconomics.

The beginnings of respectability
What might be referred to as Keynesian doctrines and practices did not begin to become accepted as part of government policy and respectable thinking until Roosevelt's second term, beginning in 1937 and lasting until the expansion of defence and World War II expenditures in the early 1940s. Concerning this stage, I would identify four major influences on governmental thinking: (1) the Great Depression itself; (2) Keynes's *The General Theory of Employment, Interest and Money*, published in 1936, which influenced young instructors and graduate students in the economics departments of the leading universities, mainly Harvard, combined with the recruitment of many of them into governmental agencies that had responsibilities for or influence on fiscal and monetary policies; (3) the development of systematic data on national income and

expenditure, at that time not yet developed into the present system of integrated national income and product accounts, and other important economic variables; (4) the effect of the 1937–8 recession on thinking about what we now call macroeconomics; and (5) economic expansion in World War II.

The Great Depression

The influence of the Great Depression itself is in one sense obvious. It shook faith in the idea that the economy was self-adjusting, or at least that market-forces alone could be relied on to restore high employment quickly enough to avoid an unacceptable amount of human suffering and loss of production.

The General Theory

The second major influence, publication of Keynes's *General Theory*, was followed by several years of critical reviews by the most eminent members of the economics profession. These adverse reviews included one by Alvin Hansen, written before he moved from the University of Minnesota to Harvard and before he was converted into Keynes's most eminent senior supporter. Since many policy ideas that were expressed in the *General Theory* and could be deduced from it had been advanced earlier by others inside and outside the USA, it may well be asked why this book was so influential and is so widely regarded as revolutionary.

The explanation that I find most plausible arises from the view of Thomas Kuhn about how paradigms are replaced. Prevailing paradigms may become subject to question as facts inconsistent with them come to light, and the questioning intensifies as such facts accumulate, but they are rarely overthrown unless some alternative theory that accounts for those facts is advanced. In 1971, when Kenneth Galbraith asked me to organize a session of the 1971 Annual Meeting of the American Economic Association on 'Keynesians in Government', Alvin Hansen threw cold water on the idea of such a session. One of his objections was that it was hard to know whom to identify as a Keynesian; he said: 'You mention Eccles for whom I have great respect – a brilliant and original mind – but by no stretch of the immagination [*sic*] a Keynesian. He never knew anything about Keynesian economics. He strongly favoured public spending in the deep depression, but that does not make him a Keynesian.' And similarly, about Ickes, Wesley Mitchell, and others. He then quoted a statement which he attributed to James Conant: it takes a theory to kill a theory. That idea points to an interpretation, one that I am inclined to accept, of why the *General Theory* was so important: it provided an alternative to the classical and neo-classical theory, which most of the other supporters of countercyclical fiscal policies did not do. Advocates of those heretical policies thereby had a theory that they could bring to bear against the theoretical objections of the orthodox.

The perceived lack of correspondence between classical and neo-classical theory on the one hand, and the disastrously deep depression on the other, had created an appetite for a more satisfactory explanation of what was going on in the world, an appetite that was until then unsatisfied.

To put it in other words, the *General Theory* made respectable what seemed obvious to common-sense observations of the lay observer but was rejected by sophisticated theorists as fallacy indulged in by amateurs.

I have mentioned two of the fallacies in which the orthodox thought the heretics were indulging. One was the amateur's ideas that because an increase in one person's money income increases his real income, this conclusion can be generalized: that an increase in everyone's money income will raise total real income. The classical economist 'knew' that a general increase in money incomes would simply raise the price level.

Again, as noted earlier, the naïve view was that acts of saving might cause underconsumption and thereby reduce aggregate demand. The more sophisticated view denied that; it asserted instead that saving merely diverted some demand for consumption to demand for investment (i.e. spending on capital goods or on increasing inventories).

The *General Theory* made clear that the classical conclusions on these points were not true or not wholly true when resources were unemployed. The idea that 'there is no such thing as a free lunch', i.e. that an increase of one kind of output involves forgoing another, is now often referred to as something recently learned. Actually it is what economics had been teaching for approximately two centuries. What Keynes argued, and what was actually new, was that under some conditions there *is* a 'free lunch'. In short, Keynes showed that what classical economics found naïve and wrong was sometimes correct. Thus he made the disreputable respectable.

Some of the rebels against orthodox economics were already in the government, although few of them had been students of macroeconomics. By far the most notable of these as a macroeconomist was Lauchlin B. Currie, an independent-minded and creative economist who in 1934 had become the main economic adviser to Marriner Eccles, chairman of the Board of Governors of the Federal Reserve System. This activist economist, whose intellectual fertility is still insufficiently recognized, had independently developed ideas that were not greatly different from those of Keynes before the *General Theory* was published, although his first published reaction to the *General Theory* was negative. Earlier than most, perhaps including Keynes, Currie had become discouraged about the possibility of obtaining economic recovery through expansionary monetary policy alone and had become convinced that on expansionary fiscal policy involving a government deficit was needed. With his assistant, Martin Krost, at the Federal Reserve, he continued and further developed a statistical series begun at the Treasury designed to measure the montly net contribution of the federal government's fiscal operations to the flow of money income or purchasing power (on this, see Alan Sweezy, 1972).

Largely through the recruiting efforts of Currie and others, or independently through the attractions of the New Deal, young pro-Keynesian economists, mostly graduate students and young instructors from Harvard, were brought into strategic places in the government.

The 1937–8 recession

Another influence on official and unofficial thinking about macro-economic policy was the 1937–8 recession. The Federal Reserve's index of industrial production plunged 29 per cent in the five months between September 1937 and February 1938 and 33 per cent in the ten months between July 1937 and May 1938, still the fastest fall on record.

Both monetary and fiscal actions in 1936 and 1937 were major causes of that recession. The budget deficit fell over $3 billion from 1936 to 1937. That may sound small to us now, but it was about $3\frac{1}{2}$ per cent of 1936 GNP, a fraction of GNP that would amount to roughly $150 billion now.

That decrease did not reflect either adherence to Keynesian policies or repudiation of them. It was accounted for mainly by two things. One was that expenditures in 1936 had been swollen by the payment of the veterans' 'bonus' and none was paid in 1937. The other cause was the coming into effect for the first time in 1937 of the payroll taxes under the new Social Security legislation.

The administration had opposed the bonus and Roosevelt had vetoed the Bill, but it was passed over his veto. His veto message offers an answer to the question of how 'Keynesian' the administration was during FDR's first term. The message denied the efficacy of 'mere spending' for the sake of recovery (Stein, 1969a, p. 58).

The payroll taxes were of course part of the long-run Social Security plan, entirely unrelated to recovery policy; they were not offset in their effects by payment of social security benefits, which did not begin in substantial amount until 1938.

Federal Reserve policy in 1936–7 also bore some responsibility for the 1937–8 recession. In the spring of 1936 the price level began to rise sharply, although unemployment, despite its great decline since 1933, was still probably between 16 and 18 per cent of the labour force. The Federal Reserve was greatly concerned that the rise of prices would continue and that the huge expansion of bank reserves, which greatly exceeded legal requirements, and the money supply might later become too hard to control. Because of this concern, in August 1936 the Federal Reserve raised reserve requirements for member banks by 50 per cent, announcing at the same time that the existing easy money policy was still unchanged. Then it raised them another one-third through equal increases in March and May of 1937. These increases in legal reserve requirements greatly reduced the excess reserves of member banks, but it left them at what was then still a large amount, leading the Federal Reserve again to express confidence that the increase in requirements would have little effect on credit conditions; apparently the Fed did not recognize that reserves that were 'excess' in a legal sense may not be excessive in an economic sense, although the mere fact that banks held them instead of investing in more earning assets should have suggested that they were not excess in an economic sense, that the demand of banks for liquidity was high.

Perhaps the failures (a) to recognize that banks have a demand for liquidity, and that it may exceed levels that satisfy legal requirements, should be regarded as evidence that Keynes's analysis of liquidity had not been completely absorbed, (b) to appreciate that large unused capacity would make a general demand-induced rise of prices temporary or at least limit it and (c) to recognize that such a rise may reflect a movement in the aggregate supply curve may all be symptoms that acceptance of Keynesian views remained incomplete for many years after the 1936–8 episode.

The 1937–8 recession undermined the theory that increased government spending need only get recovery of the economy started; that the resulting expansion would revive private investment; and that output and employment would then continue to expand without benefit of the expanded government spending, and the economy could maintain prosperity on its own, and government spending could then return to its normal level. This is the idea underlying what was felicitously called 'pump-priming'. The recession persuaded many supporters of this theory that it was incorrect.

The 1937–8 recession happened to have occured when macro-economists were debating Keynes's *General Theory*. One of the book's main themes (the distinguished economist, D.H. Robertson, thought its *main* theme) was that in a market economy involuntary unemployment could persist. Economists who doubted that the classical and neo-classical theory was applicable to the real world and who supported expansionary fiscal policy as a means to prosperity took the reversal of the recovery as support for this anti-classical idea; the economy's decline when the fiscal stimulus was withdrawn could be interpreted as a relapse to its 'normal' state of underemployment equilibrium. A symptom of this new view was Alvin Hansen's book, *Full Recovery or Stagnation?*, published in 1938.

The discouraging and frustrating recession of 1937–8 led the administration to abandon 'some moves in a budget-balancing direction'. In the spring of 1938 Roosevelt was persuaded by his advisers to embark on what Stein calls 'the first major and single-minded use of the budget to stimulate the economy' (Stein, 1969a, p. 465).

The displacement of the pump-priming idea may be regarded as another step in acceptance of Keynesian doctrine.

Perhaps the first official expression of the government's responsibility for maintenance of full use of the nation's resources, but with an optimistic rather than the pessimistic tone so often associated with the stagnationist hypothesis, is to be found in the Annual Report of the Secretary of Commerce for the Fiscal Year 1939 (pp. v–xiv). This first official expression was written by the late Richard V. Gilbert, Director of the small Division of Industrial Economics in the Office of the Secretary, with the assistance of his colleague, Roderick H. Riley.

Economic expansion in World War II
When in 1939 war broke out in Europe, the USA began to increase its exports to the Allies and build up its own defences. As US participation in the war became increasingly likely, some research units in the government began studies of US production potential, which was still far from being realized. The Keynesians in government, led by Robert Nathan and Richard Gilbert, pressed hard for increases in the defence programme unaccompanied at this early stage by curtailment of public and private civilian spending. Indeed they supported incentives to expand plant capacity so as to realize the still large unused potential. The size of this potential became the subject of intense controversy and, as defence expenditures rose, so did the question of when it was desirable to begin limiting the expansion of demand to avoid or minimize inflation.

It is not necessary here to go into those controversies; it is sufficient to note that the most optimistic views, Gilbert's and Nathan's, as to how large output could be if the economy were operating at full blast were actually exceeded by a wide margin at the peak of wartime production, and that the government economists were miles ahead of those in the universities in efforts to quantify the variables that Keynesian models emphasized. Unemployment, which was later estimated to have been 25 per cent of the civilian labourforce in 1933 and 17 per cent in 1939, was brought down to less than 2 per cent in 1943, 1944 and 1945 under the combined pressure of the great increase in the armed forces and the government's largely loan-financed war expenditures. This economic expansion was widely interpreted as showing how effective an expansion of government spending could be in putting unemployed resources to work. At the same time, of course, it showed the danger of inflation from excessive demand if prices were not controlled.

The elimination of unemployment during World War II may have been one of the greatest influences on postwar views about the role of government in attaining and maintaining high employment and production, and the possibility of avoiding serious depressions in the future. The ideas that this was a responsibility of government had, by the war's end, become widespread enough to result in passage of the Employment Act of 1946. Although that legislation, as finally enacted, did not specify the policies by which its goals were to be attained, it did represent a consensus that the government not only had the obligation to try to achieve the Act's objective, but implied that it also had the power to do so.

After World War II

By the end of World War II, Keynesian theoretical ideas had become much more acceptable to the economics profession. The violent controversy among academic economists during the first few years after publication of the *General Theory*, to a large extent intergenerational, had died down, not because many anti-Keynesians had died – they had not – but because many had been won over.

In addition, the generation of rising undergraduates – both those going into business and other professions – were increasingly being brought up on Keynesian theory. Although the first postwar college textbook in economics written along Keynesian lines, Lorie Tarshis's *Elements of Economics*, was not published until 1947, he and other economists had been teaching and drafting their textbooks and trying out their drafts on their students for several years before they were actually published. Paul A. Samuelson's *Economics: An Introductory Analysis*, also a Keynesian text, was not published until the following year. Samuelson's textbook has gone through twelve editions as of 1985 and sold several tens of millions of copies in more than twenty-five languages, so it may be regarded as having educated students all around the world for several decades. Those books were supplemented by Alvin Hansen's *A Guide to Keynes* (1953). Thus college and university students of economics, from whom the rising generations of government officials, businessmen, journalists and other opinion leaders would come, were being educated along Keynesian lines. This fact was another important part of the tide towards, first, the adoption, and then the increasing entrenchment, of Keynesian views about macroeconomic policy.

If the term 'Keynesian doctrine' is used in the loose sense of belief that government has both the ability and the obligation to iron out major fluctuations in output and employment, enactment of the Employment Act of 1946 marked a major step in its official acceptance.

Whether that is also true on a narrower intepretation of the term 'Keynesian doctrine' as reliance on fiscal policy to stabilize employment and output is more arguable. Most of those who originally conceived it were Keynesians in that sense too. But the early versions of the Bill, which called the proposed law a Full Employment Act, were strongly and successfully resisted. The legislation that was enacted set targets – 'maximum employment, production, and purchasing power' – but did not specify any substantive means of attaining or maintaining them; it only prescribed organizational means for giving the President and the Congress economic advice. If 'Keynesian doctrine' is interpreted to mean fiscal policy, and still more if it is interpreted to mean only countercyclical fiscal policy, it may be argued that the Employment Act 1946 was not a step in the progressive adoption of Keynesian doctrines and policy.

On a broader view, however, I think it was. For one thing, the government's acceptance of responsibility for seeking to achieve the specified economic goals can be interpreted to imply that many of the members of Congress who favoured the legislation thought that the government had the ability, not merely the desire or obligation, to achieve those goals.

A second reason for considering the Employment Act 1946 as 'Keynesian' is that it is not concerned merely with stabilizing the business cycle. Stability might be maintained at or around levels, including rising trends, of production that are less than the 'maximum' potential of the economy on anyone's definition, but the Act sought the 'maximum'. In that respect, it is like the *General Theory*, the main concern of which is the level of output and employment, not cyclical fluctuations.

The emphasis on maintaining maximum employment rather than merely stabilization and the explicit emphasis on growth first came with Truman's Council of Economic Advisers. That Council, the first one, was organized by Edwin Nourse, but the emphasis on growth reflected the initiative of Leon Keyserling, one of the original members and Nourse's successor as chairman. Members of the Kennedy Council have thought that emphasis on growth, as opposed to dampening cyclical fluctuations, was one of their acomplishments, which is correct, but they did not initiate that emphasis.

If the shift of emphasis in policy from stabilization of the cycle to continuing maximum employment is regarded as part of the absorption of Keynesian doctrines and policy into governmental thinking, it should be dated as having occurred during the Truman Administration, been reversed or ignored during the Eisenhower administration and then as having been restored during the Kennedy administration. These shifts may then be regarded as evidence that long-term change in doctrine occurs through a succession of steps, first, several in one direction, then a lull or a few steps in the opposite direction, and then more in the first direction, and so on.

Aside from restoring the focus of policy to continuing high production and employment, the most important contribution during the 1960s to institutionalizing Keynesianism in government policy was probably the tax cut of 1964. That has been heralded as the beginning of a 'new fiscal policy'. But Herbert Stein evidently did not think that could be regarded as one of the first applications of Keynesian doctrine, or even any application of it at all; he observes that 'nothing was less in need of a sophisticated theory to explain it than the willingness of Congress to reduce taxes'. This observation, however, ignores the fact that there was then a large budget deficit, and the proposal to reduce taxes in such a situation met considerable opposition because it was so contrary to fiscal orthodoxy.

From the point of view of 1986, it appears that economic policy ideas and practices in the 1960s represented a high point in the acceptance of Keynesian doctrines by government and private opinion in the USA. Since approximately the mid or late 1960s it has been under increasing attack, first, by academic monetarists, whose views found increasing acceptance, then by rational-expectations theorists and, more recently, by 'short-term supply-siders'. (I add 'short-term' to their usual label, to distinguish them and what they say that is new and almost unanimously rejected by trained economists, from supply-side considerations that are widely accepted by the profession but are hoary with age.) All these groups have been anti-Keynesian and, with the entry of the Reagan administration into office, Keynesians have on the whole been displaced from government positions having macroeconomic responsibilities.

The increase in the acceptability of monetarism does not appear to have been related to economic developments in the real world so much as to the persuasiveness of its leading proponents, but the intensified criticism of Keynesian theory and the increase in the influence of the other schools of thought were related to actual developments. Some of these developments were indeed different from what Keynesian theory led its proponents to expect. First, there was the increasing rise in the general price level. If, as is widely believed, this was initiated by excessively expansionary policy when output was at or near its potential, it offered no challenge to Keynesian doctrine; it was a failure to apply that doctrine. But the continuation of that inflation when output was below capacity and there was significant unemployment, and indeed even when both were actually becoming worse (i.e. stagflation), was a challenge to Keynesian doctrine and not at all what was expected by Keynesians, who tended to think mainly of changes in aggregate demand. The role of the sharp increases in oil prices in 1973–4 and 1979–80 on the general price level had not then been fully taken into account. By the time it was, Keynesianism had already been discredited in the eyes of many economists and probably most laymen.

Secondly, after 1981 those doubts were further intensified by the election and entry into office of a new administration that vigorously repudiated such doctrines. During 1983 and 1984 the rate of inflation declined when the budget deficit was not only increasing, but was surpassing all previous peacetime records in relation to the GNP. This raised further questions in people's minds about the validity of Keynesian doctrines.

Concluding observations
Reviewing the past half-century of experience in the USA, several things stand out:

(1) The 'Keynesianizing' of governmental thought and practice and of opinion leaders was a gradual, evolutionary process. It was not a steady one, however; it included not merely differences in the rates of movement in one direction, but at least one reversal of direction.
(2) In the USA the intellectuals in government, especially in the civil service, were more important influences on thought about economic policy than politicians, political parties or non-governmental interest groups.
(3) From approximately the mid-1930s to the end of World War II economists in the government were ahead of those in the universities in developing the policy aspects of Keynesian macroeconomic theory and especially in its application to empirical data, to the sources of which the government economists were much closer and which they were even in a position to generate (see Jones, 1972; Stein, 1969b; Sweezy, 1972; Duncan and Shelton 1978.)
(4) Peacetime government before 1933 was so small that it could not have done much to stabilize the economy by use of fiscal policy even if it had intended to do so. In 1929 the federal government's purchases of goods and services were about 1.3 per cent of GNP and its total expenditures about 2.5 per cent. In 1983 these figures had grown to 8.2 and 24.8 per cent respectively.
(5) It is clear that Keynes had no direct influence and, until perhaps 1938 or 1939, very little indirect influence. His influence later was on the intellectual atmosphere.

(6) The development of quantitative economic data – the national income and product accounts, unemployment statistics and other statistical information – permitted increasing application of theoretical concepts. Even in the second Roosevelt administration, there were no reliable figures on unemployment and, in the absence of figures on the amount of capital expenditure, their amount was taken to be indicated by the volume of new security issues until an article by George Eddy showed that to be a very misleading indicator. By now, data have been developed to a degree unknown and unimagined before World War II.

References

Baffi, P. (1985), Rivista di storia economica, 1; title of essay not available, but subject is influence of Keynesian thought on Italian economic policy in the early postwar years.

Brown, D.V., Chamberlin, E.H., *et al.* (1934), *The Economics of the Recovery Program*, New York: McGraw-Hill, 1934; reprinted, New York: Da Capo Press, 1971.

Currie, L.B. (1934), 'The failure of monetary policy to prevent the depression of 1929-1932'. *Journal of Political Economy*, **42**, April, 145-77; reprinted in *Landmarks in Political Economy*, ed. Earl J. Hamilton *et al.*, Chicago: University of Chicago Press, 1962, 168-98.

Currie, L.B. (1935), 'Comments on pump-priming' (memo *c.* February-March), *History of Political Economy*, **10** Winter, 525-33.

Currie, L.B. (1938a), 'Causes of the (1938) recession' (memo, 1 April), *History of Political Economy*, **12**, Fall, 316-35.

Currie, L.B. (1983b), 'Some theoretical and practical implications of J.M. Keynes: *General Theory*', in National Industrial Conference Board, *The Economic Doctrines of John Maynard Keynes*, New York: 1938, 15-27.

Currie, L.B. (1940a), Testimony before the Temporary National Economic Committee, 16 May 1939, 'Investigation of concentration of economic power: savings and investment', 9, US Congress, Senate, Seventy-sixth Congress, first session, Washington, DC: GPO, 3520-38.

Currie, L.B. (1940b) Statements submitted to the Temporary National Economic Committee, 'Investigation of concentration of economic power: recovery plans,' Monograph No. 25, US Congress, Senate, Seventy-sixth Congress, third session, Washington, DC: GPO, 28, 29, 31.

Currie, L.B. (1972), Discussion of papers presented by Byrd L. Jones and Alan R. Sweezy, in *American Economic Review, Papers and Proceedings*, **62**, May, 139-41.

Currie, L.B. and Krost, M., (1978), 'Federal income-increasing expenditures, 1932-35' (November 1935), *History of Political Economy*, **10**, Winter, 534-41.

Davis, J.R. (1971), *The New Economics and the Old Economists*, Ames, Ia.: Iowa State University Press.

Duncan, J. and Shelton, W. (1978), *Revolution in United States Government Statistics, 1926-1976*, Washington, DC: US Department of Commerce.

Eddy, G.A. (1937), 'Security issues and real investment in 1929', *Review of Economic Statistics*, **18**, May, 79-91.

Galbraith, J.K. (1965), 'How Keynes came to America', *New York Times Book Review*, 16 May; also in *Economics, Peace and Laughter*, Boston: Houghton Mifflin, 1971.

Garvy, G. (1973), 'Keynes and the economic activists of pre-Hitler Germany', *Journal of Political Economy*, **81**, April, 391-405.

Gilbert, R.V., and others (1938), *An Economic Program for American Democracy*, New York: Vanguard Press.

Hansen, A.H. (1938), *Full Recovery or Stagnation?*, New York: Norton.

Hansen, A.H. (1940a), Testimony before the Temporary National Economic Committee, 16 May 1939, 'Investigation of concentration of economic power: savings and investment', US Congress, Senate, Seventy-sixth Congress, first session, Washington, DC: GPO, 3495–520, 3538–59, 3837–59.

Hansen, A.H. (1940b), Statements submitted to the Temporary National Economic Committee, 'Investigation of concentration of economic power: recovery plans', Monograph No. 25, US Congress, Senate, Seventy-sixth Congress, third session, Washington DC: GPO, 28, 32, 41, 43, 98.

Hansen, A.H. (1953), *A Guide to Keynes*, New York: McGraw-Hill.

Hayek, F.A. von (1931), *Prices and Production*, London: Routledge and Kegan Paul.

Jones, Byrd L. (1972), 'The role of Keynesians in wartime policy and postwar planning, 1940–1946', *American Economic Review Papers and Proceedings*, **62**, May, 125–33.

Jones, Byrd L. (1978), 'Lauchlin Currie, pump-priming and New Deal fiscal policy, 1934–36', *History of Political Economy*, **10**, Winter, 509–24.

Jones, Byrd L. (1980), 'Lauchlin Currie and the causes of the 1937 recession', *History of Political Economy*, **12**, Fall, 303–15.

Kuhn, T.S. (1970), *The Structure of Scientific Revolutions* (2nd rev. edn), Chicago: University of Chicago Press/International Encyclopedia of Unified Science.

Lerner, A.P. (1943), 'Functional finance and the federal debt', *Social Research*, February, 38–51.

Patinkin, D. (1977), 'The process of writing the *General Theory*', in D. Patinkin and J. Clark Leith (eds), *Keynes, Cambridge and the General Theory*, London: Macmillan, 3–24.

Salant, Walter S. (1973), 'Some intellectual contributions of the Truman Council of Economic Advisers to policy-making', *History of Political Economy*, **5**, Spring, 36–49; also Brookings Institution Reprint No. 269, 1973.

Salant, Walter S. (1976), 'Alvin Hansen and the fiscal policy seminar', *Quarterly Journal of Economics*, **90**, February, 14–23.

Salant, Walter S. (1977), in Don Patinkin and J.Clark Leith (eds.) *Keynes, Cambridge and the General Theory*, London: Macmillan, 43–48.

Salant, Walter S. (1980a), 'How has the world changed since 1929?', in *The Business Cycle and Public Policy 1929–80*, Washington, DC: US Congress Joint Economic Committee.

Salant, Walter S. (1980b), Essay (untitled) in Francis H. Heller (ed.), *The Truman White House: The Administration of the Presidency 1945–1953*, Lawrence, Kans.: Regents Press, 196–200.

Salant, Walter S. (1983), Comments on Donald Moggridge's 'Keynes and our current discontents', Brookings Institution Discussion Paper, April.

Salant, William A. (1957), Discussion of 'Keynesian economics after twenty years', *American Economic Review, Papers and Proceedings*, **47**, May, 91–3.

Scitovsky, T. (1957), Discussion of 'Keynesian economics after twenty years', *American Economic Review, Papers and Proceedings*, **47**, May, 93–5.

Stein, H. (1969a), *The Fiscal Revolution in America*, Chicago: University of Chicago Press.

Stein, H. (1969b), 'Where stands the New Fiscal Policy?', *Journal of Money, Credit and Banking*, **1**, August, 463–73.

Stein, H. (1984), *Presidential Economics: The Making of Economic Policy from Roosevelt to Reagan and Beyond*, New York: Simon and Schuster.

Sweezy, A.R. (1972), 'The Keynesians and government policy, 1933–1939', *American Economic Review, Papers and Proceedings*, **62**, May 116–24.

US Commerce Department (1939), *Twenty-seventh Annual Report of Secretary of Commerce for the Fiscal Year Ended June 30, 1939*, Washington, DC: GPO, v–xiv.

Wright, D. McCord (1940), 'The economic limit and economic burden of an internally held national debt', *Quarterly Journal of Economics*, **54**, November, 116–29.

6 Keynes and public policy: a comment
Alistair Dow

The Glendon Conference marked fifty years from the publication of *The General Theory of Employment, Interest and Money*. Can we today learn anything about economic policy from the close historical examination of how Keynes's ideas had their impact in Britain in the 1930s and 1940s? An examination of any one of the chapters presented in this book should convince the doubter that we can. I should like to draw attention to a couple of themes, implicit or explicit in these contributions, which have, I believe, a general interest.

There are some economists who pursue the discipline for their own aesthetic pleasure, self-styled artists subsidized by a credulous public which thinks of economics as useful. Many economists, though, are still concerned with political economy, in the sense that they aspire to influencing economic policy through their theories. (This aspiration may span the political spectrum from left to right.) For all such, the question arises: how does the author of a particular theory, or a school espousing a particular theory, achieve the implementation of an economic policy based on their theory?

We see how Keynes attempted it from the chapters presented here. He talked to Labour politicians and their advisers, as Elizabeth Durbin has documented. He argued his case on countless government committees with senior civil servants, as Sue Howson has shown. For the purpose of effect he adopted for a time a tendentious style of argument, seen in the *General Theory*, simply to provoke response. So Don Moggridge has concluded. Finally, he presented his position in such a way as to enrol not one but two political parties, the Liberal and Labour parties, in his service. Robert Skidelsky reminded us that Keynes fully understood economic policy to be dependent on a political process.

Keynes stated his belief that ultimately 'the gradual encroachment of ideas' was the main influence on policy decisions (rather than sectional interest, or in modern terms 'rent seeking'), but he was prepared to hammer people over the head with the ideas he believed to be most apt. Robert Skidelsky emphasized that there was nothing ethereal about the transmission mechanism Keynes saw from economic ideas to economic policy. Strategic thinking and hard work were required in equal measure.

It is most unlikely that Keynes's strategy for achieving from his theorizing the maximum policy impact in the 1930s and 1940s suits the different institutional and political setting of the present day. But what is the equivalent strategy for, let us say, modern Post-Keynesians? The need for such strategic thinking on how policy is formed, and influenced by ideas, is something to be learned from Keynes's promulgation of the ideas in the *General Theory* some forty to fifty years ago in Britain.

In addition, I should like to gnaw on a bone I have already tried to bite elsewhere.[1] The nature of probability was important to Keynes not as an empirical concept, but as a logical concept. His concern with probability in this sense was central to his analysis of business confidence in the *General Theory*, that is to say, central to the behaviour of those who made investment decisions. Such business attitudes – animal spirits, if you will – were particularly important, Keynes believed, for economic policy. He was not alone. The famous Treasury View on crowding out, it has been argued, was not simply financial, but rather was based on an assessment of the behaviour of business confidence.[2] The politicians, of whom Elizabeth Durbin wrote, and the civil servants, considered by Sue Howson, were vitally concerned with business confidence. I would perhaps go further than Don Moggridge does in considering the probability notion, in his chapter, to express the hope that the rising interest in Keynes's concept of probability, looked at in the ethical and historical context of Keynes's Cambridge, might lead to a re-examination of business confidence in a modern setting in relation to economic policy.

Notes and references

1.   A. Dow, and S. Dow, 'Animal spirits and rationality', in T. Lawson and H. Pesaran (eds), *Keynes' Economics Methodological Issues* (London, Croom Helm, 1985), pp. 46–65.
2.   Roger Middleton, *Towards the Managed Economy* (London, Methuen, 1985), pp. 92–4.

PART II

KEYNESIAN ECONOMICS PAST AND PRESENT

7 Keynes and the classics revisited
Robert W. Clower

'The thing can be done,' said the Butcher, 'I think,
  The thing can be done, I am sure.
  The thing shall be done! Bring me paper and ink.
  The best there is time to procure.' (Lewis Carroll, *The Hunting of the Snark*)

Macroeconomics has been in a muddle longer than anyone now cares to remember. The muddle began with the *General Theory* when Keynes failed to identify 'a fatal flaw in that part of ... orthodox reasoning that deals with the theory of what determines the level of effective demand and the volume of aggregate employment' (*CW*, XIII, p. 486). It was exacerbated by the failure of Keynes's interpreters – Hicks, Hansen, Klein, Samuelson, Modigliani, Patinkin, Leijonhufvud, and others – to make sense of arguments that Keynes had bungled. The accompanying tumult of controversy produced a plethora of models and a babel of conclusions, all more or less plausible, none sufficiently compelling to command widespread acceptance – an enormous superstructure of macroeconomic knowledge in search of a unifying theory.

How best to bring this body of practical knowledge together within the framework of an intellectually satisfying theory, no doubt will remain an open question for a long time to come. My purpose here is merely to give focus to future work in this direction by taking a fresh look at the much-discussed issue of 'Keynes and the classics'. I start (as Keynes started) with a simplified aggregative model of classical theory which can plausibly be claimed to represent an essentially self-adjusting monetary economy, and I ask (as so many economists since Keynes have asked): what characteristics of the classical theory might plausibly be altered to yield a model consilient with Keynes's 'vision'? In answering this question, I think we shall find materials that are indeed helpful in suggesting fruitful directions for future macroecomic research.

The classical tradition
No classical theory of short-run adjustment is to be found in the pre-Keynesian literature,[1] probably because no classical writer thought it purposeful to attempt to reduce the complexities of real-time trading processes to analytical order. So my version of short-run classical theory is less a description of what any pre-Keynesian writer actually said than an

account of what I think a nineteenth-century 'true believer' in the self-adjusting capabilities of the economic system might have said had he been trained in modern theory.

Taking our cue from John Hicks's influential 1937 paper on 'Keynes and the Classics',[2] let us start by considering a fiat money economy with just four classes of non-money commodities: consumption goods (c), capital goods (k), labour (n) and loans (b). Suppose that the number of traders and the physical volume of trading in each commodity is sufficiently great that, even in the very short run, no seller or buyer either imagines himself or is in fact capable of significantly influencing the terms of trade by his own actions. More succinctly, *assume that any trader can buy or sell any desired quantity of any commodity on short notice at the "going" price.* For future reference, let us call this assumption the Thick Market hypothesis. Then, whether we regard the typical trader as one of many transactors in an organized auction market or as a market-maker in his own right, we may suppose that short-run sale and purchase decisions are governed at every point in time by the prevailing (average) market prices, p_c, p_k, $p_n = w$, and $p_b = 1/r$.

Still following Hicks, let us further assume that the money wage rate, w, is given and that capital goods already in use are specialized to particular trades and have no second-hand market. Then we may set out our 'classical' model as a system of three price-adjustment equations:

$$dp_c/dt = a_c \left[d_c(p_c, p_k, w, r, Y_n, M) - s_c(p_c/w)\right] \tag{1}$$
$$dp_k/dt = a_k \left[d_k(p_c, p_k, w, r, M) - s_k(p_k/w)\right] \tag{2}$$
$$dr/dt = a_b \left[x_b(p_c, p_k, w, r, M)\right] \tag{3}$$

where d, s and x stand for 'demand', 'supply' and 'excess demand', M represents the quantity of money and Y_n represents the realized money earnings of workers.[3]

On the Thick Market hypothesis, it is plausible to suppose that the motions of this system in the neighbourhood of an equilibrium point are stable and heavily damped; hence the average 'observed' values of the dependent variables p_c, p_k, and r may be presumed to be given as reduced-form solutions of the excess demand equations. The qualitative properties of these solutions are standard. Here it will suffice to remark that, assuming no money illusion, relative prices and the rate of interest – hence output and employment – will vary with changes in the quantity of money. Monetary neutrality holds only if we assume flexible money wage rates and add a wage-adjustment equation to the system.[4]

This model captures the essential flavour of classical theory. Except as a 'temporary abode of purchasing power', money has no significance as an asset because in normal circumstances it offers its holder no return and is no more 'liquid' than any other commodity. Money plays a special role in the economy only because it enters into one side of every exchange transaction and so – through real balance effects – directly influences the absolute level of money prices. Individual economic activities are coordinated by 'the price system'. If changes in underlying parameters ('animal spirits', the 'propensity to hoard', etc.) produce temporary inconsistencies in consumption, production or trading plans, these inconsistencies are quickly reconciled through movements in prices, any consequent changes in output and employment being incidental.

There are extreme cases of course in which the system could get into trouble. A sudden collapse in the marginal efficiency of capital, for example, might yield so low a price for capital goods that gross real investment would go to zero and remain there pending the elimination of excess capacity through gradual wear and tear. Similar consequences might ensue if trading in loans came to be dominated by speculative 'bulls' and 'bears' whose gambling proclivities pushed the real rate of interest to a level where new investment was chronically unprofitable. Notice, however, that in both these cases the underlying source of delayed adjustment is the absence of a market for second-hand capital goods. In effect, the assumption that existing capital goods can't be traded (as also the assumption that the money wage rate is given) is a violation of the Thick Market hypothesis. Thus our discussion of extreme cases merely reinforces earlier indications that the classical conception of the economic system as naturally self-adjusting is intimately connected with the validity of the Thick Market hypothesis.

Keynes's *General Theory*

Turning now to the *General Theory*, we have no need to invent a model; we can start with Keynes's summary of the analytical core of his argument, as set forth in chapter 18 (pp. 247–9) of the *General Theory*. This summary has been formalized in various ways by later interpreters and critics; but John Hicks's 1937 'interpretation' sets out the nearest thing to a canonical representation of the Keynesian model, so let us settle for that (Modigliani's 1944 model has achieved much the same status, but is less general because it treats capital goods and consumption goods as identical rather than distinct commodities.)

First, we need some additional notation. Let Y denote total income, defined as the sum of income produced in the consumption goods industries, $Y_c, = p_c s_c (p_c / w)$, and income produced in the investment goods industries, $Y_k = p_k s_k (p_k / w)$:

$$Y = Y_c + Y_k$$

Similarly, let E_c and E_k denote total expenditure on consumption and investment goods: $E_c = p_c d_c$ (.); $E_k = p_k d_k$ (.).

Then continuing as before to treat the money wage rate and the quantity of money as given parameters, we may express Hicks's schematic model of Keynes's *General Theory*[5] as:

$$M = L(r, Y) \tag{4}$$
$$Y_k = E_k(r, Y) \tag{5}$$
$$Y_k = Y - E_c(r, Y) \tag{6}$$

This system of three equations may be presumed to determine solution values of Y, Y_k and r from which – taking account of earlier definitions and underlying production functions – we can work out corresponding solution values of employment and output. But in what sense can the system in equations (4)–(6) be said to represent a 'theory of output and employment' rather than a 'theory of price'?

To answer this question, let us first rewrite the system to reveal the price variables that are suppressed in the present formulation. Making use of earlier definitions of Y, Y_k, E_k, and E_c, and carrying out appropriate simplifications (specifically the cancellation of price variables that appear on both sides of the last two equations), we obtain:

$$M = L(r, p_c/w, p_k/w)$$
$$s_k\{p_k/w\} = d_k(r, p_c/w, p_k/w)$$
$$s_c\{p_c/w\} = d_c(r, p_c/w, p_k/w)$$

This system, though formally equivalent to the system in (4)–(6), is more naturally regarded as a 'theory of price' than a 'theory of output and employment'. We may clinch the issue by expressing the model as a set of differential equations:

$$dr/dt = b_r[M - L(r, p_c/w, p_k/w)] \tag{1a}$$
$$dp_c/dt = b_c[d_c(r, p_c/w, p_k/w) - s_c\{p_c/w\}] \tag{2a}$$
$$dp_k/dt = b_k[d_k(r, p_c/w, p_k/w) - s_k\{p_k/w\}] \tag{3a}$$

This system differs from our earlier 'classical' model in just two major respects. First, the excess demand for bonds is expressed in terms of 'liquidity preference' rather than the demand and supply of 'loanable funds.' But this is merely a matter of form, for since money enters into one side of every transaction, we might also express the excess demands for consumption and investment goods in 'liquidity preference' terms ('The reward for parting with liquidity is immediate gratification through consumption, or the expectation of a stream of future profit, or...').[6] Secondly, the money variable is omitted from the excess demand functions in (2a) and (3a); but this merely reflects an implicit specification error in the underlying Hicks model. From a conceptual standpoint, therefore, the Keynesian system in (1a)–(3a) is formally indistinguishable from our earlier classical model in (1)–(3) and cannot plausibly be regarded as possessing behaviour properties that would permit us to reach any but 'classical' conclusions.[7]

Now there can be no doubt that to accept the system in (1a)–(3a) – and so the system in (1)–(3) – as a model of Keynes's *General Theory* is equivalent to imputing to Keynes a faith in the efficacy of the price system that is utterly at variance with his actual beliefs. But neither can there be serious doubt that Hicks's simple model of the *General Theory* accurately reflects the substance – the letter if not the spirit – of Keynes's formal analysis. The crux of the matter is that Keynes in the *General Theory* not only failed to reject, but positively embraced, an essentially classical (more accurately, neo-classical) theory of short-run output determination, and thereby implicitly adopted the Thick Market hypothesis as a basis for his own theory of aggregate supply.[8] Keynes's theory of aggregate demand, though outwardly novel because it makes the current level of total expenditure depend upon the prevailing level of output and employment, actually involves no significant departure from classical tradition. So the theoretical foundations of the *General Theory* are incompatible with the beliefs that led Keynes to write it albeit unintentionally.

Salvaging the *General Theory*

Evidently the central message of Keynes's *General Theory* can be salvaged only by discarding the conventional theory of short-run supply. But we cannot discard the conventional theory of short-run supply unless we also discard the conception of market organization on which it is based; for the conventional theory merely expresses how rational sellers would behave if their trading activities were confined to thick markets.

The *General Theory* contains no hint that Keynes was in any way dissatisfied with the conventional theory of supply; indeed the conventional theory plays a central role in his claim that real wages generally move in the same direction as output over the trade cycle. It was not until 1939, in his response to criticisms of this claim by Dunlop and Tarshis,[9] that Keynes explicitly voiced doubts about the assumptions underlying his earlier analysis of aggregate supply and, more particularly, questioned the validity of what I have called the Thick Market hypothesis by linking producer discretion in short-period pricing policy with trading in thin rather than thick markets.[10]

A thick market, as noted earlier, is one in which traders can be presumed to know within narrow limits the price at which any desired quantity of a commodity can be bought or sold on short notice. A thin market is one in which the opposite presumption holds: trading volume is too slight to permit traders to gauge, even within broad limits, the price at which desired sales or purchases can be completed on short notice. The crucial difference is that for thick markets it makes sense to suppose that the short-run revenues of individual producers are determined by their output choices, while for thin markets the same supposition makes no sense at all. Let us explore the implications of the second case.

Consider a representative producer whose short-run average variable and average total costs are represented by the curves AVC and ATC in Figure 7.1.

By hypothesis, the producer has no usable information about his probable short-run sales at alternative asking prices, so there can be no question of choosing a combination of price and output that maximizes short-run profit. Over the longer run the producer can hope to influence sales by appropriate market manoeuvres (advertising, temporary price cuts, etc.), but more immediately he is largely at the mercy of impersonal (and predetermined) market forces. Under these conditions probably the simplest and most sensible strategy is for the producer to set his asking or list price at a reasonable level and hope for the best in the way of sales volume. What seems 'reasonable' to the producer will depend of course on past sales experience, on present and prospective costs and on present and prospective competition. Here, let us interpret 'reasonable' to mean a price (P_0 in Figure 7.1) high enough to ensure that average total costs are covered for a range of sales levels significantly less than capacity output, $s*$.[11]

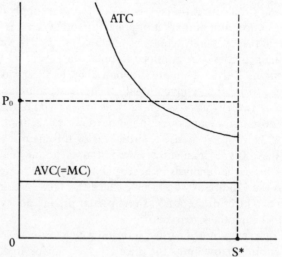

Figure 7.1

Then since the 'asking' or 'list' price exceeds average variable (and marginal) cost for all outputs less than s*, the producer will be *willing* to produce and sell any less-than-capacity output at his posted price. But the amount that can *actually* be sold will depend upon customer demand at that price, which will depend on a host of conditions over which the producer has no short-run control. In these circumstances it is plausible to argue that the producer will adjust output passively to match average sales at the posted price, holding buffer stocks of inventories to avoid frequent transient adjustments of output. Thus, on average, short-run output will move in the same direction as realized sales.

Taking account of the preceding argument, but referring now to an economy in which all produced goods are traded in thin markets, let us suppose that aggregative short-run output and interest rate behaviour may be characterized by the adjustment equations:

$$dq_c/dt = h_c[d_c(.) - q_c] \tag{7}$$
$$dq_k/dt = h_k[d_k(.) - q_k] \tag{8}$$
$$dr/dt = h_b [x_b (.)] \tag{9}$$

where q_i (i = c, k) represents current output as contrasted with 'supply' and (.) = (p_c, p_k, w, r, Y, M) – argument Y rather than Y_n appearing in (.) because, under our present assumptions, producers as well as workers may be 'income-constrained' in the short run.

The system in equations (7)–(9) accurately portrays what has come to be rgarded as the distinctive feature of Keynesian economics: aggregate output is determined by aggregate sales and prices play no role in the short-run adjustment of income to changes in effective demand. This of course is the route to salvage of Keynesian economics that is taken in most textbooks, usually without notice to the reader that the underlying assumptions concerning short-period output variations are completely at odds with the conventional profit maximization model of supply presented in later microeconomic sections of the same text. It also corresponds to the extreme case of what Hicks has dubbed 'fix-price theory'.[12]

Apart from being a crude caricature of Keynes's analysis, the system in equations (7)–(9) seriously misrepresents the role of prices in the short-run adjustment process. In situations involving significant unused capacity, producers can be expected to engage in competitive selling activities (temporary discounts, rebates, prize contests, etc.) in an effort to boost short-run sales, so average transaction prices will tend to fall. Similarly, in situations involving little unused capacity, producers can be expected to compete for factors in ways that increase both variable and fixed costs, and some of these increases will be passed on in the form of higher asking prices. Arguing heuristically, we may suppose that both sorts of adjustment are adequately described by the aggregative equations:

$$dp^*_c/dt = g_c[d_c(.) - s^*_c] \tag{10}$$
$$dp^*_k/dt = g_k[d_k(.) - s^*_k] \tag{11}$$

where p^*i is an index of transaction prices and s^*i is an index of production capacity.[13] Combining these relations with equations (7)–(9), we obtain a system of five adjustment equations to describe short-run movements in quantities, transaction prices and the rate of interest.

The equation for dr/dt in this system calls for no special comment; we may view the loan market as 'thick' and rapidly self-adjusting even in a Keynesian model. But the remaining four equations – two dealing with adjustments in output quantities, and two dealing with movements in average transactions prices – pose problems whose solutions are distinctly problematical.

To see this, suppose that the system starts in temporary equilibrium with capacity fully utilized and sales occurring only at posted list prices. Next suppose that the equilibrium is disturbed by a decline in 'animal spirits', 'confidence', or what have you, causing investment expenditure to fall. Then investment goods output will quickly decline, because the speed of adjustment coefficients in equations (7) and (8) are, by hypothesis, large numbers. Prices will not decline noticeably in the short run because the adjustment coefficients in equations (10) and (11) are – again by hypothesis – relatively small. Both 'workers' and 'capitalists' are income-constrained, because neither goods nor services are particularly 'liquid' (though prices are 'administered', and therefore known, quantities sold are unpredictable). So as investment output drops, the demand for consumption goods will also decline via the familiar multiplier process.

Now, initially at least, no counteracting forces will operate to stem the decline. Real balance effects will have no bite, because transaction prices will not fall noticeably, and though the money volume of transactions will decline, the potential effect of this on spending will be attenuated by rising uncertainty about future needs for cash to meet payrolls, etc. – hence a rise in the demand for precautionary balances. There will perhaps be some tendency for spare cash to go into loans; but this tendency will not be strong, because with sales falling and becoming more uncertain, producers will find it increasingly difficult to synchronize purchases with sales, and this will mean that average money balances will tend to increase even at lower volumes of monetary transactions (cf. Clower and Howitt, 1978, in Clower, 1984, pp. 168–70). Nor are matters likely to improve as the decline continues, for in thin markets trade credit (mainly in the form of bookkeeping entries) is likely to play a prominent, and perhaps dominant, role as a short-run means of payment.[14] As sales decline and business confidence weakens, trade credit outstanding will shrink, possibly by substantial percentage amounts, even though currency and deposits subject to check are largely unchanged.

There is no need to carry the story further. Notice that nothing of substance in the above argument is changed if we relax the assumption of fixed wage rates and add a 'thin' market for labour services to our model.

In that more general case, as for the more restricted model in equations (7)–(11), 'observed' short-run behaviour cannot be adequately characterized by static, reduced-form solutions of the adjustment equations. In effect, the normal state of the economy is one of Brownian motion; the system, even if asymptotically stable is so lightly damped that the probability of ever being in the neighbourhood of equilibrium is close to zero. This being so, we cannot expect to advance much further in studying Keynesian problems – problems associated with short-run adjustment processes – using the kind of analytical conventions and mathematical techniques that have served us so well during the past fifty years. What is needed if we are to make further progress in macroeconomics is a radical reconstruction of microeconomics along lines that are only dimly foreshadowed in the existing literature – a reconstruction that will deal seriously with the central unresolved theoretical issues of short-run competitive analysis – which is to say with the Economics of Thin Markets.

Conclusion

No doubt, more might be said about Keynes and the classics, about the reasons why the *General Theory* ultimately failed to convey Keynes's intended message and about alternative ways in which Keynes's essential 'vision' might be salvaged, but this is not the place to say it. Instead, let me offer a few concluding reflections on the rhetoric of the *General Theory*.

Keynes of course proceeded throughout the *General Theory* on the presumption that short-run behaviour could be adequately handled with static models, thereby adopting an analytical procedure that runs directly counter to some of his more distinctive claims, e.g. that there generally exists some 'involuntary' unemployment, that the economic system, if left to itself, tends to attain a state of full employment only by accident, if at all, etc. It is interesting to speculate whether the *General Theory* would have had a longer run, or indeed any run at all, had Keynes adopted an analytical procedure more in keeping with his implicit beliefs.

I have little doubt that Keynes made the right rhetorical decision a half-century ago; anything resembling an explicitly dynamical account of short-run behaviour in thin markets would surely have fallen to blind eyes and deaf ears in 1936. But I do not believe he made his decision consciously or with a clear view to some of its consequences such as the subsequent albeit delayed rejection of the formal analysis of the *General Theory* by the great majority of professional economists. In retrospect, it seems clear that the essence of Keynes's message was not that labour markets, but that virtually *all* markets, are thin and fail to operate efficiently in a classical sense. But only now, with macroeconomics again in a state of disarray, is it conceivable that such a blanket denial of the Thick Market hypothesis might be accorded a sympathetic reception.

Notes

1. One finds numerous threads of such a theory, particularly in Hume, Thornton, Tooke and Mill (cf. Hicks, 1967), but that is all.
2. The full title is 'Mr Keynes and the classics: a suggested interpretation'.
3. Y_n is included in d_c because, with the money wage rate given, the earnings of workers cannot be presumed to correspond to the money value of services offered for sale, i.e. the demand function for consumption goods is not independent of the current level of output. But this is just a Keynesian (or Marshallian) flourish, for since Y_n may be presumed to depend on prices via the demand for labour, it need not be included as an explicit argument in d_c.
4. In the augmented system, equilibrium money prices and the money wage rate are directly proportional to the quantity of money, as implied by the 'classical' quantity theory. This merely indicates the redundancy of the quantity theory in any model for which the classical invariance proposition holds; it does not validate the quantity theory – or the quantity equation – as a 'behavioural' relation. Hicks's 1937 version of classical theory is flawed in this respect.
5. Hicks also has a model of Keynes's 'special theory' in which the liquidity preference equation takes the form $M = L(r)$, but that will not concern us until later.
6. Cf. Boulding (1944), pp. 55–63.
7. This is essentially the conclusion Hicks reached in his 1937 paper, though he studiously refrained from stating it explicitly either in that paper or in his 1957 *Economic Journal* review of Patinkin's *Money, Interest and Prices* (reprinted with minor revision as ch. 8 of Hicks (1967), pp. 143–54).
8. Patinkin disputes this in various of his recent writings, but (to my mind) not at all convincingly. On this, see Patinkin (1976), p. 93, and Tarshis (1978), pp. 60–3 (in Patinkin and Leith, 1978).
9. Reprinted in *CW*, VII, appendix 3 (see esp. pp. 406–8).
10. Curiously, Keynes seems to have been more aware of the difficulties of the 'theory of short-period supply' in the early 1930s than during the writing of the *General Theory*. In a letter to Hawtrey of 28 November, 1930, for example, responding to Hawtrey's criticisms of the *Treatise*, Keynes says: 'I repeat that I am not dealing with the complete set of causes which determine volume of output. For this would have led me an endless long journey into the theory of short-period supply and a long way from monetary theory; – though I agree that it will probably be difficult in the future to prevent monetary theory and the theory of short-period supply from running together. If I were to write the book again, I should probably attempt to probe further into the difficulties of the latter; but I have already probed far enough to know what a complicated affair it is' *CW*, XIII, pp. 145–6.
11. Cf. P.W.S. Andrews, 'Competitive prices, normal costs and industrial stability', in Andrews and Brunner (1975) pp. 29–31. This is not the place to review recent work on so-called 'customer markets'; suffice it to say that there is little dispute among economists about the 'stylized facts', though there is (of course) much dispute about how they should be interpreted. For some recent comments on this topic see A. Okun (1981),

ch. 4, esp. pp. 138 ff.; E.S. Phelps (1985), pp. 383–404; R.E. Hall and J.B. Taylor (1986), pp. 389–94; R.J. Gordon (1981), pp. 502–4.

12. See Hicks (1966), chs 7–9; Hicks (1982), pp. 231–5.

13. This is no more than a rough schematic representation. The microeconomic theory of price adjustment in thin markets is still in its infancy. For discussion of some of the difficulties that confront us in this area see Bushaw and Clower (1957), ch. 7, pp. 185–9; Phelps *et al.* (1970), pp. 309–37 (Phelps and Winter) and pp. 369–93 (Gordon and Hynes).

14. This is a direct consequence of the desire of makers of thin markets to attract a clientele of 'regular' customers in order to reduce sales uncertainty; trade credit as distinct from bank credit, plays little of a role in thick markets precisely because there is no significant sales uncertainty in this case.

References

Andrews, P. W. S. and Brunner, E. (1975) *Studies in Pricing*, London: Macmillan.

Boulding, K. (1944), 'A liquidity preference theory of market prices, '*Economica*, **11**, May, 55–63.

Bushaw, D. W. and Clower, R. W. (1957), *Introduction to Mathematical Economics*, Homewoood, Ill: Irwin.

Clower, R. W. (1984), *Money and Markets*, ed. D. Walker, Cambridge: Cambridge University Press.

Gordon, R. J. (1981), 'Output fluctuations and gradual price adjustment', *Journal of Economic Literature*, **19**, June, 493–530.

Hall, R. and Taylor, J. (1986), *Macroeconomics*, New York: Norton.

Hicks, J. R. (1937), 'Mr Keynes and the classics: a suggested interpretation', *Econometrica*, **5**, April, 147–59.

Hicks, J. R. (1966), *Capital and Growth*, Oxford: Clarendon Press.

Hicks, J. R. (1967), *Critical Essays in Monetary Theory*, Oxford: Clarendon Press.

Hicks, J. R. (1982), *Money, Interest and Wages*, Oxford: Blackwell.

Keynes, J.M. (var. dates), *Collected Works* (cited as JMK, London: Macmillan/Royal Economic Society.)

Modigliani, F. (1944), 'Liquidity preference and the theory of interest and money', *Econometrica*, **12**, January, 45–88.

Okun, A. (1981) *Prices and Quantities*, Washington, DC: Brookings Institution.

Patinkin, D. (1976), *Keynes's Monetary Thought*, Durham, NC: Duke University Press.

Phelps, E. S. (1985), *Political Economy*, New York: Norton.

Phelps, E. S. et. al. (1970), *Microeconomic Foundations of Employment and Inflation Theory,* New York: Norton.

Tarshis, L. (1978), 'Keynes as seen by his students in the 1930s', in D. Patinkin and J. Clark Leith (eds), *Keynes, Cambridge and the General Theory*, Toronto: University of Toronto Press.

8 The evolution of Keynesian economics: from Keynesian to New Classical to New Keynesian
David Colander

...To have been born as an economist before 1936 was a boon – yes.
But not to have been born too long before!
  'Bliss was it in that dawn to be alive,
    But to be young was very heaven!'
The *General Theory* caught most economists under the age of thirty-five with
the unexpected virulence of a disease first attacking and decimating an isolated
tribe of South Sea Islanders. Economists beyond fifty turned out to be quite
immune to the ailment. (Paul Samuelson, 1964)

Paul Samuelson's reflection on the Keynesian revolution captures the
excitement that young economists felt about Keynesian economics in the
1930s and is a harbinger of the enormous creative development in
macroeconomics and Keynesian economic thinking that occurred in the
period from 1936 to the mid-1960s. During this period Keynesian
macroeconomics moved from being a radical idea of a few young Turks to
being the mainstream view of the profession.

In the mid-1960s the theoretical Keynesian revolution began sputtering
and by the mid-1970s it came to a complete halt; Keynesians under thirty-
five became the endangered species; only those economists over fifty
remained Keynesians and many of them went into the closet. The 1970s
disease which infected the under-thirty-five economists was New Classical
economics and by the early 1980s the press had declared Keynesian
economics dead and New Classical economics the mainstream macroeconomic view.

New Classical economics did not remain mainstream for long. By the
mid-1980s New Classical economics was itself on the verge of being wiped
out by a new strain of Keynesianism, New Keynesian economics, which
was immune to the New Classical virus. This chapter recounts this
evolution, considering the questions: why did the evolution occur as it did?
And: what is the future evolution of macroeconomic theory likely to be?

For those who don't follow closely the theoretical debates in
macroeconomics, the labels New Classicals and New Keynesian probably
have little meaning so, first, I shall briefly describe what I mean by them.[1]

In the mid-1970s New Classicals replaced monetarists as the main opposition to Keynesians. Whereas monetarism is a semi-formal analysis, New Classical economics is highly formal. Their analysis blends in assumptions of rational expectations and market clearing within a general equilibrium framework. It initially was called 'rational expectations' theory, but as it became apparent that the other elements were necessary to their analysis and policy conclusions, the nomenclature changed from rational expectations theory to New Classical theory. Leading New Classsical economists include Robert Barro, Robert Lucas, Thomas Sargent and Neil Wallace.

The rise of new Keynesian economics is, in part, responsible for the change in nomenclature. New Keynesian theory uses the same formal general equilibrium methodological framework as New Classical theory uses, but it does not use the market clearing assumption. A New Keynesian article looks similar in form to a New Classical article, but because it does not assume market clearing, the conclusion New Keynesians come to is that there is a potential role for government policy. New Keynesians see individual decisions leading to macroexternalities, so that individual decisions do not necessarily lead to socially optimal results. The policy question New Keynesians ask is how to internalize the macroeconomic externality.

Their research programme includes consideration of such issues as implicit contracts and price signalling problems which provide justification for their non-market clearing assumption. Some leading New Keynesians include economists such as John Taylor, Joseph Stiglitz, George Akerlof, Meir Kohn and Peter Howitt.

In considering the evolution of macroeconomic thinking most commentators have focused on what I call the external approach to paradigm shifts: how well paradigms have accorded with reality and how well the theories predict (or predicted). While not denying the importance of external criteria, given the nature of empirical proof in economics and the need for data interpretation, many theories can accord with reality. To choose among the set of acceptable theories (a set which is, in my view, quite large) another explanation is necessary.

The additional explanation that I want to focus on is what I call the internal approach to paradigm shifts. This internal approach, in my view, plays a key role in the evolution of macro-economic thinking.[2] The internal approach is simple: it suggests that researchers' needs and incentives determine which theory researchers use. For economists, two needs stand out.[3] The first, which I call the article criteria, is a need to publish. To succeed graduate students need topics upon which to write 'good' dissertations and professors need topics about which to write. These topics must be simple enough to be 'do-able' but sufficiently difficult to impress advisers and reviewers. The more article and dissertation topics which can be extracted from a theory, the better it meets the 'article' criteria.

A paradigm which is article laden is contagious; it will generate enormous interest and will spread quickly among the profession. However, over time the contagiousness of a paradigm will diminish as the earliest researchers use the richest topics (easy topics which seem hard), leaving later researchers with an increasingly difficult task. Without internal evolution which generates new do-able articles and dissertations, over time a theory will become sterile and will no longer be the subject of research.

Whether a theory will have a lasting effect depends on a second internal need. To have a lasting effect a theory must be teachable. The teachability criterion follows from the organization of economic research. In addition to publishing, most economists interested in theory must teach. Given current US teaching institutions, teachability means that the theory must be reducible to a simple model that captures its essence and can be conveyed to students at beginning and intermediate levels.[4] Only theories that are teachable will be integrated into textbooks. Once a theory is integrated in the textbooks, it will continue to have influence, and will form the basic understanding of the majority of students and lay public.

The Keynesian theory (1930s style) fulfilled these internal criteria superbly; it provided numerous dissertation and article topics as can be seen by the outpouring of simple models which filled the journals in the late 1940s and early 1950s. In these early years the simultaneous development of national income accounts and econometrics led to an enormous number of empirical questions the new theory could explore and answer.

Throught the mid-1960s the evolution of macro models was sufficiently fast to offset the diminishing returns in article production, keeping articles relatively easy to come by for new researchers. Articles continued to flow from the models relatively easily as the simple consumption function model of the 1950s evolved into the IS/LM-Aggregate Supply/Demand models of the 1960s and 1970s. But it was becoming more and more difficult.

Keynesian economics also nicely met the teachability criterion. It was eminently reducible to simple neat models, as is demonstrated by the rapid acceptance of Lorie Tarshis's and Paul Samuelson's texts, which provided simple models of Keynesian thinking. Even today, after Keynesian models have been discarded on the high theoretical level, they form the basis of what is taught at the beginning and intermediate levels of macroeconomics.

As the Keynesian revolution progressed, it diverged from a less well-publicized revolution in economics, the general equilibrium revolution.

This revolution also began in the 1930s, as research shifted away from Marshallian economics and partial equilibrium analysis toward a Walrasian general equilibrium framework. This general equilibrium pradigm offered a variety of research topics, although they were on a recognizably higher level of difficulty than Keynesian research topics, and required more technical skills to undertake. Thus fewer researchers considered it, but those who did found publication easy. Because it was difficult, economists working in the area acquired respect. However, in part because of its complicated nature, general equilibrium theory did not meet the teachability criteria. It was difficult to translate the ideas in it into a simple model that could be taught at the undergraduate level. Thus the general equilibrium revolution remained a theoretical revolution and never significantly affected textbook economics. What is still taught at the beginning and intermediate levels of economics is largely grounded in Marshallian economics, while what is done on the higher level is generally Walrasian.[5]

In the 1950s the Keynesian revolution advanced independently of the general equilibrium revolution with only minimal interaction. But in the 1960s macroeconomics was losing its researchers to microeconomics and to the more technically impressive general equilibrium models. By this time mathematical techniques used in economics had progressed to the point that work on algebraic Keynesian models, even relatively large ones solved by determinants, no longer was sufficiently impressive to generate dissertation topics or articles. This contributed heavily to the demise of theoretical neo-Keynesian economics.

The decline of Keynesian economics was exacerbated by a compromise between Keynesians and neo-classicals.[6] This compromise based the difference between neo-Keynesians and classicals on the fixed-wage assumption of neo-Keynesians. The Keynesian models were awarded the practical laurels; while the classicals, basing their models on some version of price flexibility caused by the admittedly unrealistic real balance effect, were awarded the theoretical laurels.

While many Keynesians believed that the fixed-wage neo-Keynesian model did not capture the true problem that Keynes had identified, the classical/Keynesian debates simply died, in large part because of internal criteria. Neither the Keynesian research programme nor the alternative monetarist research programme (which was making the classical case) was appropriate to use the new mathematical techniques which were developing this time. In fact, if anything, monetarists used less sophisticated techniques than did Keynesians. Thus, even though the debate was still relevant and the issues unresolved, it was dropped.

Rather than work on extending the neo-Keynesian model, theoretically inclined economists and gruadate students worked on incorporating macroeconomic models with general equilibrium models and on finding microfoundations for macroeconomics. This work had little or no relation to neo-Keynesian models.[7] The mid-1960s brought about a burgeoning literature in two areas: (1) microfoundations as exemplified by Phelps's book (1970), which considered the theoretical foundations of the Phillips Curve; and (2) translating Keynesian models into general disequilibrium models, exemplified in the work of economists such as Robert Barro and H. Grossman, and E. Malinvaud.

Combined, these two literatures undermined the Keynesian hold on macroeconomic theory. The general equilibrium models cemented the need for fixed nominal wages as the key to the Keynesian conclusion. Within the context of Barro and Grossman's general disequilibrium model that assumption was crucial. The microfoundations work provided alternative explanations of underemployment based on search models. Such models offered far more dissertation topics and articles than did the Keynesian model. Thus by the late 1960s the Keynesian model was doomed.

Real-world events in the 1970s finished the job and allowed the new work to gather momentum; inflation undermined all but the teaching purpose of the neo-Keynesian model. Here was the open wound that allowed New Classical economics, which emerged from the micro-foundations work, to enter.

The evolution away from Keynesian economics began before there were significant empirical problems with the Keynesian model, suggesting that that evolution was primarily fuelled by internal rather than external criteria. Were the movement not directed by internal criteria, rather than fuelling New Classical economics the inflation could have provided an opening for a resurgence of monetarism since New Classical policy conclusions differed little from monetarist ones.[8]

New Classical economics emerged from the theoretical work in the 1960s by an interesting chain of events. The microfoundations work provided an intuitive story of unemployment. At the same time, the Keynesian story of unemployment caused by fixed wages which emerged from the neo-Keynesian model was undermined by adding rational expectations to the model. New Classicals showed that by adding the idea of rational expectations, assuming long-run wage flexibility but not short-run wage flexibility in a competitive model did not make theoretical sense. As long as there are no constraints on an individual's action (and the formal neo-Keynesian competitive model had none), anything that will happen in the long run will also happen in the short run, as long as people have rational expectations. Using variations of this simple argument, New

Classicals argued that to assume fixed nominal wages, without explaining why wages were fixed, was unacceptable.

The argument convinced Barro, one of the two Keynesian researchers who had developed the general disequilibrium Keynesian model. His conversion played an important role in the New Classical revolution, and brought about a major change in macroeconomics. Economic journalists figured that if this bright former Keynesian believed it, there must be something in it. Thus he became a leading New Classical theorist, and wrote the first New Classical textbook.

The New Classical revolution initially met the article criteria nicely and thereby spread fast. It also died relatively fast because of those same internal criteria. Its use of high-level mathematical and econometric techniques contributed to its early success, but those same high-level mathematical and econometric techniques were also damaging to its longevity. Quickly the New Classical modelling was carried to such heights that it was beyond the range of almost all graduate students and economists. Combined with the fact that the empirical results flowing from New Classical economics were both difficult to interpret and inconclusive, New Classical economics soon exhausted the good dissertation topics.

The New Classical theory also failed on teachability criteria. While there was a nice metaphor to describe the New Classical idea, there was no simple model which could be taught and built into the textbook. Barro's book attempted to codify New Classical economics, but the result was a macroeconomic textbook which, if taught generally, would reduce the number of intermediate macro courses across the country by at least 50 per cent. Because it lacked a textbook model, New Classical economics was destined for a blaze of glory that would forever change the theoretical macroeconomics terrain, but could not become mainstream macroeconomics. All successful macroeconomic textbooks except Barro's are organized around an IS/LM framework, and there seems little chance of change in the near future.[9]

New Classical economics did, however, make a difference. It shocked Keynesians out of their complacent acceptance of the fixed-wage neo-Keynesian model and provoked a new consideration of the underpinnings of Keynesian thought and policies. A major response was the development of alternative Keynesian models, written in the style of New Classical models and including rational expectations, but which came to Keynesian conclusions. This work is what I call 'New Keynesian'. New Classical economics also provoked a reconsideration of the historical foundations of Keynesian economics (as this Conference testifies). Finally, it led to a modification of neo-Keynesian models, so they are less dependent on assumptions of wage inflexibility. Combined, this work suggests that

Keynesian economics is making a comeback and some version of it is likely to be the mainstream in the late 1980s.

Empirical evidence that Keynesian economics lives can be seen in survey results by Frey *et al.* (1984) and Colander and Klamer (forthcoming). In both these surveys only about 10 per cent of the economists surveyed believed fiscal policy was not an effective policy (a New Classical would take the position that fiscal policy is totally ineffective), and only 17 per cent of all graduate students saw the rational expectations assumption (a key element in New Classical economics) as very important. Forty per cent saw the New Keynesian assumption of imperfect competition as very important and only 10 per cent saw it unimportant.

Given the variety of Keynesian responses to New Classical economics, the current state of Keynesian macroeconomics is one of confusion. Which direction it will likely take in the future is unclear, but by considering internal criteria, some speculation is possible. New Classical economics was short lived because it failed to meet the article and teachability criteria. New Keynesian economics, because it uses the same models as do New Classicals, faces many of the same problems that New Classical economics did, and unless it changes, it too is likely to be as short lived. The typical new Keynesian model takes a New Classical model and demonstrates how, if one slightly modifies an assumption about information or about institutional constraints on individuals, the model leads to Keynesian results. That provides some easy dissertations and articles, but since there are limited New Classical models, there are limited possibilities for New Keynesians. There are only so many times you can show that rational expectations does not necessarily lead to equilibrium.

The New Keynesian school is, however, in a better position than the New Classical school in regard to teachability. It seems to have reached a compromise with neo-Keynesians. Advanced work is done using New Keynesian models; lower-level textbooks teach neo-Keynesian models.[10] But this is a tenuous marriage which continues only because there is no better alternative. If New Keynesian economics is to have staying power, it must develop some method to modify the simple textbook model to demonstrate and contrast its arguments with alternatives. To date, it had not done so, and thus on internal criteria New Keynesian economics has a limited future.

The neo-Keynesian model is in a stronger position in regard to teaching, but it does not meet the article criteria. Unless the model evolves further and incorporates dynamic considerations, it too has a limited future. The historical approach has similar problems on article criteria, but the confusion will likely allow more historical articles to be published than otherwise, especially if the articles can relate to modern developments.

My conclusion, then, is that even though Keynesian economics is in current disarray, its future, although uncertain as to the direction it will go, looks relatively strong in the short term, and somewhat less certain in the longer term. Because of its deep penetration into the textbooks, Keynesian economics will likely dominate the theoretical work of the 1980s, but its domination will be nothing like the blissful days of the 1930s and 1940s.

Notes

1. Elsewhere (see Colander, 1986) I have described these theories in more detail.
2. Obviously the issues are much more complicated than I can discuss in a short paper. External and internal criteria interact in complicated ways that I do not have space to explore.
3. There is a third set of criteria somewhere between internal and external criteria, and it consists of the 'political' (how well does the theory fit practical needs?) and 'funding' (can economists get paid for doing their theory?) criteria. While these are interesting and relevant, because of shortage of space I do not deal with them here.
4. The importance of teachability depends upon the nature of the profession and the type of job researchers earn their money from. In the USA most theoretical economists are teachers, hence teachability is extremely important. Moreover, the nature of the teaching method determines how that simple model must be reduced. As teaching methods change, a theory that was teachable may become unteachable.
5. These two revolutions threw off track another revolution which began in the 1930s – the development of monopolistic or imperfect competition – in part because they were both firmly based in Marshallian tradition. Off track, it simply died, with Joan Robinson forsaking hers for Keynesian economics, and much to the consternation of Chamberlain.
6. This compromise is nicely described by Leijonhufvud (1968) in one of the works that furthered the theoretical breakdown of the neo-Keynesian synthesis.
7. Although the Keynesian theory was not grounded in general equilibrium theory, attempts were made to give it a presence of a general equilibrium grounding. Don Patinkin's real balance effect provided a semblance of general equilibrium grounding which, although incomplete and inappropriate from a formal general equilibrium standpoint (see Hahn), served the purpose of the time.
8. New Classical economists were not especially concerned with practice; it was a theoretical revolution. To the degree that it was concerned with practice, it simply borrowed monetarist policy prescriptions.
9. Having recently completed a macroeconomic textbook in which I tried to not focus on IS/LM analysis, I can attest from experience to the strong push by reviewers to structure macroeconomic books around IS/LM analysis. My compromise with the reviewers was a historical approach where I include IS/LM analysis, but it is not the only model presented.
10. A recent text by John Taylor and Robert Hall, whom I would call New Keynesians, presents the neo-Keynesian model as the core of macroeconomics and throws in discussions of New Keynesian propositions; they do not point out the problem in connecting the two.

References

Barro, R. (1984), *Macroeconomics,* New York: Wiley.
Barro, R. and Grossman, H. (1976), *Money, Employment and Inflation,* New York: Cambridge University Press.
Colander, D. (1986) *Macroeconomics,* Glenview, Ill.: Scott, Foresman.
Colander, D. and Klamer, A. (forthcoming) 'The making of an economist'.

Frey, B. Ginsburgh, V., Pestiau, P., Pommerehne, W. and Schneider, F. (1984), 'Consensus and dissension among economists: an empirical enquiry' *American Economic Review*, **74**, March, 986–94.

Leijonhufvud, A. (1968), *On Keynesian Economics and the Economics of Keynes*, London: Oxford University Press.

Malinvaud, E. (1974), *The Theory of Unemployment Reconsidered*, Oxford: Blackwell.

Phelps, E. et al. (1970), *Microeconomic Foundations of Employment and Inflation Theory*, New York: Norton.

Samuelson, P. (1964), 'The *General Theory*: 1936', in R. Lekachman, (ed.), *Keynes' General Theory: Reports of Three Decades*, New York: St Martin's Press, 315–47.

Taylor, J. and Hall, R. (1986), *Macroeconomics*, New York: Norton.

9 What happened to Keynes's economics?
Sheila C. Dow

Now it seems that the bastard Keynesian era is coming to an end in general disillusionment;
...The Keynesian revolution still remains to be made both in teaching economic theory and in forming economic policy. (Robinson, 1973, p. 177)

Introduction

In Keynesian circles it is now conventional wisdom that, in so far as there was a Keynesian revolution, it has been eclipsed by a counterrevolution which has reinstated the pre-Keynesian orthodoxy in a modern guise. Certainly economic theory developed an aggregative macroeconomic branch, and economic policy became more interventionist at the macrolevel during and after World War II. But the more revolutionary aspects of Keynes's theoretical system, and indeed way of thinking, made little impact on the discipline. It is for this reason that Joan Robinson argued that the Keynesian revolution had still to be made.

That this understanding should now be so widely held among Keynesians is itself a major achievement. It is due to the untiring efforts of those contemporaries of Keynes who held out against the neo-classical synthesis, and to the subsequent generation of economists, whose re-examination of Keynes has been aided by the publication of the collected writings, and supported by publishing outlets (such as the *Journal of Post Keynesian Economics*), and by Conferences. But what are the prospects of this growing understanding and interest in Keynes for the looked-for Keynesian revolution? It is the purpose of this chapter to consider this question in the light of the fifty years since the publication of the *General Theory*.

One major impediment to effecting a Keynesian revolution is that, for the majority of economists, the Keynesian revolution has come and only recently gone. For them, bastard Keynesian economics (to use Robinson's expression) *is* Keynesian economics. The economic problems facing Western governments since the mid-1970s are now conventionally blamed on Keynesian policies applied in the 1950s and 1960s. (See, for example, Buchanan *et al.*, 1978, p. 27.) However, 'unscientific' the basis for this claim (by the conventional criteria for science), it has given Keynesian economics an aura of failure; thus a recent sympathetic account of Keynesian economics (all the more pertinent for being written out of academia) starts with the perception that 'Keynesian economics is on the defensive' (Hutton, 1986, p. vi).

Even more worrying, perhaps, than the dismissals of Keynesian economics on the basis of knowledge (e.g. by Hayek, 1972) are the candid professions of ignorance on the subject by major figures in the younger generation of economists, such as Sargent and Townsend (see Klamer, 1984, pp. 76, 84). For such economists, it is not so much a question of the validity of Keynes's arguments as one of whether anything can be gained from finding out what they are. We must start, therefore, with the issue of whether we should still be so concerned with Keynes's writing of fifty years ago if our goal is Keynes's goal: to 'revolutionise the way the world thinks about economic problems' (*CW*, XIII, p. 492); can Keynes be subjected to his own charge of being a 'defunct economist' (*CW*, VII, p. 383)? Should we instead be starting afresh?

After considering the rationale for studying Keynes in the second section, we proceed to consider what specifically can be learned from Keynes's own experience in trying to revolutionize economic thinking. In the process a Kuhnian framework is employed to explain the 'bastardisation' of Keynes's thinking and its absorption into the neoclassical synthesis. The concluding section draws some threads together from this discussion in order to consider the prospects for Keynes's ideas in the next fifty years.

Why should we still be interested in Keynes?
For many economists, the history of economic thought is irrelevant to contemporary theory formulation and appraisal. Lucas, for example, introduces a rare reference to history of thought into a discussion of rational expectations as follows: 'There is, I know, a growing feeling that such skeleton rattling is becoming tiresome and old hat' (1980, p. 698). Such a view is perfectly consistent with the traditional (incrementalist) philosophy of science implicit in most of economics, which holds that knowledge progresses unidirectionally: the current state of knowledge contains all that is useful or true from the past. Furthermore, the logic of theory appraisal or justification is independent of the historical context of theory formulation (see Dow, 1985, ch. 2, for a discussion of this position). Indeed in the article drawn from above, Lucas proceeds to describe rational expectations theory as a technical progression from the Keynesian theory of expectations, just as Friedman (1956) expressed his restatement of the Quantity Theory as synthesizing Keynes's monetary theory with what had gone before. According to this view, modern Keynesians should

simply present their theory in testable form to see how it fares relative to orthodox theory.

There is a wide gulf between this traditional philosophy of science and the practice of its adherents – a gulf which has much to do with what happened to Keynes's economics. Theories cannot be compared by straightforward testing if they arise from different ways of thinking about the economy, which is precisely what Keynes tried to revolutionize.

Both the rationale for and content of Klamer's (1984) conversations with leading new classical economists are highly pertinent. Klamer's starting-point was that economic theory evolves more by means of the art of persuasion rather than by the logical characteristics of models, or their correspondence with reality. This is borne out by his conversations, particularly when he elicits views on Keynes. Lucas objects to the *General Theory* because of 'the bullying tone. I don't like the sort of British aristocratic stuff' (see *ibid.*, p. 50). Elsewhere he likens Keynes to Lewis Carroll (Lucas, 1980, p. 700). Townsend puts it less picturesquely: 'I have a hard time mapping what Keynes is saying on neoclassical economics into concepts with which I am familiar' (Klamer, 1984, p. 84). There is no mention of questioning Keynes's logic or of testing Keynesian results, the only professed means of appraisal within orthodox economics.

The importance of persuasion for the success of economic theories was very familiar to Keynes; it was of even more immediate significance in his debates with policy-makers than in his debates with other economists. Like other persuasive economists, Keynes used 'purple passages' in order to persuade; this is just as true of the *General Theory*, addressed to an academic audience (*CW*, XXI, p. 344), as of his more populist writing. In what seems to have been an early draft of the Preface to the *General Theory*, Keynes writes:

> In economics you cannot *convict* your opponent of error; you can only *convince* him of it. And, even if you are right, you cannot convince him, if there is a defect in your own powers of persuasion and exposition or if his head is already so filled with contrary notions that he cannot catch the clues to your thought which you are trying to throw to him. (CW, XIII, p. 470)

Keynes explicity recognized the limitations of logic in his auto-biographical essay, 'My Early Beliefs', written in 1938 (*CW*, X, pp. 433–50). In this essay he also described his realization of the virtue of rules and conventions in thought. This was in reaction to the partial influence of G. E. Moore in favour of treating every case on its merits, where precision of questioning, combined with rational logic, was sufficient for establishing correct answers. (This inner debate of Keynes, between rationalism and realism, is echoed in Coddington's, 1975, critique of Hahn,

1973.) In other words, Keynes came to understand that ideas are not plucked by rationality out of a vacuum, but emerge as a result not only of logic but also of 'springs of feeling' (*CW*, X, p.448) juxtaposed to the conventions of the time. Indeed, Parsons (1985) argues that Keynes's epistemology provides a much more robust basis for understanding the development of disciplines in terms of paradigms than does Kuhn's (1962) more sociological framework.

An immediate corollary of this view, and the first to provide a good reason for studying Keynes, is that theory is capable of wrong turnings; it is not a cumulative accretion of knowledge. What is persuasive in one context according to one way of thinking need not be persuasive in that or any other context according to another way of thinking. Thus if, as Keynesians, we find Keynes's theory most persuasive from our way of thinking, then there is every reason to study his work.

The second reason for studying Keynes, a reason why he is still persuasive, is that his theories incorporate the epistemology outlined above. (The direct influence of Keynes's epistemology on his economics has been traced through his work on probability; see Carabelli, 1985; Dow and Dow, 1985.) Economic agents face the same difficulties as economists in acquiring knowledge on which to base decisions. It is the resulting uncertainty surrounding investment decisions and financial behaviour which characterizes Keynes's monetary theory of production. Keynes (*CW*, XIV, p.115) argued that abstraction from this uncertainty rendered orthodox economics a 'pretty, polite technique'. All theory by definition must abstract – the danger, Keynes argued, was that orthodox economists did not understand the significance of their abstraction, in particular, that it precluded persistent unemployment. Indeed, since the epistemology of orthodox economists does not allow for uncertainty in their own behaviour, it is not surprising that they should fail to understand its significance with respect to their objects of study.

The third corollary of Keynes's epistemology is that his theory is not something which can be understood simply in terms of its logical structure. Just as acceptance or rejection of a theory is not simply a matter of logic, so the understanding of it for application to new situations is not simply a matter of logic. Keynes was presenting not so much a theory, but a different way of thinking about economic problems, one which involved 'returning to an age-long tradition of common sense' (*CW*, XIII, p.552). Unless an economist already fully shares a way of thinking, the best way of understanding it is to study its application to a range of problems. In Keynes's own work we have a prodigious number of applications of his way of thinking, and as well explicit discussions of the constituents of that way of thinking. Such study is particularly apt when the way of thinking emphasizes the significance of habits, conventions and institutions, and the irreversibility of historical time, so that any application of the theory will require some adaptation to particular circumstances.

Since the *General Theory* is now fifty years old, and these fifty years represent a period of rapid institutional and behavioural change, it might be supposed that the task of adaptation to modern conditions is a hopeless one. But the fourth major reason for studying Keynes is that so many of his arguments, at both the theory and policy levels, still hold good. Clearly there have been important changes in industrial structure, in income distribution, in financial sophistication, and so on. But the fact remains that many economies are once again in recession, with mass unemployment due in large part to deficient effective demand, with government policy geared to monetary control and balancing the budget, and with the majority of academic economists engaged in a type of theorizing which distracts attention from involuntary unemployment. Keynes's economics, even in its 1930s form, still has a lot to contribute. Adapted as it has been by Keynesians to modern conditions, it seems to offer an attractive alternative to the current orthodoxy.

What happened to Keynes's economics?

Ultimately, for all his consciousness of the importance of persuasion, Keynes failed to persuade the economics profession to adopt his way of thinking. Even before the final version of the *General Theory* was published, Keynes was aware of the obstacles he faced. The first was the insistence of economists on appraising new theories (if not the old) purely in terms of logic, i.e. it stemmed from epistemological differences:

> It is, I think, a further illustration of the appalling state of scholasticism into which the minds of so many economists have got which allow them to take leave of their intuitions altogether. Yet in writing economics one is not writing either a mathematical proof or a legal document. One is trying to arouse and appeal to the reader's intuitions; and if he has worked himself into a state when he has none, one is helpless! (*CW*, XXIX, pp. 150–1)

The second difficulty, which Keynes had already encountered with the *Treatise on Money*, was the difficulty of understanding a new way of thinking in terms of the old:

> Not only is the angle of approach different, but it is difficult to see just what the relationship is between the new view and the old. Thus those who are sufficiently steeped in the old point of view simply cannot bring themselves to believe that I am asking them to step into a new pair of trousers, and will insist on regarding it as nothing but an embroidered version of the old pair which they had been wearing for years. (*CW*, XIII, p. 247)

This is precisely how many economists reacted to the *General Theory*, although his efforts to avert such an outcome led Keynes into a further difficulty, of distracting from the novelty of his new theory by continual reference to the old:

> What some of you think my excessively controversial method is due to the extent that I am bound in thought to my past opinions and to those of my teachers and earlier pupils; which makes me want to emphasise and bring to a head all the differences of opinion. But I evidently made a mistake in this, not having realised either that the old ones would be merely irritated, or that to the young ones, who have been, apparently, so badly brought up as to believe nothing in particular, the controversy with older views would mean practically nothing. (*CW*, XIV, p.87)

The import of the wealth of literature on Keynes in recent years has been that those steeped in the prevailing orthodoxy failed to understand Keynes's revolutionary way of thinking, so that the limited aspects of his work which could be understood in terms of orthodox economics were incorporated therein, notably by Hicks (1937) and Modigliani (1944). But for those who *were* receptive to Keynes's way of thinking, the continual reference to orthodox economics (which required Keynes himself to express some of his arguments in terms of the orthodox framework) was a major impediment to making the final break with the orthodoxy (see Chick, 1983).

For all Keynes's way of thinking was not widely adopted, it is certainly the case that economic theory and policy changed as a result of his work. There was a burgeoning of aggregative analysis bolstered by advances in data availability, empirical techniques and computer technology. At the policy level there was a new awareness of the scope for stabilization policy reinforced by the political commitment to full employment.

Paradoxically, it can be argued that it was partly because of these changes that Keynes's alternative way of thinking about economic problems did not enjoy similar success. The economic environment of the 1950s, 1960s and early 1970s was one of relatively stable growth with low inflation and low unemployment. There has been much debate as to how far this was due to the implementation of Keynesian policies (see e.g. Bleaney, 1985). But whatever its causes, such an environment distracted attention from the specific problems which Keynes's way of thinking was designed to address. Stable financial markets and stable, and optimistic, long-run expectations minimize the power of uncertainty to reduce effective demand and thus raise unemployment. Even if more economists had been receptive to Keynes's way of thinking, therefore, it would not have been too surprising if it had slipped out of use under the conditions of the 1950s and 1960s, which differed so markedly from the 1930s. It is therefore, among other things, ironic that now that economic conditions much more clearly require Keynes's theoretical approach, so many economists have turned away from the last vestiges of Keynesian economics which had survived in the neo-classical synthesis.

But in any case, Keynes's way of thinking encountered such difficulties at the outset that its future survival was in danger. Its fate can most usefully be analysed in terms of Kuhn's (1962) theory of scientific revolutions (see Mehta, 1977, ch. 1; Dow, 1985, ch. 2). The key feature of Kuhn's paradigms is their incommensurability: there are no criteria for appraising paradigms outside of particular paradigms. Thus the majority of economists, who understood Keynes's theory from the standpoint of the orthodox paradigm at that time, failed to grasp the essence of his alternative paradigm.

The *General Theory* can be understood as an exercise in extraordinary science, challenging the dominant paradigm on the basis of handling what for the orthodoxy was an anomaly: persistent unemployment. The reaction of the orthodoxy was to appraise the challenge by their paradigm's own criteria, and to engage in paradigm defence. This required adapting the dominant paradigm in such a way as to incorporate the new theory, so as to deal with the anomaly, but retaining the orthodox position on theory appraisal and epistemology. With the emergence of high, persistent unemployment, the dominant paradigm is again reacting to the possibility of scientific crisis, this time by returning to a fixation with individual behaviour, and denying that economics can say anything about unemployment at the macrolevel, i.e. by defining the problem away. For example, on macroeconomics in general, Hahn (1977, p. 39) admits, 'How we are to give it a theoretical foundation I do not know', while Lucas states, 'I don't think that unemployment is at the centre of the story' (Klamer, 1984, p. 420). General equilibrium theory is justified as the best mechanism for handling macroeconomic interdependencies. But as soon as it is adapted to include any information difficulties (experienced atomistically), it ceases to yield any macroeconomic solutions.

Prospects for a Keynesian revolution

The impediments in the 1980s to a Keynesian revolution are perhaps greater than Keynes himself faced. The institutional structure of the community of economists, a factor on which Kuhn places much emphasis, is better entrenched than in Keynes's day. In particular, the role of formal teaching of postgraduates and the reliance on textbooks at all levels of teaching have increased the scope for propagating the orthodoxy by exemplars. It is, after all, through the education system that an intellectual revolution is most likely to occur. This was clear from the conversations in

Klamer (1984), referring to the burgeoning of the rational expectations revolution among graduate students. Similar observations have been made about the influence on the profession at different times of teaching at Cambridge, the London School of Economics and Chicago.

The question of how far alternative theories should refer to the existing orthodoxy and aim to persuade the adherents of the orthodoxy is not a straightforward one. Certainly cross-paradigm comprehension is bound to be limited. This is all the more true given that the current orthodoxy does not recognize communication difficulties as being inherent in different, equally legitimate, paradigms. Hahn, for example, specifies one of the characteristics of a good theory as being: 'that it can be communicable to others in a language and grammar that is common ... uncommunicable truths or modes of understanding concern the inner processes of an individual and not the theory of a subject' (1985, p. 4). It is this type of view which makes communication extremely difficult. But Joan Robinson (1977) insisted that attempts should still be made. As I have argued elsewhere (Dow, 1985), *as long as* there is an awareness of and respect for methodological differences, some communication is possible and there is scope for creative cross-fertilization of ideas.

But in the quotation from Keynes (*CW*, XIV, p. 87) given above, it was clear that Keynes concluded that it had been a mistake to try to express his departure in terms of the orthodoxy; and further:

> I am conscious that this, like a great deal else in the book, is largely the product of the old associations of my mind, the result of always trying to see the new theory in its relation to the old and to discover more affinities than really exist. When one has entirely sloughed off the old, one no longer feels the need of all that. I should like some day to endeavour to restate the whole matter, not controversially or critically, or in relation to the views of others, but simply as a positive doctrine. (*CW*, XXIX, pp. 246–7)

It is an indication of the power of the current orthodoxy that many of us still make these references, as indeed I have done here. But so much work in Keynesian economics is already expressed positively, as a self-contained, coherent, viable alternative to the orthodoxy. What more can be done to bring about a revolution in thinking?

Some argue that it is a mistake even to refer to Keynes, that the alternative paradigm should be put forward as new, not shackled by Keynes's own ties to the orthodoxy of the 1930s. Keynes himself did not stress the origins of his ideas (although he did acknowledge his debt to the pre-Ricardians: *CW*, XIII, p. 552). But perhaps Keynes missed an opportunity here for helping his readers understand his 'new' way of thinking. Forming or changing a world-view in general, and a way of thinking about economic problems in particular, is a complex process; the presentation of the logical structure of a new theory cannot by itself be persuasive. The intellectual, educational, political, economic and general institutional environments all have a part to play. Thus studying the experience of the 1930s, and Keynes's way of dealing with it, will help an economist coming new to Keynesian economics to grasp the way in which modern Keynesians can deal with contemporary problems. The logical structure of Keynesian theory (relative to the logical structure of orthodox theory or not) is not enough. It is for this reason that so much of the recent reinterpretations of Keynes have stressed the methodological significance of his contribution. But since explicit methodological discussion, in turn, is unlikely to persuade, by itself, that too is not enough.

All this suggests that the institutional environment for the creation and propagation of Keynesian ideas is of fundamental importance for the prospects for a new Keynesian revolution. The rational expectations 'revolution' has been presented as a technical revolution. A Keynesian revolution will require, rather, a return to political economy, that is, a broadening of perspective, as well as the adoption of a particular perspective within political economy. Ultimately the strengthening of broader perspectives in economics, as in other disciplines, requires a change in educational philosophy and practice. But meanwhile the strengthening of the particularly Keynesian form of political economy will occur through the various fora in which ideas are already expressed and exchanged: journals, presses promoting Keynesian literature, conferences and graduate programmes taught from a Keynesian perspective.

The lesson to be learned from the experience with the *General Theory* over the last fifty years is that 'changing the way the world thinks about economic problems' is an extremely difficult task, and proved to be beyond the persuasive skills even of Keynes. Thus, while Keynesians will have done well to have completed Keynes's unfinished task of presenting the theory 'as a positive doctrine', attention must at the same time be paid to the institutional mechanisms by which 'ways of thinking' are generated and reinforced. Only then will the 'positive doctrine' reach a receptive audience.

References

Bleaney, M. (1985), *The Rise and Fall of Keynesian Economics*, London: Macmillan.
Buchanan, J. M., Burton, J. and Wagner, R. E. (1978), 'The consequences of Mr Keynes', *IEA Hobart Paper*, 78, 1.
Carabelli, A. (1985), 'Keynes' idea of the possible: his concept in cause', in T. Lawson and H. Pesaran (eds), *Keynes' Economics: Methodological Issues*, London: Croom Helm, 151–80.
Chick, V. (1983), *Macroeconomics after Keynes*, Oxford: Philip Allan.
Coddington, A. (1975), 'The rationale of general equilibrium theory', *Economic Inquiry*, 13, December, 539–58.

Dow, A.C. and Dow, S.C. (1985), 'Animal spirits and rationality', in T. Lawson and H. Pesaran (eds), *Keynes' Economics: Methodological Issues*, London: Croom Helm, 46–65.

Dow, S.C. (1985), *Macroeconomic Thought: A Methodological Approach*, Oxford: Blackwell.

Friedman, M. (1956), 'The quantity theory of money: a restatement', in M. Friedman, *Studies in the Quantity Theory of Money*, Chicago: Chicago University Press, 3–21.

Hahn, F.H. (1973), 'The Winter of our Discontent', *Economica*, **40**, August, 322–30.

Hahn, F.H. (1978), 'Keynesian economics and general equilibrium theory', in G.C. Harcourt (ed.), *The Microeconomic Foundations of Macroeconomics*, London: Macmillan, 25–40.

Hahn, F.H. (1985), *In Praise of Economic Theory*, London: University College London.

Hayek, F.A. (1972), *A Tiger by the Tail: A Keynesian Legacy of Inflation*, London: IEA, Hobert Paperback Series.

Hicks, J.R. (1937), 'Mr Keynes and the classics: a suggested interpretation', *Econometrica*, **5**, April, 147–59.

Hutton, W. (1986), *The Revolution that Never Was: An Assessment of Keynesian Economics*, London: Longman.

Keynes, J.M. (1972), *Essays in Biography, Collected Writings*, Vol. X, London: Macmillan/Royal Economic Society.

Keynes, J.M. (1973a), *The General Theory of Employment, Interest and Money, Collected Writings*, Vol. VII, London: Macmillan/Royal Economic Society.

Keynes, J.M. (1973b), *The General Theory and After. Pt I, Preparation, Collected Writings*, Vol. XIII, London: Macmillan/Royal Economic Society.

Keynes, J.M. (1973c), *The General Theory and After. Pt II, Defence and Development, Collected Writings*, Vol. XIV, London: Macmillan/Royal Economic Society.

Keynes, J.M. (1979), *The General Theory and After: A Supplement, Collected Writings*, Vol. XXIX, London: Macmillan/Royal Economic Society.

Keynes, J.M. (1982), *Activities 1931–9: World Crises and Policies in Britain and America, Collected Writings*, Vol. XXI, London: Macmillan/Royal Economic Society.

Klamer, A. (1984), *Conversations with Economists*, Totowa, NJ: Rowman and Allanheld.

Kuhn, T. (1962), *The Structure of Scientific Revolutions*, Chicago: Chicago University Press.

Lucas, R.E., Jr (1980), 'Methods and problems in business cycle theory', *Journal of Money Credit and Banking*, **12**, November, 696–715.

Mehta, G. (1977), *The Structure of the Keynesian Revolution*, London: Martin Robertson.

Modigliani, F. (1944), 'Liquidity preference and the theory of interest and money, *Econometrica*, **12**, January, 45–88.

Parsons, D.W. (1985), 'Was Keynes Kuhnian? Keynes and the idea of theoretical revolutions', *British Journal of Political Science*, **15**, October, 451–71.

Robinson, J. (1973), 'What has become of the Keynesian revolution?' in J. Robinson, *Collected Economic Papers V*, Oxford: Blackwell, 168–77.

Robinson, J. (1977), 'The relevance of economic theory', in J. Schwartz (ed.), *The Subtle Anatomy of Capitalism*, Santa Monica, Calif.: Goodyear, 16–21.

10 The hidden microeconomics of John Maynard Keynes
David McQueen[1]

As we all know, Keynes did not give us a reconstructed microeconomic theory to mesh with the new macroeconomics of the *General Theory*. Had he done so, economic theory, and I daresay economic policy also, would likely wear a different and happier aspect today.

How interestingly different a full, Keynesian microeconomics would have been from contemporary textbook fare! Much less cut-and-dried, for a start. This is the author who held that in economics and other 'psychics', as contrasted with physics and its 'atomic hypothesis': 'We are faced at every turn with the problems of organic unity, of discreteness, of discontinuity – the whole is not equal to the sum of the parts, comparisons of quantity fail us, small changes produce large effects, the assumptions of a uniform and homogeneous continuum are not satisfied' (*CW*, X, p. 262). The author also who argued that the economist: 'who tried to avoid all vagueness and to be perfectly precise', would never succeed in guiding his reader all the way to the matter in hand (*CW*, XXIX, p. 36).

But to castigate Keynes's spirit for failing to produce a companion, 'micro' volume to the *General Theory* would be churlish indeed towards one who has already left us so giant a legacy. If the brilliantly seductive but dangerously flawed concubinage of the neo-classical synthesis has in due course opened the door to a massive counterrevolution – to a latter-day pre-Keynesian economics, on its surface far more sophisticated, but in its fundamentals far more mechanistic and rigidly anti-empirical, than the views to which someone like Pigou was coming by the early 1930s (Hutchinson, 1978) – that is our problem. Keynes unfortunately was taken from us before he could comment on that ultimately so costly intellectual misalliance.

To be sure, in the *General Theory* itself, and some of the correspondence surrounding it, are to be found derogatory statements about the 'standard' microeconomics of Keynes's day – chiefly the Marshallian, partial equilibrium variety with which he was most familiar. And we know, from such sources as the Keynes–Harrod correspondence (*CW*, XIII, pp. 533–4), that more such statements would have appeared in the book had Keynes not been persuaded that to gain acceptance of what he regarded as his most important new ideas, he must not overstrain our profession's high valuation of intellectual sunk cost, and its consequently limited tolerance for novelty. As, for example, by following Sraffa (1926), and asserting too boldly that many of the most important pairings of supply and demand curves that we like to conceive do not in fact represent independent symmetric fuctions.

But while Keynes did not construct a complete new microeconomics, he nevertheless through the 1920s and early 1930s consistently and repeatedly employed a number of microeconomic propositions fundamentally at odds with the assumptions (see Hahn, 1984) of a latter-day Arrow–Debreu model of perfectly competitive general equilibrium. I am not normally drawn, any more than I suspect was Keynes himself (one can imagine his deadly aphorism!), to the detailed, biblical exegesis of the works of defunct economists. By this method, especially when applied to the writings of so prolific an author, the sufficiently determined autopsist can 'prove' almost anything – even that the Keynes of the early 1920s was a monetarist! But study of the collected works, including notably the 'activities' writings, reveals a recurrence of certain microeconomic leitmotivs with enough contemporary relevance to merit attention here.

Why go to the activities, though? Does not an economist sooner or later put all his important thoughts about economic theory into serious academic works? Most perhaps do, but this is an exceptional case – a passionately engagé man, who did not always tidy up after himself before moving on to the next real-world crisis. Especially from 1919 onwards, was there ever an economist so continuously active in the forward trenches of contemporary policy debate? His longer works, such as the *Treatise on Money* and the *General Theory*, are in a sense catch-up works. In them he imparts to his fellow academics, in that more formal manner which they best appreciate, ideas many of which have already been substantially developed on the fly, in the heat of battle, to be added at once to that incredible torrent of expert testimony, articles and letters to the quality press and high political and financial figures as well as to his fellow economists. Some intellectual process such as this best explains how so many of the policy recommendations (both Keynes's and others') flowing logically from the *General Theory* found their way into the public domain long before the *General Theory* itself (Kahn, 1984).

Partly because of this practice of battlefield theorizing, and partly out of that earlier-mentioned desire not to overload our profession with novelty within the compass of a single book, some important 'Keynes' (as opposed to 'vulgar Keynesian') microeconomics never got tidied up, pulled together and preserved in places where it would readily attract its just share of attention from later generations of economists.

The core propositions of this 'hidden' microeconomics seem, to me, to be these:

(1) Time matters, history matters. It matters that the 'laws' of economics only take effect over time periods of varying length, and that some of them which appear to be eternal are in the event wholly or partly repealed by history.

(2) The price-driven forces of resource allocation between industries often work very slowly, with the result that they may be overtaken by other forces before they have finished their work.

(3) Uninsurable uncertainties are one of the leading facts of twentieth-century economic life and an important justification for macroeconomic policy.

(4) The downward stickiness of money wages in a modern economy is more than just an empirical observation and prudent assumption; there are important operational reasons for it. Marginal productivity, at best, sets a broad band of wage possibilities within which other forces, many of a social and traditional character, determine actual wage rates.

(5) An incomes policy is conceivable and potentially useful, but attended by severe practical difficulties of implementation.

(6) Primary and secondary producers differ greatly in their reactions to recession and depression, in a manner that testifies eloquently to the imperfectly competitive environment in which much of the second group operates.

(7) Large parts of the utility functions of consumers in advanced industrial societies are interdependent.

It will be readily enough apparent how incompatible are the above propositions (virtually all of which are today being examined by modern industrial organization, general equilibrium and game theorists) with key assumptions of a 'standard' general equilibrium model. Let us look at each of them in turn, with appropriate references to the *Collected Works*.

(1) *Time matters, history matters.* We find of course in the *Tract on Monetary Reform* (1923) the oft-quoted sarcasm about the Marshallian long run: '*In the long run* [original italics], we are all dead. Economists set themselves too easy, too useless a task if in tempestuous seasons they can only tell us that when the storm is long past the ocean is flat again'(*CW*, IV, p. 65).

The practical implication – the warning to policy – here implied emerges perhaps best in the next proposition to be examined. As to the impingement of history – of great historical disturbances – upon our perception of the 'economic laws' and processes of microeconomic adjustment underlying such phenomena as the pre-1914 gold standard, while this thread constantly re-emerges throughout the writings of the 1920s and 1930s, it is harder than are the other propositions to attach to a single quotation. But some of the opening passages of *Economic Consequences of the Peace* convey clearly enough the general message of historical irreversibility; for example:

> What an extraordinary episode in the economic progress of man that age was which came to an end in August 1914! (*CW*, II, p. 9)

> The German machine (pre-1914) was like a top which to maintain its equilibrium must progress ever faster and faster. (*ibid.*, p. 11)

> I seek only to point out that the principle of accumulation based on inequality was a vital part of the pre-war order of Society and of progress as we then understood it, and to emphasize that this principle depended on unstable psychological conditions, which it may be impossible to recreate. (*ibid.*, p. 19)

In the longer-term event Western Europe has proved better able to reconcile continued accumulation with the new mass consumption than Keynes foresaw. But he was right in so far as he held that accumulation on the basis of a pre-1914 type of social structure might no longer be possible. (2) *The price-driven forces of resource allocation are sluggish.* Sole policy reliance on them to accomplish major adjustments, such as German reparations, or Britain's return to the gold standard at the pre-1914 parity, may therefore have disconcerting results. They may simply not be tolerable politically. And often in conjunction with this, they may be overtaken before completion by history, in the form of large, new, unexpected disturbances. Before the stable cobweb of the theorem implodes to an equilibrium, something blows it apart again. If there is one thing of which twentieth-century economic life has had a surfeit, it is history, in this sense.

This theme emerges first in 1919 when Keynes asks:

> in what export trade is German labour going to find a greatly increased outlet. Labour can only be diverted into new channels with loss of efficiency, and a large expenditure of capital. The annual surplus which German labour can produce for capital improvements at home is no measure, either theoretically or practically, of the annual tribute which she can pay abroad. (*CW*, IX, pp. 12–13)

The difficulty of inter-industry resource transfer is further emphasized in 1921:

> Since capital and labour are fixed and organized in certain employments and cannot flow freely into others, the disturbance of the balance is destructive to the utility of the capital and labour thus fixed. The organization, on which the wealth of the modern world so largely depends, suffers injury. In course of time a new organization and a new equilibrium can be established. But if the origin

of the disturbance is of temporary duration, the losses from the injury done to organization may outweigh the profit of receiving goods without paying for them. (*ibid.*, p. 42)

And in 1925 we re-encounter the same theme as, in relation to the 'return to gold', Keynes considers the possibilities of shifting British resources between 'unsheltered' industries, such as coalmining, and service and other 'sheltered' industries:

> Like other victims of economic transition in past times, the miners are to be offered the choice between starvation and submission, the fruits of their submission to accrue to the benefit of other classes. But in view of the disappearance of an effective mobility of labour and of a competitive wage level between different industries, I am not sure that they are not worse placed in some ways than their grandfathers were. (*ibid.*, p. 223)

History, it is here suggested, has once again moved on irreversibly since the days of the coalminers' grandfathers.

And there is much more in the same vein through into the 1930s. Keynes clearly viewed modern economies as *not* heavily characterized by easy entry/easy exit 'contestable' markets (Baumol *et al.*, 1982). Rather he saw them as marked by heavy sunk costs and pronounced specialization of physical and human capital in particular industrial employments. Failure to recognize this causes economists and others repeatedly to overestimate the speed with which resources, moving in response to price and wage signals, transfer between employments, *especially in generally soft economies.*

In fairness, it should be noted that on the general importance of time in economic affairs, and on sluggishness in interindustrial adjustment, Keynes had been anticipated to a considerable degree by Marshall, notably in appendix H to the latter's *Principles of Economics* (Marshall, 1920)

(3) *Uninsurable uncertainties are common, so that many of the 'contingency markets' required for a full, general equilibrium model are, in real life, missing.* In a 1923 article Keynes notes the increasing length and roundaboutness of modern productive processes, which require the business world constantly to be carrying, for considerable intervals, heavy money liabilities against the expectation of money recoupment at a later date:

> Whether it likes it or not, the technique of production under a regime of money-contract forces the business world always to carry a big speculative position; and if they are reluctant to carry this speculative position, the productive process must be brought to a standstill. (*CW*, XIX, pp. 113–14)

A year later, before the Committee on the Currency and Bank of

England Note Issues, he notes the absence of organized protection for most of this speculative position:

> You have the forward exchange market ... but a forward market in commodities by means of which traders can insure against the risk of movements of prices is limited to two or three of the biggest trades. Why I want price stability is that it will minimize disastrous losses to traders through no fault of their own, through events which were quite beyond their cognizance. (*ibid.*, p. 26)

No doubt, by the early 1930s Keynes would have added greater stability in quantities demanded to his 'want' list.

To translate the proposition into contemporary, information-cost terms the greater ability of firms, as compared with networks of contractually linked individuals, to bear big speculative positions, may be urged as one of the fundamental reasons why we have firms in the first place. By entering into larger volumes of transactions, self-insuring and realizing the economies of mobilizing business information on a larger scale than can individuals they convert *some* of the uncertainties confronting them into stochastic risk arrays to which rough probability numbers, such as bad debt ratios, may be assigned. But that still leaves much uncovered uncertainty, from some of which, Keynes argues, the firm should be relieved by public macroeconomic policy.

(4) *Money wages are only loosely linked to marginal productivity, and there are reasons for their downward rigidity.* An extended disquisition on this topic occurs in a 1930 article, in which Keynes outlines two main lines of attack by dissenting economists on orthodox wage theory. The first of these interestingly anticipates Liebenstein's (1976) hypothesis of 'X-inefficiency'. The second is based on the view that by reason of historical influences, as gradually modified by contemporary social and political forces ... there is a large arbitrary element in the relative rates of remuneration, and the factors of production get what they do, not because in any strict economic sense they precisely earn it, but because past events have led to these rates being customary and usual'. 'To a large extent', says Keynes, 'I sympathize with these attacks. I think there is a great deal in what the critics say. I believe that the best working theories of the future will own these assailants as their parents' (*CW*, XX, pp. 5–7)

To relate all this to general downward rigidity it is necessary to cross-reference, first, to a statement on wages before the Macmillan Committee in 1930 (*CW*, XX, p. 64), then to the well-known passage on relative wages in the *General Theory* (*CW*, VII, p. 264). The citation in support of the proposition on incomes policy immediately following is also relevant.

(5) *An incomes policy is conceivable and potentially useful, but difficult to implement.* In 'The Economic Consequences of Mr Churchill' (1925)

Keynes considers how wages might be adjusted downwards to accord with the restored sterling parity:

> One way is to apply economic pressure and to intensify unemployment by credit restriction, until wages are forced down. This is a hateful and disastrous way ... The other way is to effect a uniform reduction of wages by agreement, on the understanding that this shall not mean in the long run any fall in average real wages below what they were in the first quarter of this year. The practical difficulty is that money wages and the cost of living are interlocked. The cost of living cannot fall until after money wages have fallen. Money wages must fall first, in order to allow the cost of living to fall. Can we not agree therefore, to have a uniform initial reduction of money wages throughout the whole range of employment, of (say) 5 per cent, which reduction shall not hold good unless after an interval it has been compensated by a fall in the cost of living? (*CW*, IX, p. 228)

The worst of the problem is the fear of employee groups that their position in the structure of *relative* incomes will deteriorate – that free-riders and holdouts in other industries and sectors will make 'mugs' of them, thus failing to produce a commensurate fall in the cost of living, and so leaving them with reduced wages on both a money and a real basis. Keynes recognizes that non-wage incomes – rents, profits and interest – present a particularly severe difficulty in this respect (*ibid.*, pp. 228–9).

(6) *As depression strikes, primary producers cut price and maintain output; secondary producers cut output and maintain price.* The reason for including this here is to note Keynes's recognition, in his observation of the behaviour of secondary producers, of the prevalence of 'imperfect' competition. Other members of his circle (e.g. Sraffa, 1926; Joan Robinson, 1932; Kahn, 1931) were much more deeply involved in this matter. Still, the recognition is there, in 1930 and 1931, that many real-life firms face non-horizontal average revenue curves (*CW*, IX, pp. 127, 135–6). Subsequently, in the *General Theory* and afterwards, both Keynes and his followers played down this aspect, out of an all-too-justified fear that many economists would conclude that Keynes's explanation of mass unemployment boiled down to no more than an aberration from the neo-classical model produced by excessive inflexibility of prices and wages. Many so concluded anyway! But now that more recent Keynesian scholarship (see e.g. Leijonhufvud, 1968; Clower, 1965; Chick, 1983) has established that the heart of the uncertainty out of which depressions are born lies elsewhere in the model, and that the dismissal of the *General Theory* as a mere special case will not do, the imperfect competition aspect can surely be brought back into the light of day. It does not move the whole model; but it contributes something; and it was demonstrably in Keynes's mind as the 1930s opened, probably as a joint result of his Cambridge associations and of his observation of some of the most

dramatic events in all economic history.

(7) *Household utility functions are interdependent.* In the 1930 article, 'Economic Possibilities for our Grandchildren', we read:

> Now it is true that the needs of human beings may seem to be insatiable. But they fall into two classes – those needs which are absolute in the sense that we feel them whatever the situation of our fellow human beings may be, and those which are relative in the sense that we feel them only if their satisfaction lifts us above, makes us feel superior to, our fellows. Needs of the second class, those which satisfy the desire for superiority, may indeed be insatiable; for the higher the general level, the higher still are they. But this is not so true of the absolute needs. (*CW*, IX, p. 326)

Economist readers will hardly need reminding that acceptance of this position drives a coach-and-four through the conventional theory of consumer demand, and through the generalizations about pervasive scarcity with which most of our elementary textbooks still begin. It also opens up fascinating new dimensions of the ongoing debate about the economic significance of advertising.

Conclusion

I hope the foregoing will not be taken as one of those tiresome, academic *jeux d'esprit*, whereby, for instance, Keynes is proven to be an unwitting Post-Keynesian. Always he must first be seen as of his own place and time, in the problems of which he was so passionately involved. But in considering how much of his legacy is relevant for *our* place and time, knowing more about what kind of microeconomics he was comfortable with as he moved forward towards the *General Theory* may help us to make *our* microeconomics one which coexists more comfortably with our macroeconomics.

Throughout these interrelated propositions drawn from Keynes's writings of the 1920s and early 1930s time and uncertainty keep reappearing as crucial elements, and as a result of this exercise, I am more than ever drawn to the view of Keynes attributed by Blaug to Clower and Leijonhufvud, and summarized thus:

> For Clower and Leijonhufvud, Keynesian economics is about incomplete and costly information, sluggish price adjustments, quantity rather than price-adjustments, the dual-decision hypothesis, income-constrained processes, and false trading at non-equilibrium prices in the absence of a Walrasian auctioneer. What is crucial in neoclassical economics, they seem to be saying, is not the assumption of perfect competition but the much less widely noted assumption that all prices adjust instantaneously to clear markets – for that is what is implied by the notion of a Walrasian auctioneer. (Blaug, 1978; see also Leijonhufvud, 1968; Clower, 1965)

At the heart of Chicago and other neo-classical microeconomics lives, I believe, a time-bomb, planted there by none other than Chicago's own (by adoption) Ronald Coase, in his seminal 1937 article on the firm (Coase, 1937). Prior to that article, we did not really have a theory of the firm; only a theory of markets containing firms too small to be individually interesting and worth internal dissection. But once Coase asked the questions: why do we have firms in the first place? Why do we bring this institution into the system to supersede part of the market's price mechanism?, the bomb started ticking. Following through the great volume of post-Coaseian literature of the firm, via such authors as Coase again, H. A. Simon, Alfred Chandler, Jr, and Oliver Williamson (see e.g. Chandler, 1977; Williamson, 1985) we are drawn more and more, as it seems to me, to the view that one of the biggest reasons we have firms, in a remarkable variety of sizes and complexities, is to deal somewhat better with time, uncertainty, sluggish price adjustment, big outstanding speculative positions and all those dark forces which envelop our future.

Which of course brings us back to the heart of Keynes. Somewhere about here is where a *true* marriage of micro and macro might at last be arranged. And since the firm *is* an institution, and one which, as Chandler shows in his masterly *The Visible Hand* (1977), has evolved mightily through time, for reasons perfectly well susceptible to economic analysis, we might even expand the marriage ceremony to include some measure of reconciliation with those long-lost relatives, institutional economics and economic history.

Notes

1. As someone returning to Keynes after a longish exposure to industrial organization, I am much indebted to Geoff Harcourt and Omar Hamouda for suggested improvements to my original draft, but responsibility for this text rests of course with myself. Another major debt must be acknowledged: without the work of Don Moggridge and others in assembling and editing Keynes's *Collected Writings* (referred to in the text as CW), the task of researching and composing this paper would have been infinitely more laborious.

References

Baumol, W., Panzar, C. and Willing, D. (1982), *Contestable Markets and the Theory of Industry Structure*, San Diego, Calif.: Harcourt Brace Jovanovitch.

Blaug, Mark (1978), *Economic Theory in Retrospect* (3rd edn), Cambridge: Cambridge University Press.

Chandler, Alfred, Jr (1977), *The Visible Hand – the Managerial Revolution in American Business*, Cambridge, Mass.: Harvard University Press.

Chick, Victoria (1983), *Macroeconomics after Keynes*, Cambridge, Mass.: MIT Press.

Clower, Robert (1965), 'The Keynesian counter-revolution: a theoretical appraisal', in F. Hahn and F. P. R. Brechling (eds), *The Theory of Interest Rates*, London: Macmillan/International Economic Association.

Coase, R. H. (1937), 'Nature of the firm', *Economica*, n.s. 4, 386–405.

Hahn, Frank (1984), *Equilibrium and Macroeconomics*, Cambridge, Mass.: MIT Press.

Hutchinson, T.W. (1978), *On Revolutions and Progress in Economic Knowledge*, Cambridge: Cambridge University Press.

Kahn, Richard (1931), 'The relation of home investment to unemployment', *Economic Journal*, 41, June, 173–98.

Kahn, Richard (1984), *The Making of Keynes' General Theory*, Cambridge: Cambridge University Press.

Leijonhufvud, Axel (1968), *On Keynesian Economics and the Economics of Keynes: A Study in Monetary Theory*, London: Oxford University Press.

Liebenstein, Harvey (1976), *Beyond Economic Man*, Cambridge, Mass.: Harvard University Press.

Marshall, Alfred (1920), *Principles of Economics* (8th edn), London: Macmillan.

Moggridge, D. E., and others (eds) (1972), *The Collected Writings of John Maynard Keynes*, London: Macmillan/Royal Economic Society.

Robinson, Joan (1932), *The Economics of Imperfect Competition*, London: Macmillan.

Sraffa, Piero (1926), 'The laws of return under competitive conditions', *Economic Journal*, 36, December, 535–50.

Williamson, Oliver (1985), *The Economic Institutions of Capitalism*, New York: The Free Press.

11 The development of Keynes's theory of employment
Robert W. Dimand[1]

The development of John Maynard Keynes's theory of the level of employment in a monetary economy can be observed in the lectures he gave at Cambridge University from 1932 to 1935. Keynes gave a series of eight lectures each year on the subject of whatever book he was then writing. Students' notes on his lectures from the autumn of 1932 to the autumn of 1935, supplemented by Keynes's own notes for two lectures in the spring of 1932 and two that fall, record the state that Keynes's theory of a monetary economy had reached, year by year. The extent of the notes and their reliability are discussed in Dimand (1986b). Apart from the incomplete coverage of spring 1932 lectures, these notes cover all the lectures given by Keynes at Cambridge between the publication of his *Treatise on Money* (1930) and the *General Theory* (1936). The lectures reveal distinct changes in Keynes's thought, with the changing nature of the lectures reflected in changes of title from 'The Pure Theory of Money' (the same title as the first volume of the *Treatise*), in the Lent term of 1932, to 'The Monetary Theory of Production', in the Michaelmas term of that year, and then to 'The General Theory of Employment' in 1934.

Keynes was motivated to develop his theory by his belief that fluctuations in aggregate demand had raised the level of unemployment, and that the government could restore full employment by appropriate demand management. His theory thus has to answer several questions. He had to provide an explanation of 'effective demand or, more precisely, of the demand schedule for output as a whole', together with an explanation of why the level of effective demand should be subject to fluctuation in a monetary economy. Next he had to explain why fluctuations in effective demand affect employment and output by analysing the supply schedule for output as a whole. For government intervention to be justified, Keynes had to show that the downward pressure of unemployment on money wage rates could not be relied upon to restore full employment. The principle of effective demand could then be used to determine what policy the government should pursue to produce full employment. Keynes's lectures reveal the process by which he developed answers to these questions and combined them in an integrated theory.

121

The four crucial elements of Keynes's theory are the multiplier theory of effective demand, the liquidity preference theory of the demand for money as an asset, the marginal efficiency of capital theory of investment and the analysis of the inability of workers to negotiate a market-clearing real wage by bargaining for nominal wages. In this chapter, I will examine the evolution of these elements and their integration into a coherent theory, as seen from the notes on Keynes's lectures.

Wages and employment: the *Treatise* and after

The *Treatise on Money* presented no formal theory of employment and output. Instead it presented a theory of price level change based on a concept of windfall profits (Q), which was identified with the difference between investment and saving. Because earnings (E) of the factors of production were defined to exclude unanticipated windfalls, positive profits (I greater than S), meant that the price level exceeded the earnings per unit of output. Positive profits also meant that entrepreneurs would become more optimistic about the future, since they had received a favourable surprise, and so they would increase investment, resulting in even higher profits next period. This model separated investment decisions from saving decisions since entrepreneurs had to choose the volume of investment based only on an expectation of household's saving decisions (Dimand, 1986b). What the model lacked was an equilibrating effect of changes in the level of income on the rate of saving, with the result that a profit inflation or deflation could continue without limit instead of coming to rest at an equilibrium level of income with saving equal to desired investment.

While the *Treatise* left the link between changes in investment and changes in output vague, it included two isolated passages foreshadowing later developments, On pages 206 and 207, Keynes explained that windfall losses (Q less than zero, I less than S) would cause entrepreneurs to reduce 'the volume of employment which they offer to the factors of production at the existing rate of earnings ... Finally, under the pressure of growing unemployment, the rate of earnings – though, perhaps, only at long last – will fall'. On page 271, however, without referring back to his earlier remarks, Keynes observed: 'If the money-rates or remuneration of the *different* factors of production could be reduced simultaneously and in equal proportion, no one need suffer ... But there is generally no means of securing this.' These two passages, when joined, provide an explanation of money wage rigidity in terms of a rational concern with relative wages, without money illusion, and show how this can cause unemployment when there are demand shocks, in a manner resembling chapter 3 of the *General Theory*.

In spite of the change of title for his lectures in the autumn of 1932, Keynes still retained much of the analysis of the *Treatise*. In his opening lecture on 10 October, Keynes argued that 'So long as there is an excess of S over I – entrepreneurs will incur a loss at whatever level E/O is fixed' and that in a closed economy E/O, the earnings of the factors of production, will not affect the excess of S over I.[2] While the derivation of a finite multiplier had been forcefully brought to Keynes's attention by Ralph Hawtrey's critique of the *Treatise* and by Richard Kahn in his 1931 article,[3] Keynes's 1932 lectures made no use of the leakages into personal saving analysed by Hawtrey. Instead Keynes clung to the *Treatise* analysis of why Q would not be affected by changes in E.

Keynes criticized Marshall and Pigou for discussing the supply of labour solely in terms of real wages and for forgetting that workers must bargain for money wages. Despite faulting the older Cambridge economists for this oversight, Keynes did not offer any analysis of the labour market in his 1932 lectures. Keynes's lack of such an analysis is of considerable importance. If he had dropped the *Treatise* argument that a reduction in the money wage bill would reduce entrepreneurs' receipts by the same amount without altering profits, he would not have had any explanation for the failure of money wage cuts to restore prosperity. This is a possible explanation for the surprising absence of the multiplier from the 1932 lectures. A clue can be found in Kahn's article. Kahn examined the effect of a change in investment spending on the equilibrium level of output on the assumption that the money wage rate was fixed, and promised a second article in which this restrictive assumption would be dropped.[4] The second article never appeared. Keynes's reluctance to switch from the *Treatise* framework to the multiplier theory in 1932 may be due to the fact that such a switch would have left him without a theory of the effect of wage cuts on employment. In the 1932 lectures Keynes did not even discuss the causes and consequences of money wage rigidity.

On 14 November, Keynes summarized the parameters of a monetary economy as the quantity of money, the state of liquidity preference, the expectation of quasi-rents, the state of time preference and 'the supply schedule – the response of supply ... to state of profits etc'. In his next lecture he presented the equations of his theory, including two versions of the supply function. One version resembles the treatment of windfall profits in the *Treatise*, except that it relates the level of output to profits rather than the change in output. The other, which had entrepreneurs producing until the marginal cost of production equals the price of their product, given supply conditions, is much closer to the *General Theory*'s treatment of supply. There is no hint in the lecture notes that Keynes then realized that the two approaches to supply functions were inconsistent.

In his lecture of 21 November 1932, Keynes argued at length that output and investment tend to vary in the same direction, but instead of using the multiplier to relate changes in output to changes in investment, he relied on the *Treatise* definition of profit as investment minus saving.[5] According to Tarshis's notes, Keynes concluded this lecture with an argument that relied on windfall profits as the determinant of output:[6]

> Output increases when disbursement increases faster than costs. Generally safe to assume that changes in investment (ΔI) are the same in sign as changes in disbursement relative to costs. Generalizing then whether or not Output is increasing depends on whether or not Investment is increasing. ('Problem of curing unemployment is a problem in monetary economics').

The theory of effective demand in the 1932 lectures was built on Q, not the multiplier. Keynes limited himself to arguing that changes in output and investment have the same sign, but did not analyse the quantitative relationship between the changes. Keynes's lectures in the autumn of 1932 were sufficiently different to shock Lorie Tarshis, who had arrived in Cambridge as the *Treatise*'s most devout believer after studying it under Wynne Plumptre in Toronto. Despite this, Keynes had not yet broken away from the windfall profit theory of changes in output and investment.

Another striking feature of the 1932 lectures is the concept of a minimum nominal interest rate, which later became known as the 'liquidity trap'. On 31 October, Keynes explained that because of the zero own-rate of interest of money, the nominal interest rate could not fall below zero. Given transactions costs of buying and selling securities, and some risk that the interest rate would rise, lowering bond prices, the minimum interest rate would be some small positive amount. In his final lecture on 28 November, Keynes stated his belief that Britain had reached the minimum rate of interest.

The eighth and final lecture of the series, given on 28 November, bears a strong resemblance to chapter 23 of the *General Theory*, but only presents the window-dressing of the *General Theory*, not its essential elements. In this lecture Keynes discusses Bentham and Smith on the Usury Laws, Mandeville's *Fable of the Bees* and mercantilism. Keynes's defence of the rational basis of mercantilism thus predated his reading of Eli Heckscher's *Mercantilism*, which had not then been translated into English.

Keynes's lectures in October and November 1932 did not satisfy all his listeners. Both Lorie Tarshis and Robert Bryce actually decided to leave economics at the end of that academic year, though fortunately for the economics profession, neither followed through on this decision. Their disappointment is understandable, since in the 1932 lectures Keynes recognized the need for a theory of a monetary economy without being able to provide one.

The monetary theory of production, 1933

In the Michaelmas term of 1933, Keynes gave eight lectures on 'The Monetary Theory of Production' which contrasted sharply with his lectures of the previous year. The 1933 lectures dealt explicitly with the failure of the labour market to clear in the face of demand shocks, and integrated the multiplier, the saving function and liquidity preference into his theory. Of the building-blocks of the *General Theory*, only the marginal efficiency of capital was missing.

On 16 October 1933, Keynes told his audience that the *Treatise* had been primarily interested in prices, even while claiming to provide a clue to movements of output. Now Keynes would be concerned with the volume of output and employment in a monetary economy. He began by presenting the two fundamental postulates of the classical theory, as exemplified by Pigou's *Theory of Unemployment*: the real wage equals the marginal product of labour under perfect competition, and the marginal utility of the wage equals the marginal disutility of labour. Keynes explained that there could be no excess supply of labour if these two conditions hold, but that seasonal, transitional and voluntary unemployment were consistent with the classical postulates. Keynes accepted the first classical postulate but not the second, so that involuntary unemployment was possible in his theory.[7] Keynes cited the example of the USA in 1932 to show that labour had accepted money wage reductions in the depression, but had not been able to adjust real wages to clear the labour market because prices had fallen along with money wages. Keynes returned to criticism of the classical theory of employment in his next lecture, on 23 October, and insisted that 'the struggle over money wages is really over distribution of total wages among earners'. This was a recognition of the significance of a passing remark in the *Treatise* that nominal wages could be sticky because overlapping contracts meant that not all nominal income could be reduced by the same proportion at the same time.[8]

On 6 November, Keynes redefined Q as expected quasi-rents, the excess of expected sales proceeds over E, 'the cost to which the entrepreneur commits himself when he makes a short period decision to employ people'. This definition was consistent with the one passage in the *Treatise* which recognized that anticipated profits are relevant for investment decisions, not ex-post realized windfalls. Y, the income of the community, was defined as E + Q, the expected sales proceeds. This resembles the *General Theory* discussion of aggregate demand. 'Profits', in the *Treatise* sense, reappeared in Keynes's 6 November lecture as windfall appreciation, A, 'the excess of actual sales proceeds of goods selling in the period plus the change in the value of capital', over the cost of production. According to the notes taken by Lorie Tarshis, but not those taken by Bryce, Fallgatter or Salant, Keynes then presented a consumption function stated as C = f(Y,A), where Y = C + I. This is the first appearance of the consumption function in Keynes's lectures, and differed from his later versions by the inclusion of windfalls.

The notes taken by Bryce, Fallgatter, Salant and Tarshis all agree that on 20 November Keynes expounded the 'psychological law' that consumption changes by less than income, and discusses the propensity to spend. Fallgatter's notes on this lecture record the consumption function as C = f(Y), omitting windfall appreciation. The four sets of notes also agree that on 27 November Keynes derives the multiplier from the marginal propensity to consume, and showed that it was equivalent to Kahn's ratio of the change in total employment to the change in primary employment.

In his final lecture on 4 December 1933, Keynes summarized his monetary theory of production in these equations:

$M = f(W,p)$ money supply = liquidity preference;
$C = \phi_1(W,Y)$ consumption function;
$I = \phi_2(W,p)$ investment function;
$Y = C + I$ aggregate demand

where W is defined as the 'state of news',[9] and p is the interest rate. Liquidity preference and the marginal efficiency of capital remained sensitive to the state of news in Keynes's later lectures and writing, responding to changes in long-period expectations, but the consumption function became dependent on the level of income alone. Thus, while volatile expectations and uncertainty about the future could cause fluctuations in the level of effective demand by changing investment, the multiplier for fiscal policy to offset these fluctuations, derived from the marginal propensity to consume, would remain stable.

Keynes's 1933 lectures were a decisive advance beyond those he gave a year earlier. The 1932 lectures called for a theory of output rather than prices, and of a monetary economy as distinguished from a neutral money economy, but failed to provide this theory.

The 1933 lectures provided an explanation of involuntary un-employment, arguing that nominal wage rages could be sticky without money illusion, and liquidity preference, the consumption function and the multiplier appear in forms very close to those of the *General Theory*. The marginal efficiency of capital was mentioned but was not developed or explained until 1934. In the 1933 lectures Keynes did not yet derive a supply function, although he remarked on 6 November that since marginal costs normally rise with output, there would be an inducement to increase output only if the price level was expected to rise. There were also approaches Keynes tried out and then abandoned, notably the appearance of windfall appreciation, A, and the state of news, W, in the consumption function.

Marginal efficiency of capital and rate of investment

Keynes's theory of investment was the last part of the *General Theory* to reach its final form, appearing in his Michaelmas 1934 lectures on 'The General Theory of Employment'. This theory has had a bad press over the years, but the evidence of the lecture notes supports the contention of Stephen LeRoy (1983) that Keynes's theory of the rate of investment in the *General Theory* is a refinement of the *Treatise*'s portfolio balance approach to the pricing and production of capital goods, and that the marginal efficiency of capital is not the same as the marginal product of capital. According to LeRoy:

> Keynes's model does not involve theoretical error, and Keynes's statement of the model is precise and complete. The general failure of the profession to understand what Keynes had done is due primarily to the difficulty of the material; Keynes was presenting the first analysis of temporary general equilibrium under a two-sector technology with nonshiftable capital.

In his lectures, as in the *General Theory*, Keynes defined the marginal efficiency of capital as the internal rate of return equating the present value of a stream of expected quasi-rents to the supply price of new capital. On 26 November 1934, Keynes criticized Irving Fisher for having the rate of return over costs, Fisher's equivalent of the marginal efficiency of capital, equate the present value of the stream of expected earnings to the demand price of capital, rather than the supply price. Keynes condemned this as a confusion of the marginal efficiency of capital with the rate of interest, and his cry of protest appears in Bryce's notes for that day underlined and separated by blank lines from the preceding and following sentences: 'Fisher's solution is just nonsense.'[10]

The lecture notes thus confirm LeRoy's argument that the marginal efficiency of capital schedule reflects portfolio preferences and the conditions of supply of new capital goods, so that its slope is determined by the elasticity of substitution between capital and labour in capital-producing firms, not capital-using firms. In the *General Theory* bonds and capital are treated as close substitutes, so that the price of such securities will be such as to induce the public to hold the existing volumes of securities and money. Firms in the capital goods sector then maximize profits by producing new capital goods until their marginal cost equals the price of capital assets (assuming perfect competition). This determines the flow rate of investment, not the stock of capital. The two points of substance on which the theory of investment in the lecture notes differed from the *Treatise* were the recognition that the price of newly produced capital goods must coincide with the greater of the two sectoral prices of existing capital, and the derivation of an upward-sloping supply curve for capital goods in the short period.

In the *General Theory* Keynes wrote that the marginal physical product of capital 'involves difficulties as the definition of the physical unit of capital, which I believe to be both insoluble and unnecessary'. His wariness of problems of defining a unit of capital might well be due to the issues raised in Gerald Shove's biting 1933 *Economic Journal* review of J. R. Hicks's *Theory of Wages*, attacking the use of the marginal productivity of capital in distribution theory. Keynes avoided this by using the marginal efficiency of capital, which depended on costs of producing new capital goods rather than the marginal product of capital. However, as Bliss (1975) has noted, calculations of Keynes's marginal efficiency of capital, like those of Fisher's rate of return over costs, can have multiple roots.

Conclusion
Students' notes on Keynes's lectures at Cambridge from 1932 to 1935 offer a fascinating opportunity to study the development of his theory of a monetary economy. The Michaelmas 1932 lectures point the need for an explanation of how nominal demand shocks can have real effects, but do not provide such an explanation. The multiplier and the consumption function appear in the 1933 lectures, when the windfall profits of the *Treatise* disappear. The *Treatise's* portfolio approach to the rate of investment was refined into the marginal efficiency of capital in the 1934 lectures. The liquidity preference theory of the rate of interest, which has strong roots in the *Treatise*, was already present in 1932 in a form resembling the version in the *General Theory*. By 1933 the downward rigidity of money wage rates was explained in Keynes's lectures by reference to relative wage concerns. Even if money wage rates could be reduced, Keynes argued in 1933, this could fail to adjust the real wage rate to clear the labour market because of the effect on prices of reductions in money wages.

On 31 October 1932, Keynes explained that the nominal interest rate could not fall below some minimum because of the zero own-rate of return on money, and on 28 November he argued that Britain had reached this minimum. Once the expected rate of deflation had lowered the nominal interest rate nearly to zero, price declines could not lower the interest rate further. The aggregate demand curve would then be vertical, and money wage reductions would cause prices to fall in the same proportion.

Study of the students' notes on Keynes's lectures at Cambridge from 1932 to 1935 illuminates not only the stages of development of his theory of the level of output and employment in a monetary economy, but also the nature of this theory. Until the publication of empirical papers by John Dunlop in 1938 and Lorie Tarshis in 1939, Keynes fully accepted the first classical postulate, which implied that involuntary unemployment could exist only if the real wage rate was above the market clearing level. Keynes was thus concerned in his lectures on the *General Theory* to derive a theory of effective demand to account for demand shifts which, by lowering prices with a given money wage, could raise the real wage above its market clearing level, and then to explain why bargaining for money wages could fail, in the absence of government intervention, to restore full employment.

Notes

1. I am grateful for helpful comments to Basil Moore, and my colleagues Eric Davis and T. K. Rymes. For the use of unpublished notes on Keynes's lectures, I am indebted to Robert B. Bryce, Walter S. Salant and Lorie Tarshis, and to T. K. Rymes, who is editing the notes for publication.
2. Bryce and Tarshis notes, 10 October 1932.
3. Hawtrey, in Keynes (*CW*, XIII, 1973), pp. 150–62; Kahn (1972), ch. 1; Davis (1979).
4. Kahn (1972), p. 3 and n.
5. Bryce and Tarshis notes, 21 November 1932.
6. Tarshis notes, 21 November 1932.
7. Bryce, Salant and Tarshis notes, 16 October 1933.
8. Bryce notes, 23 October 1933. Salant notes: 'Struggle over money wages is one over *distribution* of real wage, not its size' (Salant's emphasis: Keynes, I, 1930, p. 271).
9. Bryce, Fallgatter and Salant notes, December 4, 1933. Tarshis missed this lecture and copied Bryce's notes for it.
10. Bryce notes, 26 November 1934.

References

Bliss, C. J. (1975a), 'The reappraisal of Keynes' economics: an appraisal', in J. M. Parkin and A. R. Nobay (eds), *Current Economic Problems*, Cambridge: CUP.

Bliss, C. J. (1975b), *Capital Theory and Income Distribution*, New York and Amsterdam: North Holland.

Dimand, R. W. (1986a), 'The macroeconomics of the *Treatise on Money*', *Eastern Economic Journal*, **XII**, **4**, 431–41.

Dimand, R. W. (1986b), 'The road to the *General Theory*', ms.

Johnson, E. S. and Johnson, Harry G. (1978) *The Shadow of Keynes*, Oxford: Basil Blackwell.

Kahn, R. F. (1972), *Selected Essays on Employment and Growth*, Cambridge: CUP.

Keynes, J. M. (1923), *A Tract on Monetary Reform*, London: Macmillan.

Keynes, J. M. (1930) *A Treatise on Money*, London: Macmillan.

Keynes, J. M. (1933), 'National self-sufficiency', *Yale Review*.

Keynes, J. M. (1936), *The General Theory of Employment, Interest and Money*, London: Macmillan.

Keynes, J. M. (1973–81), *Collected Writings* (general editor Sir Austin Robinson, individual volumes edited by Donald E. Moggridge and Elizabeth S. Johnson), London: Macmillan.

LeRoy, S. (1983) 'Keynes's theory of investment', *History of Political Economy*, **15**, **3**, pp. 397–421.

Patinkin, D. (1980), 'New materials on the development of Keynes' monetary thought', *History of Political Economy,* **12, 1,** pp. 1–28.
Rymes, T. K. (ed.) (forthcoming) Notes on Keynes' lectures taken by Robert B. Bryce, 1932–4, Marvin Fallgatter, 1933, Walter S. Salant, 1933 and Lorie Tarshis, 1932–5, London: Macmillan.

12 Keynesian economics, or *Plus ça change*
Brian Bixley

I

I do not propose in this chapter to ask what Keynes 'really' said or 'really' meant in the *General Theory*. We all know what more poets and painters say when asked to explain what they 'really' mean, and the gap between art and science is frequently narrow and, as McCloskey has reminded us,[1] often artificial. Even 'real' scientists stress the role of imprecise intuition in their work, particularly in the formulation of hypotheses. One senses that something must be the case, and then sets out to demonstrate it. Mathematicians, I am told, typically sketch out the lines that a proof might follow, without providing a formal proof. And when the formalizations, the demonstrations, the proofs, the tight little theorems are provided, do these necessarily correspond to what the proposition's first exponent 'really' meant, even when the proof is undertaken by the exponent himself? The answer is, I believe, obvious. Such a conclusion must make any distinction between a legitimate 'economics of Keynes', on the one hand, and 'Keynesian economics' (or bastard Keynesianism'), on the other, highly speculative.

Until recently, I had not looked at all seriously at the *General Theory* for twenty years. My interests in economics do not lie in macro theory. True, once or twice I have been required to teach Introductory Macro, but Samuelson or Lipsey, Sparks and Steiner[2] served to remind me of what I knew of Keynesian economics. What did I know? Or better, since Aver reminds us that one of the conditions for 'knowing' something is that 'it be the case', what did I imagine to be the central arguments of the *General Theory*?

The answer was simple, perhaps alarmingly so. I believed that Keynes had argued that, in a closed, no-government economy, the level of employment could be written as a more or less linear function of output (at least up to, or approaching, 'full-employment output'), that a level of output (and therefore a level of employment) was only sustainable if there were adequate demand for it and that this demand – effective demand – was made up of consumption and investment expenditures. Household consumption expenditures were normally less than household incomes, investment decisions were made largely by firms and not households, and there was no reason why corporate I together with household C should produce a level of effective demand adequate to call forth a full-employment output. Effective demand could be deficient, and if it were, output and employment would tend towards an analytical equilibrium at less than full employment. Indeed that was the definition of deficient.

Of course, there were many qualifications and extensions of this broadest of sketches. The employment–output ratio only held up to a certain employment level; money 'really mattered' since investors compared the rate of return on real investment, financial investment and liquidity; expectations were important in shaping investment decisions, and therefore in determining the level of effective demand. There was the slippery question of wage rates. Keynes's 'classical' predecessors had admitted the possibility of departures from full-employment equilibrium if prices and particularly the price of labour were not flexible downwards, but it was easy to argue that this was an illegitimate extension of a micro argument to a macro proposition. I lead my unwary students through MPSs and APCs, through autonomous this and endogenous that, through gaps and multipliers, through saving paradoxes and liquidity preference functions. None of these 'qualifications and extensions' were intended to conceal the essential message, that the levels of employment and output were crucially determined by expenditures on consumption and investment goods and services, and that these levels might well be 'stable equilibrium' levels at less than full-employment output.

These simple – and doubtless simplistic – sentiments have been evoked by a recent reading of an article by Harcourt and O'Shaughnessy (1985),[3] in which it is argued 'that there are some interesting convergences in the debate over the *General Theory*' (*ibid.*, p. 3), the convergences being found in Meltzer's 1981 *Journal of Economic Literature* article,[4] in Patinkin's *Anticipations of the General Theory* (1982)[5] and in Eatwell and Milgate's *Keynes's Economics and the Theory of Value and Distribution* (1983).[6] I have already indicated that I do not propose to consider what Keynes 'really' meant, nor do I intend to ask what Meltzer, Patinkin and Eatwell and Milgate 'really' meant. I wish rather to focus attention on what Harcourt and O'Shaughnessy perceive as being the common developments in those three essays. I do that because, unlike Rip Van Winkle who fell asleep for twenty years and woke up to find that everything had changed, I feel something like a man who had been asleep for thirty years and has now woken up to discover that nothing has changed. Of course, I may have misunderstood what Harcourt and O'Shaughnessy 'really' mean!

II

The major shared element in the three essays under discussion is the notion of effective demand providing a theory of unemployment equilibrium:

The three views converge ... in the seriousness with which they take Keynes's[7] claim to have formulated a theory of unemployment *equilibrium*. In doing so they reject those standard interpretations that assign unemployment in the *General Theory* (and in the real world) to various 'imperfections' that prevent the economy arriving immediately at a ... full employment equilibrium. (Harcourt and O'Shaughnessy, 1985, p. 4)

Meltzer's main points, as summarized by Harcourt and O'Shaughnessy, are:

(1) That 'private investment decisions produce an equilibrium rate of investment lower ... than the rate required for maximum output, [and thus that] aggregate demand is deficient – that is, less than the amount required to maintain full (maximum) employment' (*ibid.*, p. 5).

(2) 'Nothing in the market economy adjusts. The equilibrium is stable' (*loc. cit.*).

(3) It is hence inappropriate to 'interpret the *General Theory* as a theory of an economy in persistent disequilibrium' (*loc. cit.*).

(4) There will be (real-world) fluctuations around the (analytical) underemployment equilibrium.

(5) Money wage rigidity is not 'the explanation of the failure of the markets to clear' (*ibid.*, p. 6).

(6) Volatile expectations do not 'account completely' for involuntary unemployment, but are important for understanding fluctuations around a less then full-employment position (*ibid.*, p. 7).[8]

Patinkin, we are told, has changed his position. Whereas in 1976 he claimed 'the state of unemployment *qua* market disequilibrium [was Keynes's] major concern in the *General Theory* (*ibid.*, p. 12), it now (1982) appears 'that for his project of investigating "anticipations" of the *General Theory*, just what is the book's innovation, comes down to the principle of effective demand as the determinant of the (in general less than full employment) equilibrium level of output' (*ibid.*, pp. 12–13).

And here are Harcourt and O'Shaughnessy on Eatwell and Milgate:

Like Meltzer and Patinkin ... Eatwell and Milgate argue against interpreting Keynes as a theorist of *disequilibrium* ... They are critical of the way the neo-classical synthesis assimilated Keynes to be a special case of a more general theory in which equilibrium took place at full-employment, but where various 'imperfections' or 'rigidities' delayed or prevented this equilibrium being attained ... They see Keynes's principles of effective demand – the proposition that it is changes in income and employment, rather than changes in the rate of interest, that equilibrate saving and investments – as his real contribution. (*ibid.*, p. 13)

The common threads, discerned by Harcourt and O'Shaughnessy in these essays are then:

(a)   saving and investment will be equilibrated by changes in income rather than by adjustments in the interest rate;

(b)   equilibrium can be attained at less than full employment (allowance being made for voluntary unemployment). Of course, this is an analytical equilibrium; nature will only approximate art;

(c)   this equilibrium does not depend on 'imperfections' or 'rigidities' in the system.

These propositions represent for Harcourt and O'Shaughnessy the 'interesting convergence in the debate over the *General Theory*'. Can I deny experiencing a *frisson* of pleasure on learning that though I have apparently not been on the frontier of Keynesian theory for the past thirty years, the frontier is coming back to me? Unfortunately, I can lay no claim to prescient wisdom or originality. I had simply done what all undergraduates of my era had been expected to do; I had read Klein (1947), Dillard (1948), Hansen (1953) and Kurihara (1956).[9]

III

It would be tedious to document in great detail that these 'interesting convergences' formed the orthodoxy of thirty, almost forty, years ago. Nevertheless, I shall provide a sampling of views on each of the three common threads that I listed above. I will not claim that all four writers agreed on all issues, that they emphasized the same elements in the *General Theory*, or even that they were consistent in their interpretations; but the sampling should be adequate to demonstrate that none of the four would have found any difficulty with the three 'common threads'.

(1) On the equilibration of Saving and Investment through changes in income and employment rather than through the rate of interest, only Hansen fails to provide totally unambiguous statements. Klein sounded – as his whole book sounded – a declamatory note: 'It was not a new theory of the rate of interest that was needed to replace the classical saving–investment theory, as some economists seemed to think: instead it was a theory of output that was needed to replace the old theory of the interest rate' (Klein, 1947, p. 38). This theory was provided by Keynes, who:

> emphasized that his real contribution was to change the equilibrating variable from the interest rate to the level of income ... In the static Keynesian system, there can be differences between savings and investment only when the system is not in equilibrium. (*ibid.*, pp. 116–17)

Dillard appears to disagree with Klein about the relationship between S and I, but not about the equality-inducing mechanism:

> In Keynes' *General Theory* aggregate investment always equals aggregate saving. This equality is a condition of equilibrium regardless of what the level of employment happens to be. Equality between investment and saving is a consequence of change in the level of income. (Dillard, 1948, p. 59)

Dillard draws S and I schedules intersecting to determine income, so that his 'aggregate investment always equals aggregate saving' would be interpreted to mean, *ex-post*, in equilibrium. He continues:

> The novelty of Keynes' treatment of saving and investment lies not in the fact that they are equal but that they can be and normally are at less than full-employment. Whereas the classical school associates the equality between investment and saving with automatic changes in the rate of interest, Keynes associates it with changes in the level of income. (*ibid.*, p. 65).

Kurihara's language is a trifle odd, but there is no ambiguity:

> The desire to save and the desire to invest are shown to be such opposite forces which nevertheless depend on income so crucially that their mutual relation changes with income changes until their conflict is resolved by a unique level of income. (Kurihara, 1956, p. 19)

And:

> The accounting equality of S and I carries with it the implication that unless the economy as a whole is willing and able to invest at the same rate at which the general public is disposed to save, producers will have to contract or expand output and employment until the economy gains a position of equilibrium. (*ibid.*, p. 77)

Hansen's discussion is more confusing, claiming 'that while investment and saving are always equal, they are not always in equilibrium' (Hansen, 1953, p. 59). Of course, conceived as schedules, they are not always equal; when they are, the system is in equilibrium. The problem of definitions of S and I which made them inescapably equal had already been spotted by Klein, who pointed out that:

> Hicks ... gave the *General Theory* a more favourable review, although he was unable to pick out the essential Keynesian development. He [Hicks] remarked that the casual reader may take the savings–investment equality to be the innovation of the book. Then he [Hicks still] went on to say that this equality depends only upon definitions. Many of us who claim to be more than casual readers of all Keynes' more important works must side with these simple-minded folks and say that the innovation is 'S = I' but that it is not a matter of definition alone. (Klein, 1947, pp. 99–100)

(2) All four writers conceive of the *General Theory* as a theory of equilibrium. Three of them (Dillard, Hansen, Kurihara) draw upon Hicks's notion of a shifting equilibrium, though this seems to me to be a simple confusion between an analytic equilibrium – the theory yields, given the values of the independent variables, a unique equilibrium output/employment level – and a real-world 'shifting equilibrium' as the values of the variables, including the state of expectations, change. Dillard wrote:

> Thus, at any one time, there is, according to Keynes' theory, a uniquely determined amount of employment which will be most profitable for entrepreneurs to offer to workers. There is no reason to assume this point will correspond to full employment ... The aggregate demand schedule and the aggregate supply schedule will intersect at a point of less than full employment. This establishes an equilibrium from which there will be no tendency to depart in the absence of some external change ... These concepts ... are geared to the fundamental idea of a *shifting equilibrium* as distinguished from a special, full employment equilibrium. (Dillard, 1948, pp. 32, 59)

Klein, having already rejected Hicks's interpretation of the I = S equality, was in no mood for such imprecision: 'We must be brought to realize that Keynesian economics will admit full-employment or over-employment as legitimate solutions to the equations as well as the infinite number of underemployment solutions' (1947, p. 154).

It is interesting that what appears to me as the more technically precise formulations of Klein become somewhat muddied in the later works. I might also add that whatever Keynes accomplished in the later chapters of the *General Theory*, his *intention* in this respect is clearly set out in chapter 1: 'I shall argue that the postulates of the classical theory are applicable to a special case only and not to the general case, the situation which it assumes being a limiting point of *the possible positions of equilibrium.*'

(3) Finally, there is the question of whether the unemployment equilibrium – shifting or not – depends on the presence of 'imperfections' or 'rigidities' in the system. The strongest statements come from Klein. He begins with a reference to Joan Robinson's 1933 *Review of Economic Studies* article: 'It is also interesting that she did not need ... to appeal to lower limits to the interest rate, or rigid money wages, or imperfections in competition to explain the phenomenon of unemployment' (*ibid.*, p. 40).[10]

Klein then makes two important distinctions; first, between the *classical system* and the Keynesian *system*:

> The classical system can explain unemployment which is due to frictions or market imperfections and to unwillingness of workers to be employed. For our tastes, this is clearly insufficient because even a perfectly competitive, frictionless system need not always have full employment. In order to show that

full employment is not automatic in a world subject to the Keynesian conditions, it is necessary to assume nothing whatsoever about rigidities in the system. (*ibid.*, pp. 80, 89)

And then, secondly, a distinction between the model (system) and the 'real world'. He admits that 'the assumption of rigidities will become very useful in explaining how an underemployment situation can be one of equilibrium' (*ibid.*, p. 90), but it turns out that he is distinguishing between 'Keynesian economics' where 'wage flexibility does not correct unemployment' and the 'real world' where in fact wages are sticky. The introduction of imperfections will give the unemployment results of Keynesian equilibrium, but they are not necessary for it:

> It is not true... that the Keynesian equations in conjunction with a perfect, frictionless system will always yield a full-employment solution ... The long familiar observation about the stickiness of wages *supplement* the results of Keynesian economics and brings the student into contact with actuality. (*loc. cit.*)

The other writers all deny that wage stickiness is crucial, and Kurihara, in particular, has a long discussion of why wage cuts are likely not to be effective, even when Pigovian 'real value of cash balances' is introduced (1956, pp. 162–70).

Overall, I believe the conclusion is clear. In forty years we have come full-circle with respect to our perceptions of the essential message of the *General Theory* (though Harcourt and O'Shaughnessy write rather depressingly of 'the principle of effective demand [as] a theory of unemployment equilibrium' that 'there are difficulties for such an interpretation that must be faced'). As a teacher of the history of economic thought, I can simultaneously applaud the continuing scrutiny of Keynes's writings, and regret that it is possible to hail as 'recent interpretations' positions set out not in obscure journals, but in widely used textbooks over thirty years ago. The proposition that 'those of us who do not study history are destined to relive it' may be amended to read 'who do not study the history of their discipline are destined to rewrite it'. Perhaps 'applaud' too is the wrong word. It is not time to reduce investment in 'a hagiographic Keynes industry devoted to producing publications in commemoration of the master' (Johnson, 1976)[11] and increase investment in a macro theory which will help the victims of unemployment equilibrium? My recent reading suggests that this is a proposal for which I could have counted upon Keynes's support.

Notes and references

1. D. McCloskey, 'The rhetoric of economics', *Journal of Economic Literature*, **XXI** (2), 1983, pp. 481–517.

2. See P.A. Samuelson, *Economics* (New York, McGraw-Hill, 1948), and R. Lipsey, G. Sparks, and P. Steiner, *Economics* (New York, Harper and Row, 1979).

3. G.C. Harcourt and T.J. O'Shaughnessy, 'Keynes' employment equilibrium: some insights from Joan Robinson, Piero Sraffa and Richard Kahn', in G.C. Harcourt (ed.), *Keynes and his Contemporaries* (New York, St Martin's Press, 1985).

4. A.H. Meltzer, 'Keynes' *General Theory*: a different perspective', *Journal of Economic Literature*, **XIX**, 1981, 34–64.

5. D. Patinkin, *Anticipations of the General Theory, and Other Essays on Keynes* (Chicago, University of Chicago, 1982).

6. J. Eatwell and M. Milgate (eds), *Keynes' Economics and the Theory of Value and Distribution* (London: Duckworth, 1983).

7. It would be interesting to know when this disagreeable format ('Keynes's' for 'Keynes'') become orthodox.

8. Or it might be added, for understanding fluctuations around a full – or overfull – employment equilibrium.

9. See L.R. Klein, *The Keynesian Revolution* (New York, MacMillan, 1947); D. Dillard, *The Economics of John Maynard Keynes* (Englewood Cliffs, NJ, Prentice-Hall, 1948); A.H. Hansen, *A Guide to Keynes* (New York, McGraw-Hill, 1953); K.K. Kurihara, *Introduction to Keynesian Dynamics* (London, Allen and Unwin, 1956).

10. J. Robinson, 'The theory of money and the analysis of output', *Review of Economic Studies*, **I** (1), 1933.

11. H.G. Johnson, 'Keynes' *General Theory:* revolution or war of independence?', *Canadian Journal of Economics*, **IX**, November 1976.

PART III

IMPRESSIONS AND RECOLLECTIONS OF J. M. KEYNES

13 My life and times in the shadow of Keynes
Richard Goodwin

After a very good lunch, at the Conference, having no specific topic to discuss, I availed myself of the dubious privilege of old men, like myself and Lorie Tarshis, to indulge in nostalgia. I talked about how the Keynesian revolution affected me at the time, or how I now remember it. Unlike Lorie, I didn't have the great good fortune to be taught the ways of wisdom from the great man himself; but I was lucky enough to be taught by Roy Harrod at Oxford, who was his ardent disciple and admirer. Hence I did have the advantage of reading the *General Theory* before publication in galley-proof, and I was very excited by the experience.

I went first to Harvard just at the onset of the Great Depression, which had a tremendous influence on me. I was conditioned to look at the facts from the start, they were all around me as I went through my college career, and very much influenced my thinking. I was taught, as everyone else was, the beautiful simplicities of market-clearing *laissez-faire* capitalism, but I never took it very seriously. I became a sort of Marxist under the impact of seeing the near-disintegration of the American economy in that period, without any underpinnings of social security or public assistance. Keynes did not discover unemployment, it was painfully evident to anyone who cared to look at that time, people standing around selling apples or begging, or living off their friends and relatives, with really no way out.

My teachers had to face the fact of unemployment, and search for a explanation of something which did not fit their theory. The theory implied that all markets clear, including the labour market. The way out was an ingenious device, to blame it all on the peculiar nature of banking. Banks were producers, like other businesses, but they produced money and did it for profit, and the more you produce, the more you make. So they easily tend to overproduction, and then get into trouble and are forced to retrench, which then leads to underproduction. In other words, the troubles were entirely to do with the banking system, not the economy itself. Now as a semi-Marxist, I never accepted this view. I was immune from it, but I didn't know the way out. I was confused because the teaching was confusing. Somehow it didn't relate to what was going on.

These issues, I think, also explain a great deal about our concerns at the Conference, about what Keynes's theory was, how he phrased it and why he had to phrase it the way he did. He himself had been brought up in the tradition that the banking system is essential, and had made a great effort in his *Treatise on Money* to explain a credit cycle, and find the solution in laying down the basis of sound central banking. My guess is that this explains why Keynes concentrated on money, liquidity preference, the role of the central bank, the stock-market casino and such things, instead of going directly to the behaviour of the commercial and industrial sectors in reaction to uncertainty in a turbulent world. He had to counter the traditional teaching but, in my view, what he really needed to do was not to bother about Say's law, and elaborate the speculative motive for holding money, but to recur to the more Marxian concept that the *differencia specifica* of capitalism is that employment is not determined by the wishes or desires of the workers, but by employers. Of course it is. That may be simplistic, and you may not like it, but basically that is where it all leads to, even though Keynes tended to express it in the more monetary aspects of his theory. My feeling is that part of the reason for the current eclipse of Keynesianism, and the efflorescence of the half-truths of monetarism, is simply a desire to return to the traditional view that if only the banks behaved properly everything would be all right. It would not be.

All the same, when I read the *General Theory*, I was thrilled. I felt that the scales had been peeled from my eyes. I saw it as the New Jerusalem, the True Way and Path. With that innocent euphoria from my teaching in Oxford, I returned to Harvard in 1937 to carry the message to the barbarians of North America, feeling ready to explain to them how to view the economy. Instead of finding eager acceptance, I fell into a bed of thorns. The entire faculty was not only unreceptive, but basically hostile. After all, they had been teaching the orthodox theory for a long time, they were still teaching it, and they went on teaching it for many years. The exception in Harvard was Alvin Hansen, but he was an outsider, an import from the Mid-West, and he was not really part of the establishment. He was regarded with great scepticism, really to the end of his life, by most of his colleagues. It was a very noble action of them to hire him at all! But that did not mean they accepted his teachings or thought he was right. When I returned, I thought I had got the message from Harrod, and I had read the *General Theory*, and it all seemed very plain and simple. I still really think it is very simple, but I soon found I was not equipped to answer the critics in their own specialized realm of discourse. I will illustrate by a traumatic experience. I was a member of a small discussion group of both senior and junior colleagues, which met, as I remember, once a week or perhaps less often, in the evening. They were usually pleasant occasions, and one person gave a paper each time. I chose to give a paper on what was called the Food Stamp Plan. What this amounted to was the idea of taking the surpluses of some food products, and selling them at a reduced price to all families in need. This seemed to me to be an eminently simple, sensible idea. People had no resources when they were thrown out of work, they couldn't get a job, and there was not state support for them. Then there were all these farm products which could not be sold. So the sensible thing was to bring the two together, and I thought that the problem itself was not a problem. It seemed obvious common sense. What I wanted to do was to discuss the mechanics of how to design and implement such a system. So I presented the paper, and was slowly working through it, when one member of the group, Abraham Bergson, who was at that time working out his well-known theory of the Social Welfare Function, suddenly realized that what I was proposing was price discrimination on a massive scale! He interrupted my talk and wrote on the blackboard the equation for a constrained maximum, using Lagrange multipliers, saying that this means that the social optimum can only be attained with single prices. One price for each good; one price per good. And he said, 'Unfortunately that means, this paper is nonsense!' Had I been Japanese, I think I would have gone out of the room and committed hari-kari. My memory has erased what in fact I did do. Only some years later did it occur to me that he was simply repeating the essential fallacy of the neo-classical paradigm. The equation was a constrained maximum. But if you don't have full employment, there are no constraints, and a constrained maximum is irrelevant. I knew the mathematics perfectly well, but had just never thought of applying it in this situation; and it did not apply. So much for Paretian welfare economics, in a world in which full employment is the exception rather than the rule.

Having learned my Keynesianism from Harrod, I got it in a rather different form than most people, because he reformulated the *General Theory* in dynamic terms. Keynes phrased the problem in a static form; a given level of investment determines effective demand, output and hence employment. But investment is not given, nor is it solely determined by the marginal efficiency of capital (MEC) or the interest rate. There are a lot of influences, and working on it is a very complicated question. Harrod closed the Keynesian system dynamically with the accelerator, and he developed a theory of trade cycles. It was very perceptive, but marred by the lack of the mathematics of differential or difference equations. He dropped it after serious criticism by Tinbergen, and then subsequenty switched to his famous growth theory, which was a great success and dominated postwar thinking. Nevertheless, I came back to Harvard with the idea that cycle theory was the right framework to explain unemployment. There I found an ally in Hansen, who earlier had had a somewhat similar experience to Harrod. He had given a paper somewhere, asserting that the accelerator explains the cycle, only to be brusquely dismissed by Ragnar Frisch with the statement that a first-order dynamic equation will only generate exponential growth, not cycles. Hansen had to accept this criticism, but he did not really give up, and when the *General Theory* arrived, he knew he had the answer in the multiplier. He appealed to Samuelson for help in formulating it, and Samuelson added a second lag, making it a second-order dynamic equation and defeating Frisch. Thus the famous Hansen–Samuelson multiplier–accelerator theory.

However, the real intellectual muscle at Harvard, when I was there, was Schumpeter. Revered by everyone and not taken very seriously by anyone, a bit of both. I was impressed by him. After beginning with hostility for his very reactionary political opinions, I became a great admirer, and remained so all the time I was at Harvard and until his death. I always took pleasure in his company. He loved intellectual disputation, even from people like Paul Sweezy and myself whom he knew were socialists. He thought we were absolutely wrong, but he found that very interesting as we both came from banking families, and this fitted his theory of why capitalism would come to an end. The worms working from within! My effort was not to change his politics, that I could not do, but rather to try to convince him that what he needed for his own theory – because he also had a theory of the cycle – was Keynes. He needed effective demand to explain why investment comes in bursts or 'swarms'. There is a technical mathematical problem to explain how the essentially smooth growth of technological knowledge gets changed into fluctuations in innovational activity. That's what capitalism does with technological progress. To my astonishment, Schumpeter totally rejected the whole of the *General Theory*. He would never accept it. He never did and thought it was trivial nonsense and quite useless.

I also tried to convince him that he needed mathematical cycle theory (Keynesian version) to formulate his theory of development, and he was more sympathetic to that idea. He had written an article as early as 1905, saying that economists needed mathematics. He believed this all his life, but was not able to put it into practice. With his characteristic generosity of spirit, he said that if I would give a course of lectures he would attend. The lectures were the first I had given anywhere, and he did attend, but they had no effect. Mathematicians, like musicians, are born not made. The theoretical blindness, as far as the *General Theory* was concerned, baffled me then and still baffles me now. Schumpeter was an anglophile and he had met and conversed with both Keynes and Kahn. His admiration for Keynes was great. I was told that, in Bonn, he had wanted to write a treatise on monetary analysis and he always talked about it. However, the moment Keynes's *Treatise on Money* was published, he never mentioned it again. The *General Theory*, though, was a different matter.

Lord Kahn has suggested to me that Schumpeter was simply jealous of Keynes. After some reflection, I find I cannot accept this view. My feeling is that he rejected the *General Theory* because, like so many of his generation, he had taught the neo-classical theory for so long, and this required the constraint resulting from full employment to justify the whole apparatus of the standard price-market analysis. Only in such an economy can one justify the emphasis on relative prices in orthodox value and output theory. But further than this, he thought that Keynes, and more particularly Keynesians, were providing a trivial analysis which failed to embody a sense of the historic mission of capitalism; not the static version of most economists, but the creative evolution of the economy through technological change linked to human greed. His view was that tinkering with the economy through fiscal policy would transfer too much power to politicians and bureaucrats, with fatal damage to the abrasive thrust of private capitalism. This did not seem very persuasive in the 1930s, but because of the recent joint centennial of the births of Keynes and Schumpeter, I have been led to rethink the problem. Now I think I understand Schumpeter's position a bit better and I'm a bit more tolerant of it. He wrote a lot of rubbish during the Great Depression, along with most of his colleagues at Harvard, but now that we have seen so much mismanagement of various economies over so many years, his views can no longer be lightly dismissed. Even Keynes, though he felt himself a mandarin dealing with mandarins, also had occasion to feel disillusion. Nowadays, after thirty years of the greatest economic growth rates ever experienced, the USA, Britain and Germany are committed, for better or worse, to the Schumpeterian path.

Keynesian policies seemed to offer an answer to Marx's prediction of the end of capitalism in ever more violent crises. Now one may have second thoughts in view of the damaging effects of full employment in the form of wage explosions and inflation. This could be seen as Marx's revenge; recurrent unemployment may be essential for the health of private capitalism. In the midst of a grave illness of the world economy Keynes undertook a painstaking reassessment of economic analysis, until he arrived at a satisfactory diagnosis of that ailment. The nature and methods of treatment followed, and the results from 1950 to the mid-1970s appeared to confirm both diagnosis and treatment. The following decade has suggested that the success of the treatment may have secondary, damaging side-effects.

14 Keynes during the Great Depression and World War II
Robert B. Bryce

The recollections in this chapter are not an essay in theory like the other papers at the Conference. They are largely personal observations mixed in with history, and deal for the most part with my own contact with Keynes in Cambridge. In 1932, I graduated in engineering at a time when, in Canada, there was no demand for engineers. I was curious, however, to find the cause of the very severe depression that gripped us at that time, and was told the best place to look was in Cambridge. I went over there with Lorie Tarshis, and a few others from Toronto, in the steerage class of one of the oldest boats. In retrospect, I must say that my lack of knowledge of previous economic doctrine probably helped me to take on the new ideas then being produced by Keynes's Political Economy Club, despite my lack of economics training. This Club is fairly well known now by those familiar with Keynes; it met each week, on Monday nights in his rooms, and there were about twenty of us undergraduates lucky enough to belong. At each meeting, after drawing lots, seven of us had to stand up and take part in the discussion, willy-nilly, when one of us or a research student presented a paper. Keynes, at the end of the evening's discussion, talked on the subject for fifteen minutes to half an hour, and it was always a treat to hear him talking spontaneously about anything and everything! A wide range of latitude was provided to the speakers on what they were to write papers about, but Keynes always had something worth hearing on the subject.

I soon discovered in my regular work preparing for the tripos examinations that I needed more tuition than my college could offer. I was fortunate in being able to go to Joan Robinson for it. I found her argumentative, provocative; it did me good, though. I can't say that I think that it did her any good!

I studied Keynes's lectures in detail, but they did not satisfy my curiosity at that time, although looking back now I see more in them than I did at the time. I went to many other lectures, and had endless arguments with other overseas students. Lorie Tarshis was my chief support, and I would like to acknowledge his help at that stage when I was a pretty ignorant student. I must admit that when my first year was over, I did not feel that I had made much progress towards my goal of getting some clue as to what causes depressions and what could be done to end them. What was going on in 1932–3 in regard to the *General Theory* was pretty mixed up. Keynes was obviously working towards a radical revision of his theory of money, but his progress was not really visible, and while some of the dons had a fair idea, the progress being made was not obvious to me. I was tempted to drop economics. I came to the conclusion that economics was a very messy sort of subject, and I was tempted to go back into science to which I was more used; but in the end, I was persuaded by my parents against that course, and I have never regretted it.

The next year, I had made enough acquaintances that I was able to keep up with what was going on around Keynes, and its implications. Moreover, I was getting a great deal out of the discussions in the Political Economy Club in that second year. I was very much impressed with Keynes's knowledge of markets and institutions; he had an incredible memory, really, for things that mattered! His versatility was prodigious, and what I liked best was his intuition because from my earliest years I have relied a fair amount on intuition; and I found him a kindred spirit in that regard. Out of all that, I decided that I was going to stay on and take the tripos.

I did well in these examinations, and decided to stay another year and prepare myself for what I can only describe as 'missionary endeavours'. I spent some days each week during the early months of 1935 at the LSE: I thought it was good for my soul, and it gave me an opportunity to talk about what was happening in Cambridge. For my purposes there, I produced a summary account of what I called the 'Monetary Theory of Employment' which was really my idea of what we were getting from Keynes.[1] I am glad to say that Hayek kindly gave me four sessions of his seminar to explain this to his students who debated it at great length. I found that experience stimulating, and I decided to try to go to Harvard to discuss the subject there. I was lucky enough to get a Commonwealth Fund Fellowship, a very generous one. I'm glad to say, that my supervisor of studies at Harvard was none other than Joseph Schumpeter, whom I came to know very well as an individual, although I think his interest in me was largely curiosity because he wanted me to enlighten him about what he should really think about the *General Theory*, even before it had come out. I must say that I admired his scholarship. I think that he was intensely jealous of Keynes,[2] but on the other hand, he too was a great economist in his own right, and I don't think there was any reason that he needed to feel that way.

When I left for Harvard, Kahn gave me advice not to go to lectures or the seminars, just to stick to the library, which is an excellent one, and go ahead with the thesis that I proposed to write. That was not at all consistent with the plan that I had in mind. I wanted to promote an understanding of Keynes's ideas just as soon as possible. Heaven knows, North America needed them! In any case, I was interested in what Leontief, Schumpeter and several others had to offer. I wished also to mix with the graduate students among whom there were such distinguished individuals as Paul Samuelson and Ken Galbraith at the time. Consequently, I had a very active time in Harvard. I got a very good hearing from very able people, and I think it is fair to say that when I left Harvard two years later, just a few months before Professor Hansen from Minnesota arrived, there was a pretty widespread sympathy with the *General Theory*. I leave it to Walter Salant to report on that aspect. I thought that I had accomplished my objective, at the cost of doing no research work on the thesis I had originally intended to write. Indeed I was not aiming at an academic career, so that did not concern me greatly.

My real opportunity arose a year or two later when I got into the heart of the Canadian Department of Finance in October 1938. They were not worried by the fact that I was a Keynesian. However, I should make clear that Keynes's ideas were first introduced to the government of Canada half a dozen months before I got there, by W. A. Mackintosh of Queen's, who was in my view one of the greatest of all the Canadian economists, not only for his knowledge and his understanding of economics, but also for his good sense. I am no doubt biased; we were colleagues in adjoining offices almost throughout the war. He was in 1936–8 a member of the National Employment Commission which had been appointed by the new Liberal government in early 1936 to inquire into unemployment and the unemployed and the dreadful relief tangle that Canada was in at that time. The Commission brought down several interim reports that I won't mention; it brought down a final report that is a very rare document. (I don't believe that it is even in the National Library, but it is available, I think, in the Library of the Department of Labour for any who are interested in it.) The Commission reported to the Minister of Labour and was headed by Arthur Purvis, who was one of the most able and enlightened businessmen I have ever heard of in Canada. He was the main British procurement representative in Washington during the early years of the war, and when he died, killed in an air crash going back and forth between London and Washington, Henry Morgenthau got in touch with the Prime Minister of Canada and said: 'For God's sake persuade the British to send us someone like Purvis.' To revert to 1938, this report was a mixture of many subjects and different points of view, but it did diagnose the Canadian economy at that time as on a stable plateau well below full employment, though above the depth of the depression. This was the kind of equilibrium below full employment that I had studied in the *General Theory* as one of its most important contributions, a contribution contrary to the normal thinking about the business cycle in those days. The report recommended a programme of development and conservation works financed by borrowing. However, as was Mackintosh's practice, the recommendation was hedged about by careful, cautious warnings about the effects on trade and regional considerations that would have to be taken into account. It was only some twenty years later that Mackintosh revealed that he had got the idea from the *General Theory*.[3]

This report led to a severe Cabinet crisis in Canada during April and May of 1938, in which the Minister of Labour, Rogers, who was one of the best younger ministers in the Cabinet, was pitted against Dunning, the Minister of Finance, who had very strict views of financial orthodoxy. Both threatened to resign during the crisis, and in the end Prime Minister King brought about a compromise, but in fact Rogers had won – Dunning had been defeated for the first time and King decided he did not need to worry about fiscal policy any more. This episode was unknown to Canadian economists as recently as ten years ago. It was revealed by Blair Neatby in his book on the life of Mackenzie King, because the only source of the material was in King's diary, which he was one of the first to use. I was not aware of the crisis when I joined the Department, nor did my boss, W. C. Clark, ever tell me about it.

The major demonstration of the conversion of the Canadian government occurred the next year in Dunning's budget of April 1939. No doubt, Dunning had been weakened by a heart attack which reduced his resistance, but he continued in office and relied heavily on the advice of W. C. Clark, the Deputy Minister of Finance, to whom I was a new assistant. The Canadian economy remained on the unsatisfactory plateau that I have mentioned. I was working for Clark on a variety of matters but with an opportunity to advise on the budget, indeed an invitation to contribute both to the text and to the suggested measures. I do not know who really brought it about, but the result was a budget wholly consistent with Keynesian analysis and policies, in April 1939. It recognized the strong reliance of the economy on capital expenditure by business; it recognized the responsibility of the state to promote and, if necessary, to supplement such capital expenditures and the need for incentives. We brought in as such an incentive a tax credit for business capital expenditures, years before US economists began to talk about that type of measure.

The only additional thing I would like to say concerns war finance in Canada. This was carried out over six years with a very full use of the system of macroeconomic accounts that had been developed and were being analysed in terms of the *General Theory*. Then of course we were in a very different situation during the war than during the depression. There was an expansion initially, since we were to start with well below full employment, and then a period of stabilization not only by fiscal measures, but also by credit expansion, tax effects and other policies. Then when we really got to a point of full employment two years after the start of the war, we supplemented our very rigorous fiscal policy with a comprehensive and effective ceiling on retail prices, backed up by strong wage controls, rationing and priorities. We managed by 1943 and 1944 to squeeze a prodigious output from the Canadian economy, despite special difficulties with agriculture; but in the end, even the surplus wheat that we thought was going to be a drag on the market forever, helped first to solve our problem of the US dollar shortage, and later to meet the essential requirements of the Allies.

I will not try to go beyond that; I leave out an account of our discussions with Keynes in 1944, when he came twice to Ottawa as a representative of the British Treasury. I can just say that he was a very skilled negotiator, a very persuasive and fluent expositor; indeed his exercise of fluency and charm was so powerful that the Canadian ministers preferred to take their decisions *after* they had met with him rather than while they were still under his spell. However, that story is for another time.

Notes

1. See Bryce (1978).
2. See R. Goodwin, 'My Life and Times in the Shadow of Keynes', in this volume.
3. H. Aitkin *et al.* (including Mackintosh), *The American Economic Impact on Canada* (Durham, NC, Duke University Press, 1959), pp. 53–4.

Reference

Bryce, R. B. (1978), 'An introduction to a monetary theory of employment', in D. Patinkin and J. C. Leith (eds), *Keynes, Cambridge, and the General Theory*, Toronto: University of Toronto Press, 129–45.

15 Planning the postwar international system
Louis Rasminsky

My first contact with Keynes – Keynes the man – was in October 1942 when I went to London in the belly of a Liberator Bomber along with Hume Wrong, who was a senior official of the Department of External Affairs, and Bill Mackintosh, whom Bob Bryce has mentioned in his chapter, to represent Canada at the first of a long series of international discussions about plans proposed for international monetary organizations, culminating at Bretton Woods in 1944.

During the period from October 1942 until the spring of 1946, I saw a good deal of Keynes in action, and interacted with him in many ways. I therefore thought that the appropriate subject-matter for me to take, indeed the only one that I could take at a gathering of eminent Keynesian scholars, would be to say something about Keynes's role in the establishment of the postwar international financial institutions.

It seems remarkable now that the same people who were active in formulating and administering wartime economic policy were also thinking about postwar plans. And that indeed may well be one of the reasons that the postwar plans worked out as well as they did, and served their purpose for as long as they did. Nowadays I suppose this task would be hived off to a special group known as the 'Strategic Planning Group', far removed from the current battle.

In 1942 we were already talking in Canada – as later became apparent people were elsewhere – about what could be done when the war was over, to avoid the mistakes of the 1930s. Without much notice, in June or July of 1942, we received an invitation to attend, along with the other representatives of what were then called the British Dominions (Australia, New Zealand, South Africa and India), to attend the initial discussions of Keynes's proposal for a postwar International Clearing Union. These discussions went on in London for about ten days, and are probably the most pleasant recollections that I have of my professional life.

I spent the whole of the 1930s on the economic staff of the League of Nations in Geneva. I had a ring-side seat at the unfolding of the world economic depression and the fragmentation of the world economic system. Among my colleagues there were people whose names will certainly be familiar to many: Bertil Ohlin, Gottfried Haberler, James Meade and

151

Ragnar Nurske. As the depression pursued its course in the 1930s there were no coordinated international measures to try to reverse the downward trend of aggregate demand. Country after country based its main policies on trying to increase its share of a shrinking world market. In other words, the policy was one of *sauve qui peut*. The result, so far as the international economy was concerned, was a chaotic mishmash of higher tariffs, depreciating exchange rates, bilateral clearing agreements and exchange restrictions, all resulting of course in a severe contraction of world trade – by as much as 60 per cent. And naturally too in an intensification of the depression.

During the war itself there was of course no problem of demand deficiency, but there was a widespread fear that when the wartime use of resources came to an end, the transition to a peacetime economy would be very difficult, and that we would again face the problem of inadequate demand and disorganized international markets. It was this situation that we wanted to avoid after the war. Canada of course had a special interest in liberal international trade and currency arrangements on account of the great importance of foreign trade to its economy, and the lack of bilateral balance with its main trade partners. It had a large export surplus with the UK and Europe, which we had to be able to use to help pay for the large import surplus from the USA.

When we received the print of Keynes's Clearing Union plan, I think that our greatest impression was one of relief that the great man had come down, and come down so forcefully, on the side of liberal multilateral, non-discriminatory trade and currency arrangements after the war. It was by no means inevitable that he should have done so. His views on policy, as is known, were always conditioned by circumstances, and there was an important group in Britain, headed on the economic side by H. D. Henderson, and on the political side by Beaverbrook, supported by some in the Treasury and in the Bank of England, who saw in the sterling balances that were being accumulated by many countries during the war, the possibility of a captive market for British exports afterwards, through the continuation of inconvertibility and discrimination against dollar imports.

As I say, the discussions about the Clearing Union proposals in London, in October and November, were exhilarating. In the first place, the concept of the Clearing Union itself was elegant and brilliantly original. By a simple act of creation Keynes proposed, as will be recalled, the establishment of a new international currency – which he called bancor. Each member of the Union was to be given a quota or line of credit proportional to the size of its international trade in the form of bancor in the Union. When a member of the union needed foreign exchange to meet a deficit in its current account balance of payments, it would arrange with the Union, in this conception, to ask that a sum of bancor be debited to its account with the Union, and credited to the country whose currency was needed, with that country paying out the counterpart in its own currency to the debiting country. As the Clearing Union was a closed system, the sum of the bancor debits necessarily was equal to the sum of the bancor credits, so the system was always in balance.

The discussions of the Clearing Union plan were presided over by Sir Frederick Philips, a senior Treasury official. Philips was a very able man, and one of few words. The story was told that an official at the Foreign Office reporting to his chief on the results of an interdepartmental meeting at which Philips had represented the Treasury, said, when asked what Philips's attitude had been, that Philips gave a grunt of long dissent. Keynes was surrounded by a galaxy of stars: Dennis Robertson, Lionel Robbins, James Meade and others, but he was the life and spirit of the meeting. He was obviously excited and completely seized by the Clearing Union idea. And he imbued others with his enthusiasm and with the feeling that they were participating in something important. He was eloquent and accommodating. He made every effort not to vaunt his intellectual superiority, but to treat the rest of us as equals. He was never abrasive, never rude – or hardly ever. I remember one occasion on which Sir Theodore Gregory, sometime of the London School of Economics, who was at that time, I think, representing India, asked a question to which Keynes replied, 'I cannot give a sensible answer to a nonsensical question'. Recently, Bob Bryce showed me the evidence of my own excitement and enthusiasm in the form of a long letter I wrote from London to my chief, Graham Towers, who was Governor of the Bank of Canada, in November 1942. In several hundred words I told him how much I was enjoying myself, and then, as an afterthought, added that lest he draw the wrong conclusions, it was all very hard work.

The Clearing Union proposals, and the discussions that followed, clearly foreshadowed the main issues that were to dominate the discussions of international policies since that time, although the positions of the participants have changed quite frequently, often for intellectual reasons and often because their own circumstances have changed. These issues were the code of behaviour that would be accepted by members regarding exchange stability, the obligations they would undertake to avoid exchange restrictions and to maintain the convertibility of their currencies, the financial help that would be available to them to meet temporary deficiences in their balance of payments, the transitional arrangements that would be in effect until all members were in a position to assume their obligations in full and, finally, the respective responsibilities of surplus and deficit countries to restore international balance. The code of behaviour was essentially the same as that which was put forward by the US Treasury in its proposal for an International Stabilization Fund, published a few months after Keynes's document. The Clearing Union, as originally proposed, provided however for more credit to finance international deficits than did the White plan. The sum of quotas in Keynes's plan was about 30 billion, the total size of the fund proposed by the Americans was about $5 billion. Clearly, Keynes thought at the time (and remember his thinking was essentially based on the experiences of the 1930s) that the principal responsibility for correcting international balances would lay with the creditor countries, that they must be willing to extend very large amounts of credit. I recall that at the discussions in London, in 1942, an Australian official had proposed that if any deficit country used the whole of its quota to finance a balance-of-payments deficit, its resulting bancor overdraft should be forgiven. Not to be outdone, a British representative, not Keynes, suggested that if any countries' bancor credit balance with the Fund rose to the size of its quota, that country should be expelled from the Fund.

Keynes did not support these extreme propositions, but he did emphasize the need for the creditor countries to expand their domestic demand, while in the case of the deficit countries he relied mainly on exchange rate depreciation to restore international balance; and little emphasis was placed on the domestic policies of deficit countries as a possible source of international imbalance. Remember that the very widely held assumption of the time was that the main problem after the war would be to avoid deflation. No one foresaw that the twenty-five years after the end of the war would be one of the greatest periods of economic expansion that the world has seen. Nor did anyone foresee the enormous contribution to world economic reconstruction and prosperity that would be made by the generosity of the Marshall Plan. I do not suppose that the actual terms of agreement of the International Monetary Fund would have been very much different, even if these things had been foreseen. But perhaps some of the later procedures adopted *ad hoc* by the Fund, such as annual consultations with members, and the conditionality of drawings, would have been more expressly provided for and, in any case, we all would have been more aware in the early days than we were of the dangers of inflation in the future.

The Clearing Union discussions in London were followed by a whole series of meetings which culminated in the Bretton Woods Conference in July 1944. I do not suppose that any international agreements were ever as thoroughly prepared as the agreements on the International Monetary Fund and the International Bank. Nor do I suppose that Keynes got more personal satisfaction out of his participation in matters of economic policy, at least during the last few years of his life, than he did out of his participation in the establishment of these organizations. The White plan which was published by the US Treasury in 1943 was, as I say, more limited in scope, much less elegant in form than the Clearing Union plan. In it the Fund was to play a more active role in originally fixing exchange rates, and having to consent to changes, than did the Clearing Union plan. The voting arrangements were such that the USA had a veto power over very important decisions, the most important decisions of the Fund.

As regards the responsibilities of creditor countries, the Americans included one remarkable feature, a scarce currency clause, which implied if it did not actually state that if a currency became scarce in the world, as the US dollar was suspected to do, the Fund would have the right to limit sales in that currency. By implication, countries would be relieved of their obligation to maintain non-discrimination against the USA. Keynes never took this clause very seriously, although Harrod thought that it was worth every other clause in the Fund. So far as Keynes was concerned, he probably thought it too good to be true and he never attached very much importance to it, except perhaps as evidence of the goodwill of Harry White and the others who were putting the proposal forward. As things turned out, the scarce currency clause has never been invoked because, I suppose, the widespread discrimination against dollar imports which lasted until the late 1950s was organized by the European Payments Union and not by the International Monetary Fund.

By the late spring of 1943 we, in Canada, had come to the characteristic conclusion that we might help to bridge the gap between the British and the American proposals. We produced a Canadian plan which provided for more flexibility and in other ways was larger, and probably contributed to something to bridge the gap. We did not however adopt the proposal of Keynes regarding a Clearing Union; we went for the American proposal of a mixed bag of currencies. We did so not because we did not like the Clearing Union proposal, but we thought that it just was a non-starter. It meant that there was virtually no limit on the amount of credit that a country (i.e. the USA) could extend except the sum total of the quotas of all the other countries. The Congress would not buy it. At first, Keynes was rather cross. He felt that we had prematurely given way and spoilt his bargaining position *vis-à-vis* the Americans. He was very much attached to the Clearing Union, like a mother is attached to a child. But after a few months of intensive discussion with the Americans, he too came to the conclusion that it was a non-starter and he spoke later of the aesthetic qualities of the agreement as drafted.

We worked terribly hard at Bretton Woods. There were three

commissions, one on the Bank, presided over by Harry White, one on the Fund presided over by Keynes and the third on miscellaneous questions. And there were numerous subcommittees. We all worked on these committees from 9.00 in the morning till dinner-time. Then the drafting committee, of which I was chairman, met from 9.30 in the evening until about 3.00 in the morning. After a while, I noticed that the heads of some of the older members were starting to droop around midnight, and I solved that problem by taking advantage of my knowledge that there was a fourth commission, an unofficial one that met in the Blue Room at midnight, and where the members got a great deal of satisfaction out of the gyrations of Conchita, the Peruvian bombshell! So I adjourned the drafting committee every night promptly at 12.00. The members then came back after half an hour, the red blood coursing through their veins, prepared to draft merrily on until 3.00 in the morning. And though I do not think that the draft of the Fund agreement ranks with the greatest pieces of literature, it is quite readable. The world has not known until this day how much it owes to Conchita.

16 Some aspects of Keynes the man
Robert Skidelsky

On one question I would like to take issue with Keynes himself. On 13 October 1932 he wrote to his wife, Lydia, 'I have been completely absorbed in re-writing my life of Malthus, and sit by the hour at my desk copying bits out and composing sentences and wanting to do nothing else with stacks of books round me. What a relief not to be writing arguments! What an easy and agreeable life fanciful writers must lead!'

As Keynes's biographer, I can assure you that is not so. Fanciful biographers do not lead an easy life. They have their work cut out to make sense of the characters of their subjects, particularly when those characters are as fascinatingly ambiguous as Keynes's. There are basically two views of Keynes. One is that he was a magician, a dazzling performer who speculated in ideas as in money because it amused him and brought him fame and fortune. This view takes seriously Keynes's own description of himself as an 'immoralist'. The other view is that Keynes was a saint, a saviour, who brought a diseased world a new hope of health.

The first was well put by Oswald Falk, a highly cultivated actuary and stockbroker who worked with Keynes for many years in the City in the 1920s. Falk wrote of Keynes:

> He loved the footlights and was impatient if he were off the stage for a minute, almost more impatient if he was not the central figure on it. He described Newton as Copernicus and Faustus in one, and doubtless he thought he resembled him. Can those who are always in the public eye and always dramatic have any identity in solitude? Or must they, like Lord Mellifont in the Henry James story, vanish and become nothing the moment they leave the stage? To the man behind the masks of Keynes there is no clue.

There is a striking parallel between this description of Keynes and Keynes's own description of Lloyd George – 'rooted in nothing . . . void and without content'. Is it right to see Keynes just as a succession of magical moments and brilliant performances covering up the void at the heart of him? Too many people thought so for the opinion to be ignored. But we must set it alongside the passionate conviction of most of his students that Keynes – like his teacher, Marshall – worked and wore himself out in the service of humanity. James Meade always talks of Keynes as the 'great do-gooder'. On this view a high sense of duty and concern for human suffering was the key to his character.

It may be that it doesn't much matter which of the two views is nearer the truth; it may be that at some level they can be reconciled. We have, it can be said, Keynes's economics, and that stands or falls independently of whether he was a good or bad man. But it's not really so simple. We believe in fact that character has some effect on thought. We like to think that our benefactors have good characters; when we dislike their ideas, we tend to attribute them to character defects. So Keynes's character willy-nilly enters into judgements about whether his influence was good or bad. I cannot here offer a solution to the riddle of Keynes's personality. But I mention one or two facts which no student of Keynes can ignore.

Keynes does give the impression of being someone who was driven. Every nook and cranny of his life was packed with activities and projects not just in one line, but half a dozen or more simultaneously. A few weeks after his near-fatal heart attack in 1937, he was writing to his wife from hospital:

> They want to keep my body motionless for a long time – which is apparently the only remedy for heart. I fancy that the embargo on movements of the mind may be removed before the embargo on movements of the body. At least I hope so! For my mind is terribly active. They can take away drink from patients who drink too much and food from patients who eat too much. But they can't take my thoughts away from me. When the Great White Chief comes round this afternoon I shall have to confess that I have written a letter this morning to the Chancellor of the Exchequer.

Keynes was the reverse of the economist's Economic Man who is constantly balancing the advantages of doing this against that. He just did more and more. He lived his life in top gear. As Kenneth Clark once said, he never dipped his headlights. Or to put it another way, he lived his life as though he had no budget constraint. As a result, he was constantly overworked. Complaints of overwork abound in his letters – 'too much to do, no leisure, no peace, too much to think about', 'terrible excess of meetings and work', 'dulled with work' and 'no peace, no peace'. And then the questions: 'Is it necessary?' 'Why do we buzz and fuzz?' 'Why do I do it?' The answer Keynes himself gave was 'over-activity of the cells ... a kind of cancer'.

As far as mental activity goes, this is certainly true. Keynes had one of the most active, fertile minds of this century. He had an almost universal curiosity and could not touch any topic without weaving a theory about it, however fanciful. A meeting of the Cambridge Apostles in 1925, at which the philosopher Frank Ramsey talked on the 'Philosophy of Laughter', touched off a typically ingenious line of thought. As Keynes reported it to his wife: 'I said it was a social act and that we used to make different funny noises to express each of our feelings and emotions, but now, except as children, we had lost nearly all these arts except that of laughing. It is a lonely survivor of an old fashioned way of expressing oneself.'

This attractive habit of rushing in where slower minds feared to tread, and relying on quick invention to get him out of tight corners, often affronted experts and gave him the reputation of an amateur, even in economics. But it was not all after-dinner chatter. Keynes had the capacity to become totally obsessed by intellectual concerns apparently remote from the mainstream of his work. An example from earlier in his life is his attempt to work out a formula for predicting colour-blindness, based on Mendelian ratios. An example from the 1920s is his research into ancient currencies which absorbed him for weeks at a time. He tells Lydia on 18 January 1924:

> I feel little better than a lunatic this evening. It is just like three years ago – the same thing happened. Feeling rather leisurely I return to my old essay on Babylonian and Greek weights. It is purely absurd and quite useless. But just as before I became absorbed in it to the point of frenzy. Last night I went on working at it up to 2 o'clock; and today I went on continuously from the time I got up till dinner time. Extraordinary! Anyone else would think the subject very dull. Some charm must have been cast on it by a Babylonian magician. The result is I feel quite mad and silly. With a lunatic kiss and a wild eye, Maynard.

Mental hyperactivity there certainly was; but I don't think this provides the whole explanation for Keynes's crippling workload. The instinct is to ask in such cases: what is he trying to escape from? And this instinct is sound, as is the usual answer: from being alone with himself. There is a lot of self-hate in Keynes. He was not a man at peace with himself, and rather than be alone with himself, he preferred any stage, any occupation, however trivial. I have a vivid image, to my mind very sad, of the great and fascinating Keynes sitting alone in the King's College Combination Room playing patience, night after night, often till past midnight, 'very much bored and unable to stop' as he himself described it.

For the same reasons, I think, which drove him to play patience, he spent years of what he himself called 'Chinese torture' on university and college committees which he could have escaped from. With anyone else, one would be tempted to call these the occupations of a somewhat empty middle-age. His accounts of them are extremely funny. Being at one college meeting which lasted from 11 to 5 was rather, he said, like 'being with lunatics each of whom sees very small rats and mice running in every direction, but no two of them see the same rats and mice'.

The importance of Keynes's marriage and a crucial reason for its success becomes apparent in the light of all this. 'How lucky we are', he once wrote to Lydia, 'that we never bore each other'. Lydia Keynes was both logical and unpredictable, a combination which Keynes adored. To the end, he could never tell what she would do or say next. That is why he never tired of her. And she gave a centre or point of gravity to a life which was always threatening to shoot off in all directions.

There are other things which puzzle about Keynes's psychology. Take his well-known obsession with hands. Here he is writing a letter (in 1927) on bursarial business:

> The most interesting part was the negotiation with a farmer who has been in a state of violent quarrel with the College for 7 years. I had never seen him before but had been led to believe he was an impossible character. But he came up for the dinner last night, and as soon as I cast eyes on his hands I knew that all this was a complete mistake – that he was very nice and absolutely honest and capable, and that the only thing wrong with him was a violent temper which we had managed to arouse. So I proceeded ... to behave towards him as though he were perfectly sensible and nice, with the result that we came to a complete settlement ... Hands ! Hands! Hands! Nothing else is worth looking at. In ten seconds I had completely revised my idea of his character.

This was not a private joke between Keynes and Lydia. The habit of observing hands, and the idea that the appearance of hands is an outward sign of inner quality, apparently starts when Keynes is a boy and runs right through his life. And whether through Keynes or not, it became one of Bloomsbury's tests of character. We know that Keynes detested Woodrow Wilson's hands and liked F. D. Roosevelt's. He used to judge Fellowship candidates by the state and appearance of their hands, noting particularly whether they bit their nails. It is a solemn thought that appointments at Cambridge in the 1920s and 1930s may have owed more to people's hands than to their brains. Certainly, Keynes must have had an ingenious theory about it.

One way of telling the story of the Keynesian revolution is in terms of the generation war. Keynes appealed over the heads of his professional colleagues to the younger economists, and they responsed, chiefly perhaps because he was the first major authority in their profession to proclaim that governments need not and should not take the depression lying down. But there was also a personal response to Keynes as a man and as a teacher from his students. They felt he was on their side against the pompous and the stuffy and the conventional. For bright young men, Keynes was a perfect mixture of the ironic and the imaginative. He had a certain subversive quality which made them think he was more radical than he really was. Unlike many academics, Keynes always tried to bring unformed thoughts to life, and not kill them by pointing out mistakes.

Michael Straight, better known as a Cambridge spy than a Cambridge economist, nevertheless read the economics tripos in the mid-1930s (he got a First). In a letter to his mother, he has left a vivid account of a daunting evening at Keynes's Political Economy Club. Some of Keynes's former students will remember what that experience was like, and how Keynes operated in that formidable gathering:

> Then, heaven help me [Straight writes in 1935], I had to go to his Political Economy Club, full of clever dons, third year students who had gotten firsts, and we four. Some man called Zambart Lambardi . . . read a paper on The Price Level and Stabilization. But beforehand slips were taken round, half with numbers, half with blanks, and any poor devil who drew a number had to get up in front of the fireplace and make a speech saying what he thought of Mr Z. L. Needless to say I got one! So I gritted my teeth and listened, determined to tell Mr Z. L. where he got off. I felt my stomach contracting continually, in fact almost shrinking through my back. I couldn't understand one word of his wretched paper. It was all about differential movements inside the price level.
>
> I was to speak before Keynes –9th; and three others like me spoke before me. Bauer the Austrian spoke so fast that no one could understand what he said, so that he got away with it. Stamp, the son of Josiah Stamp, made a long and intricate analogy about a traveller and a map in which he never mentioned economics, and so he got away with it; and Henderson trotted out some phrase from Joan Robinson which he had obviously just learnt beforehand and sat down before anyone could ask him what he meant – so he got away with it.
>
> I tried to say something about the price level and stabilization and I didn't get away with it. After I had finished a halting pointless speech I turned to Lambardi and put in a form of a question. But he looked up with a perplexed face and said quite justifiably that he didn't see the point of what I'd said.
>
> At which point Keynes nobly rescued me by saying 'I think I know what you mean . . .' and then explaining a long and difficult theory which of course had never entered my head but with which I fervently agreed.
>
> Then he wound up brilliantly and I sneaked out before anyone had the chance to ask me to expand on my ideas.

I regret to say that Lydia Keynes did not have a high opinion of economists in general. 'Great many of them are most tiresome', she wrote to Keynes's mother, 'no wide outlooks, no touch with life, and no great ideas. They should not rule the country, except Maynard, who is more than economist'. When we have finished probing the masks of Keynes, I think we can see that it was in having so many masks, in being as Lydia Keynes said 'more than economist', that Keynes's greatness lies.

It is the greatness of Keynes which needs emphasis today. Lydia was right. Keynes deserved to rule. And his rule has been vastly beneficient, a point which needs repeating, since it has become the fashion to decry it. No profession which nurtures a human being of the stature of Keynes need feel ashamed of itself. We urgently need another.

Name index

Subject index